Ronald Dixon

One Nation Under Them

Conspiracy in America!

2

*Reclaiming our lives, property, and money
from those who conspire against us*

To my Family,

*Especially my Wife
who inspired me
to write this book*

4

*"The issue today is the same as
it has been throughout all history,
Whether man shall be allowed
to govern himself or
be ruled by a small elite."*

~ Thomas Jefferson

"Nations, like men, are travelers. Each one of them moves, through history, toward what we call progress and a new life or toward decay and death. As it is the first concern of every man to know that he is achieving something, advancing in material wealth, industrial power, intellectual strength and moral purpose, so it is vital as a nation to know that its years are milestones along the way of progress"

~James J. Hill 1909

One Nation
Under Them

this edition 2011-2013

List of Rooms

Introduction		pg 9
Chapter One	The Awakening	pg 15
Chapter Two	The Federal Reserve	pg 27
Chapter Three	Right, Wrong or Left?	pg 77
Chapter Four	The Education Plantation	pg 105
Chapter Five	Conspiracy Fast Track	pg 125
Chapter Six	The Agenda of War	pg 207
Chapter Seven	False Flag Deception	pg 241
Chapter Eight	Generational Football	pg 255
Chapter Nine	The Green Anchor	pg 267
Chapter Ten	Music, Walls & Wiring	pg 279
Chapter Eleven	Matters of Faith	pg 287
Conclusion		pg 295
Recommended Media		pg 299

Introduction:

"I came upon the dragon"

The tyrants have not faded away or withered on the vine; they have transformed themselves and altered their appearance. They used to come at us with guns pointed and swords drawn, boots marching in the streets and public executions. No more, now they carefully weave themselves into elaborate corporate power structures, government agencies and media outlets, disguising who they are and what they intend to do. They are still with us as strong as ever, and the people of the United States are perched headlong on the ultimate battle, the battle to save the nation.

It was the year 2008. Things *seemed* normal but I wondered why our home lost so much value almost overnight, and our savings devastated. The price of gas shot up to $4 a gallon. Storefronts went vacant as unemployment skyrocketed. The media machine kept humming, keeping us busy with sports and reality TV shows as the American people went about their business, but something was terribly wrong.
 The housing market had fallen to its knees when just a few months earlier President Bush bragged about home ownership being at an all-time high, *but who really*

owned those homes? Cheap loans were popping up on the internet back in 2002-2006. Money was being handed out like candy, and the loans were packaged up and sent upriver like goodie bags from a dollar store. If you fogged a mirror you could get a house. Fraud was being orchestrated on the American people.

 I received a pay cut and loss of bonuses, and saw millions of people like me, shocked by the sudden realization that all we worked for was threatened. President Obama was calling for the printing of vast amounts of stimulus money as welfare and food stamp use increased to record levels. The middle class was hit the hardest. Median household income fell 8% in one year alone. Politicians were struggling with banker bailouts and large companies were going under.

I knew the two party system was broken, but I never believed in conspiracy theories, until now. I started looking into subjects like the Federal Reserve and government cover-ups on the internet. A flood of new information came pouring out of the computer, and I entered the hidden world of the dragon.

For decades the American people have been spoiled. Every day we are shown how bad the outside world is; the war, the poverty, the human misery that exists "over there" in some other place, far away from our carefree lifestyle of excess and ease. We have ignored the lessons of history; we are asleep; unaware that hidden forces plot against the foundation of this great country.

There is a **SHADOW GOVERNMENT**, an entity that is not only in plain sight but also burrows deep into the ground, hiding its installations and infrastructure beneath the surface. It is said a person can travel across the country *underground!* What is going on beneath us? The TBMs (tunnel boring machines) are cutting through the Earth day and night. Construction is ongoing. Secret government and corporate facilities are increasing by the year, and they've been at it since the 1940s. What are they hiding and what is their purpose?

Is there a towering castle down there with black turrets and a moat full of alligators? Are there guards milling about with cloaks and daggers? I don't think so. What exists is a bureaucratic and industrial superstructure stretching across the nation, above and below the ground, here and around the world, forming a great global governance, a sort of world management system. It is not a Soviet Union style show of force; it is hidden behind corporate slogans, dollar bills and political party jargon. This monster has to be fed a steady diet of funding that is beyond Constitutional. The *black budget* is first in priority and then other allocations fizzle down to the Congress who then put on a giant display of power and authority. The truth is that they have little power and are being manipulated by a force beyond their control. We do not live in a Constitutional Republic anymore because important decisions are made behind our leader's backs and without their knowledge or consent.

Truth is turned upside down in this compartmentalized shady elitist world. It is so evasive that not even the shadow rulers and government workers know exactly what it is and what is going on. It changes form and takes up different dimensions to confuse and exasperate the most intelligent among us. We live our lives, and die without the foggiest notion of what surrounds us. They keep us within certain parameters, control our population, and then can claim our wealth, property and legacy at death. Those who venture into their world do it at their own risk. Their fist is covered by a piece of velvet. They come across as the givers, the compassionate, the protectors, but if you mess with them and try to remove the mask, the iron fist can make your life miserable in more ways than one.

Some call it a conspiracy theory, but I call it *general awareness* because it's all too real. We were once told the mafia and Bilderbergs didn't exist. As it turns out, they do exist along with the invisible *ruling class,* the power brokers, and the cabal which includes hundreds of major corporations, media outlets and world government and banking systems. They make their presence known subtlety when a President may skip over a question about the Federal Reserve or say "the Constitution is just a piece of paper" like George Bush did. A school teacher will not discuss certain political viewpoints in class. A local sheriff has found their investigation has been taken over by federal agents. A talk radio show cuts off a caller who brings up the "wrong" subject. Instead, they want you to focus on aliens, ghosts, and Bigfoot. Meanwhile the youth march off to another war while the rest of us are caught up in sports and mindless television shows. Alien spacecraft are "projected" into the sky by our own government. Environmental concerns are exaggerated. Anything that distracts and covers up the existence and operation of the shadow government is utilized. A great hologram is there for us to believe in. It's time to lift up the rug and see the truth, draw back the veil and expose them for who they are.

Within the ranks of this secret fraternity there is as attitude of self-loathing. The self-styled elitists have claimed greatness for themselves. Only through their lights and "superior knowledge" is society going to be run and organized.

Good human attributes are reserved for the "superior class" and are not thought of as universal for all people. They look at most of humanity as a waste and it is their plan to extinguish and annihilate us by the billions. The

ends justify the means. There is treachery, treason,
betrayal, double crossing, selling out, double dealing, and intrigue, plotting, scheming, and silencing any form of dissent to control the ordinary masses. The ancient crude method of boots in the streets and the brutal show of force are no longer necessary because new more effective measures have been introduced to control us. They silently manipulate education, politics, the military, science, the media, banking and money. These people make up the master empire, the cabal that we serve, but they are small in number. The vast majority of people in the world are rational, reasonable, and morally enlightened, but this vast majority is fooled to a point
that allows and perpetuates the power of the ruling class, who are themselves *inferior*. We are led down a road of perpetual poverty, war and general human suffering and ignorance on a grand scale.

  It is up to all of us to seek out the truth of our lives and the world we live in. We must not only overcome day to day challenges but open our eyes to what is happening around us and not rely on the traditional talking heads and wall speakers to base our conclusions. Look beyond what you have been told and see beyond your limits, take a peek beyond your comfort zone. Do not box up knowledge and think you know it all, let it expand. If we can throw back the curtain of deception, and defeat this enemy, there is a better world waiting for us, where life is deeper and more meaningful, and the horizons infinite. We don't have to accept their version of life. We have worked too hard and too long to throw away our hopes and dreams. We have built a great nation and we have a great people. I want to protect and defend our sacred country and all those who died for it. There exists an element that lusts for all we have and all we have built. May we work together to stop them.

This book has no footnotes or documentation; I am not trying to "prove" anything. It is conspiracy made simple, for us common folk. Society needs a healthy dose of suspicion. I simply want to increase awareness, and open minds to what is and what might be. We all have a door to access, a room to explore. Step outside of the box and journey into the all-too-real world of conspiracy.

"an enlightened citizenry is indispensable to the proper functioning of a republic"

~Thomas Jefferson

Chapter One: The Awakening

"a world of colorful thoughts is preferable to a uniform landscape of gray, monotone servitude"

Conspiracy: A secret plan, plot or agreement to carry out an illegal or harmful act.

Every day as I step up to the plate, I have to straighten my helmet and be ready for what life throws at me. There is so much to do. The world awaits like a pile of rocks to be moved. Daily routines stand in the way of my quest. Even the act of sleeping is an obstacle, a waste of time. I haven't felt boredom in years.

I have peeled back the veneer of the world and looked inside of the machine, the motor of the world. And now, it's time to recapture what was lost somewhere along the way. The small magical world of my childhood is gone, but I can get it back again.

When I was young, each day was like a year. My friends and I would wander around the neighborhood, fascinated by a telephone pole or the sound of a transistor radio, riding our bikes to the drug store to buy baseball cards and Milky Way bars. By the time the sun set at night, the morning was a far off memory, and another day loomed in front of us like a fantastic voyage. A typical summer had its usual events like hiding in the basement during a tornado warning, or flying a cheap paper kite high up into the blue sky. The delicate melody of a slow moving ice cream truck played its tune in the distance. These were the times of freedom, happiness and immortality.

   Now, the years go by like passing cars. Places, times, and events roll into each other like a TV listing for the century. I drive past an old school and wonder what happened. Maybe the Twilight Zone will take me back to the past but the call of present time always interrupts my little dream. Time goes by and the years click away like a fast rolling slot machine, mercilessly banging off the years one by one.

   What do I do now? I have my own family, they give me meaning and purpose but they have to be taken care of. Every day circumstances have to be dealt with. I work and work every day, both at my job and on the house. There is not much of a social life, I just keep working and living and living and working some more. I am caught in the machine.

   Who am I? The school never answered that question. The church tried but never really hit the right button. My parents did their best but I was a meandering soul, a roving thought machine. Now I have to dig deep within myself to find out who I am and ponder the inner workings of the world. Cigar smoke swirls into the quiet air and disappears. Something is calling out, something deep and unrevealed. Lines of poetry and songs try to capture the flow. I write stuff down on paper towels and scraps of litter. What is happening? Eventually what I found out is both fascinating, and disturbing. I have stumbled across an essence of being that no school would ever teach; the matrix of life. I have peeled back a reality given to us by our forefathers and present day sages and luminaries, but kept hidden by the "system."

  Do we really live in the shadows? Do we exist in some sort of a new dark age? Who are the people behind the scenes and what is their mission? How much do they conceal and keep locked in a secret room, far away from the prodding souls outside the wall?

  The ones who manipulate and control us lie quietly in waiting, gliding behind a veil of illusion, striking at us when we dare provoke them, and giving us distractions to help us tolerate the meandering maze of our lives.

  I was taught the basic morals of life and experienced the full range of happiness and sadness growing up in this typical American situation. There was peaceful summer sunshine and frosty winter afternoons with family, friends, and relatives, the stuff of good times and wholesome memories. I respected the older generation and the wisdom they passed along, but something unexplainable was in the air. Sunday school gave me more questions than answers. The evening news looked and sounded like a staged play. Ordinary conversation turned monotone and bland.

When I saw a leaf floating in the air or heard a car driving by, I read between the lines. There was a message, written in the sky that would vanish whenever I looked at it. Like a squirrel that was there one minute and gone the next. Or a fairy that would show her face and suddenly disappear behind a tree. I would daydream and walk through a glorious castle in my mind but it faded away as I reached out to touch it. The wind would blow flowers a certain way, back and forth. Sand swirled up in the breeze before a thundering storm. I began to realize there was something beyond what I had been taught. The world of my youth was a creation of people, not God! And now before me lay a grand tapestry, molded and carved by the smiths of Earth, a lovely veneer of lighted lines and twisting shadows running across the landscape of my miniature world. I followed the trails of my mind and they led me to the outer covering of the great façade that we live. Some of us get there but how many of us see it as it really is? It's a mask, a false front, an image, an illusion, the shell of a contrived reality. I walked slowly around this marquee for many years, inspecting, searching its exterior for clues, watching it breathe out the images and appearances, the deceptions and the mirage that we all take in and take for granted. I was given a pretense to live by and obey, and I discovered this semblance could be solved like a puzzle, and I was driven to solve it!

If this is the land of freedom and liberty, then why all the secrecy? Why the smoke and mirrors? Why the great illusion?

There is a power, a political force greater than the President and bigger than the Congress, a force that lurks in the shadows, and rules by stealth, but disappears when you speak of it and becomes as a mist when examined. It is rarely explained and never held accountable. It is the unnamed, unmasked specter living among us. It has crept between the pages of the Constitution and melts its hidden message between the lines.

I have opened a new door and here I stand, in that secret, forbidden room where the walls have folded down and the ceiling has disappeared revealing the world as it is. I would not be here but for a series of random events that lined up like dominos and happened to fall at a certain time. I could not know this unless I knew *who I was*, where I came from and what I chose to do about it.

Do you believe in conspiracies? I say it's not a matter of *what is a conspiracy,* but, *what is not a conspiracy.*
First of all, you conspire against yourself every day. You

confuse yourself with conflicting thoughts and then pretend and deceive yourself all over again. The field of psychology tries to deal with this human condition. When three people get together, two conspire against the third.

A pharmacy with ten employees may conspire against their own shoppers. They may decide to re-label expired food instead of throwing it away. Or the scanner may be set to not allow for sale prices. All life situations have some conspiratorial backdrop. There is always more than what you see and hear.

As organizations, corporations, and bureaucracies get more complex, the conspiracies within them increase proportionately. What we have in the final analysis is an existence filled with half-truths, lies, and hidden agendas. We never really know what people are thinking and doing. What we call truth is actually a thin, fragile eggshell of reality covering the endless and ever changing shroud of secrecy that we all live under, both individually and in groups.

Some of the biggest and intricate conspiracies of all time will never be known, and some of the greatest events in human history may not have happened the way we think they did.

You are lucky to even know your own self by the end of a lifetime, let alone all the complex webs woven through the centuries. History could have gone many different ways and taken many forms. Millions of leaders, artists and inventors were never born that may have been. When the curtain is thrown back to reveal the wizard, chances are there is not only a man operating the controls, but many more curtains beyond.

In 1961, John F. Kennedy summed it up this way;

"The very word secrecy is repugnant, in a free and open society, and we are as a people, inherently and

historically, opposed to secret societies, to secret oaths, and to secret proceedings. For we are opposed around the world, by a monolithic and ruthless conspiracy that relies primarily on covet means for expanding its sphere fear of influence, on infiltration instead of invasion, on subversion instead of elections, on intimidation, instead of free choice.

It is a system which has conscripted, vast human and material resources, into the building of a tightly knit, highly efficient machine that combines military, diplomatic, intelligence, economic, scientific and political operations.

Its preparations are concealed, not published. Its mistakes are buried, not headlined. Its dissenters are silenced, not praised. No expenditure is questioned. No secret is revealed. That is why the Athenian law maker Solon, decreed it a crime to any citizen to shrink from controversy.

I am asking your help in the tremendous task of informing and alerting the American people. Confident with your help man will be what he was born to be, free and independent."

Kennedy may have been assassinated for speeches like this that warn of a grave danger, yet in 1992 and 2013 Vice President Joe Biden publically supported the Wilsonian secret society; *"the affirmative task we have now is to actually create a New World Order"*

Tyranny depends on ignorance and lack of individual thought. Heed the old saying; "those who conquer themselves are the greater conquerors." Once you control your own life, you must work to expose those who would control others.

My Dad gave me a stack of political stickers back in 1968. I stuck them all over the fenders and spokes of my rusty bike. Each sticker had the name of some guy running for president. Nixon, Romney, Humphrey, Kennedy, Wallace, Reagan, McCarthy. I thought the names were cool. I liked Nixon because some kid at school was named Steve Nixon. My parents supported Humphrey, of course, the main Democrat, the working class guy. Die hard Democrats. Well my guy won, but I never knew what he stood for, until the Watergate scandal, and now even that is a mystery. Little did I know that Nixon took us off the last of the gold standard in 1971. Something I never learned in school, something we all should have known, but were never taught.

I can still hear the neighbors chatting…
"My Dads a Democrat, I guess I'm a Republican, but I don't know. Why vote for anybody? They're all the same, it doesn't matter, and they're all losers. Kick the bums out of office, who cares? Taxes go up no matter what! Why bother?"

The slick, double talking politicians we see on TV are above and beyond us. They don't know who we are and we will never know them. It's easier just to laugh at them on late night TV than to waste time finding out what they stand for, let alone vote for these hypocrites. "Maybe I'll vote for President. Is that next year or the year after? Who cares? I have more important things to do, just surviving for one. There is nothing we can do about it anyway."

Where does this attitude come from? Why have we strayed so far from the ideals of the Constitution? Yes the Constitution! You know the document that some white wigged guys wrote a long time ago? To answer this question, we need to explore the history of public schooling. After all, we had to be there, at a certain place at a certain time for eighteen years, but why? Why were we compelled to go there? Is it a place of learning, or something else?

The colonists valued education, so much in fact that well over ninety percent of the children attended school on a regular basis. The wealthy landowners of the time knew it was for the benefit of the entire community to educate all people, so they set up what were called free or charity schools. These were schools that the poor could attend and receive a free education.

The original reason given for the creation of "public" schools was that the poor were not being educated. This is not true. They were not only well educated, they were defenders of liberty and criticized their government out of expectation. Now if you criticize the government, you are labeled as mentally unstable, a right wing or left wing radical, or anarchist.

The old time one room school house was a place open to all. In fact, what went on in those stove pipe heated rooms was more or less a miracle. With meager resources, no busing, no school psychologists, behaviorists, or assistant vice principals, they were able to produce literate, critical thinking students who became inventors, scientists and leaders of the new industrial age. How did they do it? Simple, they were taught to be individuals first. Taught to value the Declaration of Independence and the Bill of Rights and sound money. They were taught to think from premise to conclusion, developing a rational thought process. They were not taught diversity, a catch word for today. They were already diverse, in age as well as their immigrant background. The older students helped the younger ones. The young ones grew to help the next generation. By fifth grade they were studying Shakespeare and physics. They learned to be independent, mature, and self-confident without a whole lot of expenditure. They were the industrious ones that took an infant group of colonies, and turned them into the greatest machine of industry and technology the world had ever seen.

The economy was driven to dizzying new heights unimaginable only a few decades past. For the first time, the poor had real opportunity and were becoming better off. It all came from the Jeffersonian premise that the common people should be literate, educated, and wise enough to keep the government small, manageable, and out of the way. So, what happened?

In chapter four, I will explain in more detail the rise of compulsory schooling in America. Suffice it to say that over the years a progressive force has instilled itself into the grain of America, and it has been eating away at the very foundation and bedrock of the country.

Now I know why the masses move through their lives without any thought of politics. The reason is clear. We do not go to school primarily to learn how to read and write. We go to be socialized and have our values inculcated, and our behavior modified. We are not taught to be individuals. We are guided to be "like" everyone else, to "fit in". We develop into groups of common cause, and common identity. We become indoctrinated. The two political parties are made to appear different, but somehow we know they are the same and they are run by the same masters. We feel the cruel vibration of peer pressure at every turn in the hallway and throughout the rest of our lives. How many leaders and innovators have been lost in the process? How much knowledge have we lost? How many students never found themselves or their individuality?

It is a tragedy to see masses of people wandering through life not knowing who they are or where they are going. A few are able to figure things out on their own and break the chains, but many fall into a primal existence of drugs, partying, and endless TV channel surfing. They look for something meaningful but end up with sand running through their fingers.

We don't question our lives anymore. The mundane public strolls by with no sense of purpose or meaning. Faces all look the same, the blank expressions, the utter emptiness, the dull thread of life drifting from one gray cloud to the next, without end.

The politics of life are hiding behind every tree, affecting us in subtle ways, even if we don't know or care, it exists. Political thought is the foundation of happiness or of serfdom. It is not dull or boring. Politics is nothing more than the act of one part of humanity controlling another part to some degree. The scene comes to life if you press the right button. This book is designed to bring it to life!

The Fairness Doctrine came into effect in 1949 when only three networks ruled the airwaves. Different perspectives had to be given for each viewpoint. The problem is that each viewpoint was limited in scope, and monitored by the government. Now, the days of Walter Cronkite telling us "the way it is" have passed. I doubt whether those old commentators were able to tell the full truth about anything to the American people. Those days are now gone. The Fairness Doctrine was repealed in 1987. Now the commentators give their own opinions, which is a far greater system of information delivery. I believe many Americans have a deep seeded suspicion of the media but never had the tools to fight it. Now, because we live in a smaller, more complex world, technology allows us to see beneath the surface like we never have before. That technology is the information superhighway. The internet has liberated the flow of real information, so each person can judge for themselves what is true and useful. The establishment is now poised to regulate it and subdue information again and we must fight against it.
  Some people in this world will not think outside of the

box. They are content with their lives and feel safe within their chosen parameters. Conspiracy theories are "out of bounds" because they pose a threat to their comfort zone, or they believe theories such as this are fanciful or belong in the archives of the mentally disturbed. Their viewpoint however is painfully responsible for allowing tyrants and other such madmen to take control throughout history. Right now is no exception. The American people of today are not exempt or too special to be taken over and fall under the control of totalitarianism. History shows us that when the good people of society choose to do nothing against their oppressors, we all lose. Looking the other direction is not an option. Some say that conspiracy theorists see the glass as half empty and not half full. What I say is that *the glass itself is cracked.* Our republic has become obsolete and most don't even realize it. In order to have a good garden grow it has to be weeded out from time to time. Right now is our time to weed the garden. Every generation needs a revolution. The country is too special and the people in it are too valuable to allow bad elements to overcome it. There are great people not only in government but in the private sector. We have worked together for a long time to build this great nation. Don't let it slip away. Educate yourself and become aware and suspicious because the bad guys are among us and working overtime to overtake us.

  As individuals, we are ignorant of many things. A person can spend their life reading every book in the library and still only know a small percentage of the vast storehouse of human knowledge and experience. I would say the same thing about the collective. We as a people know very little about the whole picture. The entire landscape of human endeavor is mostly a fog that we can only speculate about. The one thing we have is the art of suspicion and the talent of questioning things.

This activity is vital to freedom and liberty and vital to one knowing oneself. If you can somehow know and control yourself, it's not necessary to know all the inner workings of the government. The biggest threats to the collectivists are *individuals.*

The internet, talk radio, and alternative news have given us a new vision and a new voice, a way to wake up from our slumber! It's a portal for us to see the movers and shakers of the world in 3 dimensions. We are rediscovering ourselves, our history and what should be our true place in the world. Now, when we enter the polling place, we vote with passion and meaning! We now have hope. Hope for a better life and a better tomorrow. We find others with the same beliefs and values. We tell our family, friends, and co-workers. We write blogs and call the radio station. We attend functions and rallies. We read history with a new sense of fascination.

We approach the same challenges as the colonists who faced the British. Only this time it's not a war against standing armies, it's a battle against the silent, invisible forces of totalitarianism. Are you ready for the fight?

"those who decide not to participate in politics will be governed by their inferiors"

~Plato

Chapter Two: The Federal Reserve

"the abuse of fiat money is the great crime of history"

I grew up in a typical American suburb with a sprawling park across the street. Beyond the two softball fields were the swing sets and a "fat lady" tree to climb on. We used to kick rubber balls on the house and watch them roll down the other side. The ball would bounce a couple of times on the roof and fall down, landing in the soft grass. Then it rolled across the front lawn towards the street. Little did I know at the time how much work, sacrifice, and precise economic situations it took for this event to happen, to get the ball rolling across the green grass on a summer afternoon. A war of independence had to be fought. Then, an industrial revolution took place, plastics had to be invented, housing proposed and laid out, store fronts opened, delivery and mail systems coordinated, all before the rolling ball could ever be purchased. It all seemed so simple as a child, something we blindly accepted as normal and natural, like the rain falling. We grow up having no idea of the wondrous chain of events it takes to make our modern lives possible!

We have much to be thankful for in this country. It is full of hardworking, honest people who give of themselves every day, no matter what the denomination or political party. We have government workers, everyone from the nice ladies at the library, to park foresters, street sweepers, policemen, teachers, judges, bus drivers, and all the administrative clerks and planners working together to keep things in order while creating a working infrastructure for the country. Sometimes, in criticism of the government, we fail to give these people credit for their time and energy. The government falls short in many ways but we should give praise to those who, day in and day out, perform public service without complaint.

In this great land we have a lively, free people working, inventing, and prospering. I marvel at the construction of towering glass buildings and beautiful bridges, the advancements in art, higher education, health care and agriculture. We are driven to new heights of technology which benefit the entire world. The human spirit is alive and well here in America. Now our job is to protect it, like sheltering a Ferrari in a garage, out of the hail storm. We must be forever vigilant in protecting our freedoms or they will go to the wayside. There are real elements that pose a danger to us. We must find them, isolate them and minimize their power before they drag us into an abyss of fascism. Unborn Americans have the right to enjoy the same freedoms we do now. It's up to all of us to preserve liberty and protect the Constitution for them. Now, let us track down and identify those bad elements!

~Gateway to the Underworld~

We spend our formative years at school, learning the basics as we develop good work habits and skills for living. Then, as teenagers; we get our first job and start paying taxes which are used to pay for libraries, roads and infrastructure. The government protects us from crime and foreign enemies. We have the courts to settle major disputes and put the bad guys in jail while the Constitution protects our rights and liberties. It all seems ok, but we carry with us a deep misunderstanding of the system. *There is something terribly wrong.* We go about our business as usual without the least suspicion of something being off- kilter. What is it? What could this be? The answer is simple, yet hidden.

The money in your wallet is not so much an asset but is a *debt to be paid.* Dollar bills may carry the images of the original founding fathers, inscribed on counterfeit-proof parchment, but little do we know, the money is *already counterfeited with interest* by the Federal Reserve System! The one thing we strive for and rely on is the very thing that is silently stripping our lives of freedom, wealth and dignity.

I remember the days when I looked forward to getting my "take home" pay. My check stub listed all the deductions and taxes paid. My "net pay" was what was left for me to spend or save the way I wanted. Little did I know or did anyone know that the net take home pay was still <u>vulnerable to confiscation.</u> Whenever the government prints more money into existence, it automatically devalues the existing money, giving it *less* purchasing power. We are robbed by way of *inflation.* It's like a leak in a gas tank that never ends and is never repaired. It must be stopped. If you bought a new car and the dealer still had the right to drive it on weekends that is what we have with the money system. You earn money, pay taxes, and the Federal Reserve keeps spending it AFTER you have it in your possession. *Nice trick,* and that is the true cause of poverty in this country.

The field of finance and economics is sufficiently complex to the point that the ordinary person does not understand the ins and outs. That opens the door for the smart guys to step in and make money work for them *at our expense.* The temptation must be overwhelming because the potential rewards are enormous.

The Fed works as a notorious *lynch pin,* connecting our labor to the money bandits, without us knowing it. We have "debt" attached to our money from the day it is printed, something we don't think about. It's the curse of the money masters and the plague of humanity. This enemy we all have in common is the Federal Reserve System. It is the central bank of the United States founded as an act of Congress in 1913. It is essentially a private banking cartel masquerading as a branch of government.

Ok, so who cares? Well, if there is a thief in the house, you call the police. If someone stole and wrecked your car, you require compensation, same thing on a higher level. Robert Hemphill, former employee of the Federal Reserve, had this to say about the monetary system;

"It is the most important subject intelligent persons can investigate and reflect upon. It is so important that our present civilization may collapse unless it is widely understood and defects remedied."

Every day, every minute, every second, we are getting robbed. The silent hand of inflation is dipping into our savings accounts and wallets on an ongoing basis. People complain about taxation and the high cost of living but are unaware of the silent thief in the night called the Federal Reserve System. As the money burns a hole in itself; it loses value, and eventually goes broke! When a back room printing press is available to a select few, it *will be utilized* by many bad elements wishing to confiscate your earned wealth. This "fiat" money is the liquidity of corruption. It enables financial burglars to pillage our assets. As long as we have crooked money, we will have a crooked country. In order to use this money ourselves, we have to engage and partner with unsound money. Unsound money encourages corruption. Sound money, on the other hand, brings prosperity to the common people.

A very interesting time in our history was 1920. We had a depression that is rarely discussed. After World War 1, we experienced a severe financial decline. What happened next is not talked about and very neatly covered up. Unemployment was almost 12%. President Warren Harding decided to cut government expenditures drastically and not assist the private economy with bail outs and welfare. Americans were basically on their own to reorganize themselves. A funny thing happened; the country emerged out of the depression after nine months! Unemployment fell to 2.4% by 1923 and 1.9% by 1926. Calvin Coolidge continued the "stay out of the way" philosophy. Out of this came the roaring twenties and great prosperity for all. Please note that the Federal Reserve stayed on the sidelines during this crisis. When they finally decided to meddle in the economy, banking elements and the Fed scientifically created the Wall Street crash and the great depression as Rep. Lindbergh predicted. Yet Harding gets virtually no mention in the history books and FDR is made out to be the grand savior of the country. Harding gave this advice to the American people;

"Let us call to the people for thrift and economy, for denial and sacrifice if need be, for a nationwide drive against extravagance and luxury. There hasn't been a recovery from the waste and abnormalities of war since the story of mankind was first written, except through work and saving, through industry and denial, while needless spending and heedless extravagance have

marked every decay in the history of nations."

Harding meant those words not only for the people, but for the government also. He cut government borrowing, attacked wasted and fraud, and downsized the public domain. What a difference between then and now as modern presidents "stimulate" the economy with helicopter money and big spending which makes matters worse.

The Fed withdrew the supply of money in the 1930s, and refused new loans. Roosevelt called in gold coins in 1933 under the threat of fines and imprisonment. This allowed the government to confiscate gold, assets and land from the American people. The same tricky maneuvering took place in the S&L scandal and the 2008 financial crisis.

The great depression ended not because of the start of a world war but because the United States was the last power left standing after the war and had most of the world's manufacturing infrastructure still intact. We were the great producer of the world! And that created the vast middle class we are famous for.

Most people realize the act of counterfeiting is against the law because it screws up the value of everyone else's dollar. It's a serious crime. The Federal Reserve is allowed to counterfeit on a daily basis without the approval of Congress. It actually steals from you every day! They do this by printing money, a lot of it, too much of it. It causes inflation and decreases the purchasing power of the dollar. Prices then go up. And who benefits? The recipients of the created money benefit. Who are they? Let's say politicians, bankers, corporations, foreign countries and other global minded groups and individuals. It is a hidden tax with no representation. This hidden tax affects the poor and the middle class more than the wealthy and yet the Democratic Party is in full support of the Federal Reserve System! It was Bill Clinton who repealed the Glass-Steagall Act which enabled banks to sell derivatives which packaged bad loans and sent them down the road like garbage in a plastic bag. When the bag was opened, suddenly the average household had lost 40% of its assets. Low interest loans were made available from the Fed to big banks. The banks went on to invest the money in risky areas. When the stocks went up, they enjoyed massive profits and when the stocks dropped, they received bail out money from taxpayers. All the while, the American people stood by and paid no attention. We were too busy watching sports, playing video games and taking drugs. We need a wakeup call!

Good news occurred in 2010. Within the Dodd-Frank consumer bill was included a small audit of the Federal Reserve pushed by Ron Paul and others. Paul had been proposing this legislation for 35 years and finally got a small part of it through! Although watered down, the new law has exposed some inside activities of the Fed which included a massive giveaway of money to big banks, foreign countries, and corporations totally *16 trillion dollars* from 2007-2010. Predictably, little was made of this in the mainline media. The full audit the Fed bill was overwhelmingly passed by the house in 2012 but has been resisted by the Democratic Senate and Barrack Obama. In fact Obama gave the Fed even more power as a watchdog over banking activities and to be in charge of consumer protection. Yet, the Fed continues its policy of closed door meetings and independence from scrutiny. 100 years of secrecy is enough already! What are they hiding?

December 1921. Thomas Edison and Henry Ford visit Muscle Shoals, Alabama where a nitrate and water power project is proposed. They observed the way our government sold bonds to banks which would then lend the same money back to the government at interest, all to pay for the project at hand. They suggested the government come up with the money by itself and leave out the bankers, thus avoiding interest charges. They published their idea in the New York Times. Why not pay 30 million instead of 60 million? Instead, a full 30 million dollars went to the banking officials who did absolutely nothing on the project themselves, but ran off with the cash like bandits. Unfortunately, many public works projects were funded this way, and their suggestion went unheeded.

The same crony capitalism goes on today. The state of California for example is flush with corruption. Crooked public works projects are funded by the taxpayer that line the pockets of the cronies and bankrupt the state.

I find it hard to believe the Federal Reserve and its banks charge interest on what is supposed to be our own money to begin with and they get away with it year after year. Why do we pay interest on our own money? Does anyone ever ask this question? It's an easy way for the government and others to obtain funding without going through the hassle of debate, voting and a lot of public tax discussion. Is it legal? No, printing excess money is unconstitutional and illegal if not voted on. How do they get away with it? The mechanism is kept in the dark. We are not to see the machinery. The subject is never explained very well in school if at all. Students do not learn about monetary issues and the concept of sound money, the subject is glazed over at best. The media is also quiet; they are not willing to say much. So why don't the politicians do something about it? It's because they are on the receiving end, they get the laundered money! A typical politician gets this money to run campaigns and keeps on earning it throughout their time in office. They use it for pork barrel programs, bail outs, military buildups and who knows what else! Why would any politician say anything if they are paid to keep quiet and keep the funds under the table? Congressmen and Senators are then rewarded with personal wealth at the cost of society. Public service is supposed to be a part time-temporary position. Jesse Ventura, mayor and governor in Minnesota is one of the few who served the old fashioned way. Get in and get out!

In 2011, The Tea Party finally held up a standard to the good old boy network. Elected Tea Party members of congress have refused caucus appointments and other "bribes for votes" attempts to buy them off. The media has complained that the Tea Party cannot be bought off like other politicians. There is finally a movement supported by the people to cut back the levels of government and deal with the 14 trillion dollar national debt, and the establishment doesn't like it! This Libertarian movement can be attributed to all the good American people who have self-educated themselves without the help of traditional media and education. Our country is becoming informed and the mask is coming off the face of tyranny.

Our current monetary system is clearly against the Constitution. Article 1 section 7 states "all Bills for raising Revenue shall originate in the House of Representatives" This means all money to be spent must go through a voting process; it cannot just be printed into existence. Section 8 states "The Congress shall have power to Coin Money, Regulate the value thereof and fix the Standard of Weights and Measures." This duty belongs to the Treasury Dept., not the Federal Reserve which is a private company. It is curious to me how the Democrats do not take a stand against this private interest group that runs the monetary system. Democrats usually stand up to big corporations demanding higher tax rates. The Federal Reserve System is the biggest company around but pays no taxes what so ever! Where are the liberals on this one!

Section 9 states "a Regular Statement and Account of Receipts and Expenditures of all Public Money shall be published from time to time." This never happens. There are billions of dollars unaccountable every year in this country. Finally, in 2011, after the matter went to the Supreme Court, an limited audit of the Fed revealed 16.1 trillion dollars was loaned or given away between 2007-2010, none of this vast amount of money went through any screening, congressional debate or voting process! We obviously do not live in a Democratic Republic if a private bank can give themselves that much power. I call it banking fascism.

Section 10 states" No State shall make anything but Gold and Silver coin a tender in payment of debts." This means we are not allowed to print what is called "fiat" money which has no backing in gold. Thomas Jefferson, Jackson and others were very suspicious of the early central banks. The first bank was shut down because of corruption and the funneling of money overseas. Jefferson said central bankers are more of a threat to the people than standing armies. Andrew Jackson shut down the Second Bank of the United States, paid off the national debt and put central banking out of business for 78 years. 1836 was the only year in American history that we were debt free, thank you Andrew Jackson.

During the free banking era that followed, the country grew and prospered like no other in history. We were on the gold standard. Gold stayed at about twenty five dollars an ounce the whole time and prices stayed the same. It was an era of free, competitive banking. The poor got better off and opportunities abounded for all. It was a time when individuals were out of debt and saved their own money. Small and medium businesses paid for their own expansion, without taking loans. Local banking developed into an honest profession spreading across the country. The big bankers in New York were furious! J.P. Morgan, Carnegie, and the Rockefellers would have nothing to do with this outrage! After all, they were losing money, big money and big power. In 1873, in an effort to corral money, the big bankers minimized the issuance of silver and monopolized gold as much as possible and contracted the money causing a national recession for years to come. They were able to foreclose on farms and property as they called in loans. William Jennings Bryan campaigned honorably for President under the silver banner but still lost to banker supported McKinley in 1896. Bryan had this to say about reforming the money before other reforms are possible;

"There is no reform that can be accomplished until the money of the Constitution is restored. What we need is an Andrew Jackson to stand, as Jackson stood, against the encroachments of organized wealth.

They say that we are opposing national bank currency; it is true. If you will read what Thomas Benton said, you will find he said that, in searching history, he could find but one parallel to Andrew Jackson; that was Cicero, who destroyed the conspiracy of Catiline and saved Rome. Benton said that Cicero only did for Rome what Jackson did for us when he destroyed the bank conspiracy and saved America. We say in our platform that we believe that the right to coin and issue money is a function of government. We believe it. We believe that it is a part of sovereignty.

Mr. Jefferson, who was once regarded as a good Democratic authority, seems to have differed in opinion from the gentleman who has addressed us on the part of the minority. Those who are opposed to this proposition tell us that the issue of paper money is a function of the bank, and that the government ought to go out of the banking business. I stand with Jefferson, rather than with them, and tell them, as he did that the issue of money is a function of government, and that the banks ought to go out of the governing business."

President Garfield, who was wise to the banker's tricks and wanted honest money, was killed while in office. He said this in 1881;

"Whoever controls the volume of money in our country is absolute master of all industry and commerce...and when you realize that the entire system is very easily controlled, one way or another, by a few powerful men at the top, you will not have to be told how periods of inflation and depression originate."

Many of Lincoln's interest free greenbacks were called in to further contract the money supply, deepening the problems and lessoning liquidity. So even though we were on a metallic standard, the bankers were still able to manipulate the money supply by removing silver from the marketplace.

The following quote is taken from the United Bankers Magazine in 1892; it discusses how bankers dominated public opinion by distracting the masses on useless subjects to keep attention away from the money issue. The common people were known as the "inferior social strata of society" which gives their opinion of the American worker, farmer and businessman. They self-appoint themselves as rulers over others when in fact they are the inferior minority. Today's media uses the same technique, to disguise and cover up the plans of the banking and finance industry...

"We must keep the people busy with political antagonisms. We will speed up the question of tariff reform within the Democratic Party and put the spotlight on the question of protection for the Republican Party. By dividing the electorate this way, we'll be able to have them spend their energies at struggling amongst themselves on questions that for us have no importance whatsoever"

The bankers intentionally caused confusion so the public would demand change, not knowing the reforms were led by the bankers themselves.

Enter the Federal Reserve System. This private banking cartel found its way into the halls of Congress and put a clamp around the Constitution. The following quote sums up just what the early bankers thought of the common person and their knowledge of money;

"The few who understand the system will either be so interested in its profits or be so dependent upon its favors that there will be no opposition from that class, while on the other hand, the great body of people, mentally incapable of comprehending the tremendous advantage that capital derives from the system, will bear its burdens without complaint, and perhaps without even suspecting that the system is inimical to their interests".
~the Rothschild Brothers, 1863

We are not "mentally incapable" of understanding money and how it works. There is a certain language that is used in financial circles. They have a boat load of complicated terms and phrases used primarily to disguise and confuse the general public and cover up what they are doing behind the scenes. Listen to any speech by a Federal Reserve official, there is no way a common person or even a Senator can comprehend it. This is by design; the simple crime of inflation is layered under the smoke and mirrors of financial language. They continue to manipulate money for their own needs at our expense because we haven't been shown the truth. I submit it's not because we are incapable of knowing, it's because the knowledge of money and how it works is carefully kept hidden from the public. It is kept in a vault and not taught in school. It should make Americans angry. In fact, Henry Ford had this to say;

"It is well enough that people of the nation do not understand our banking and monetary system, for if they did, I believe there would be a revolution by tomorrow morning".

Charles A. Lindbergh Sr.

Charles Lindbergh Sr. was the father of the famous aviator who flew across the Atlantic. He was a strong opponent of the Federal Reserve Act. The public at the time did not understand the enormity of the upcoming legislation. Serving as congressman from Minnesota, 1906-1917, he had this to say after the act was passed December 23, 1913;

"This act establishes the most gigantic trust on Earth. When the President (Woodrow Wilson) signs the bill, the invisible government of monetary power will be legalized...The worst legislative crime of the ages is perpetrated by this banking and currency bill."

It is noteworthy that many opponents of the Federal Reserve Act were on Christmas holiday when it was hurriedly pushed through congress.

Mr. Lindbergh was well read and very much aware of what the banking interests were up to. He had been studying their history going back to the Civil War. The interest free greenbacks of Lincoln had saved the country millions of dollars of interest because the bankers were left out of the equation. For the next 25 years stocks and bonds were manipulated and watered down which eventually led to the (intentional) panic of 1907. The panic was provoked by the bankers so the public would be tricked into demanding some kind of action. Just as they planned, the government created the National Monetary Commission to "study" the situation and "recommend" new policies. This led to the Glass-Owen bill which became the Federal Reserve Act. Lindbergh said this after the passage of the act in 1913;

"From now on, depressions will be scientifically created."

Lindbergh wrote the book "Banking, Currency, and the Money Trust" and also "Why is your Country at War?" which describe cover ups and problems within banking and government. "The Economic Pinch" from 1923 reads like a book from 2003 as he describes the way the three main groups (farmers, laborers and legitimate businessmen) are deceived by a fourth group (the big banks, the press and the profiteers). In this enlightening essay, Lindbergh exposes the fourth group whom he calls the "profiteers of peace" and the "patrioteers of war" that exist above and beyond the scope of the common man. The common man being largely unaware of their existence and the extreme power they are up against. Ordinary people do not think well enough to lessen the influence of the elite and "set things straight'. The press is part of the fourth group who also work together with most politicians to create calamities of finance and war in order to steal the assets of the unassuming masses. The press never warns the people of a coming calamity but they communicate with the profiteers so they can prepare for the coming collapse and profit from it. We can get rid of the fourth group and keep the necessary three if only we were conscious of the situation.

The school system, the press and the politicians keep the truth from us and the money we make is the property of the Federal Reserve who can confiscate it back to themselves through inflation. The game is definitely rigged.

Lindbergh points out that shortly after the Civil war, a group of men formed a selfish plan to rule the world by the manipulation of finances. Then, wealthy financiers (like Carnagie) funded the education system, gearing it to keep people in the dark from then on. Many teachers were fired for speaking the truth. Jefferson had given the warning years ago. The people were being deceived by their own government.

One day Lindbergh strolled down to view the maddening rush of boxing fans waiting to see the Dempsey/ Carpentier bout. He noted how every person in Times Square was overwhelmed with excitement and how they reacted to each news bulletin about the match. It was a mad rush of ordinary New Yorkers wholeheartedly enthusiastic about the event, knowledgeable about every aspect of it. He wished they were that excited and intelligent about politics! The same goes on today as millions of Americans scramble to watch American Idol or Monday Night Football. It's a distraction, a costly one at that.

It may sound like Lindbergh was somewhat liberal but he believed in honest business, sound money and free enterprise. He said a minimum wage or a living wage would only serve to increase the price of which a company sells its goods. It's merely a ploy to calm the masses while still maintaining the dishonest money flow. The "master organizers" were (and still are) "the masters of mankind."

The bankers intensified a panic in 1913 and then demanded a bailout from the government or else "great calamity" would happen. Does that sound familiar with the panic threat and bailout of 2008? How long are we going to allow this to go on? He said;

"Election after election we have gone on voting, blind as bats in the sunshine, blind to what was necessary to the general welfare. Light dazzles the bat. Falsehoods have dazzled us. We have believed the false to be true, the true to be false in so many cases. Falsehoods have dazzled us as light dazzles the bat, only we lack the instinct of the bat to get away from what confuses. There is a cure for our confusion if we get the facts before us in the right way. Our mind was made to use at all times. We must analyze the facts into simple everyday truths, then sort the true from the false, and we shall not be confused. All of us should think".

This is good advice for what ails us today. The way out is to think and be independent. He goes on;

"Individual action is needed rather than a following. The hardships of the world are due mostly to the masses following leaders and not all having minds of their own. A great leader leads the best, when the people know what the best is".

 About money, he had this to say;

"We must at once, if we do our duty, create an honest dollar. A dollar that the Federal Reserve Bank alone controls cannot be honest. There is a key to the good things of the world. That key is the mind. It is thought that opens the way to all things".

Lindbergh did his part to uncover and expose the banking trust. His congressional investigation proved to the Congress that Wall Street and the bankers were behind the Federal Reserve Act. The bill passed anyway, became law and the rest is history. He tried to do away with the many congressional caucuses calling them "conspiratorial" meetings.

The plates of his first two books were being printed one day in Washington DC in 1918 when a group of fake government agents broke into the printing shop and demanded the destruction of all plates having to do with Charles A. Lindbergh. Some of the original books survived however. The banking interests at the time were not only spying on Lindbergh, but also harassing him with actual gunshots. He refused a bribe of two million dollars to call off the investigations. They also tried to defeat him at election time in his home district in Minnesota. The plan backfired because so much money was pumped into the district, the happy, prosperous voters didn't care about the result! The secret plans of the money manipulators had to be revised again and again because of Lindbergh's efforts. Eventually, he drew up articles of impeachment for several Federal Reserve officials including kingpins Harding and Warburg. History books fail to recognize the great contribution of effort and knowledge Lindbergh brought to the table at the dawn of the Federal Reserve. He risked his life and reputation to shine the light upon the money trust and the upcoming world order.

~Jekyll Island~

In his book, "The Creature from Jekyll Island"
G. Edward Griffin takes us on a journey back to 1910, describing the secret beginning of the Federal Reserve System.

On a cold November evening in New Jersey, a train slowly rolled out of town with a very expensive railroad car coupled to the rear, the car of Nelson Aldrich, banker and Republican whip in the Senate. The passengers in that car were worth about one quarter of the world's wealth. They traveled in secrecy, changing their names and telling no one of their journey. The public could not know that these once competitive bankers were forming a dark union.

One thousand miles away was their destination. Jekyll Island, Georgia. Recently purchased by J.P. Morgan, it was used as a vacation getaway destination, but this time it would be the site of the birth of a banking cartel that would transform America. The financiers met there for nine days. The goal was to draw up a bill that would limit competition between them and create a system to maximize profit and put independent non-national banks at a great disadvantage. It was the beginnings of the Federal Reserve.

Banking was becoming fiercely competitive, the South and Western banks were getting stronger, and taking a larger share of profit from the New York and European bank interests as they held over fifty percent of all deposits. The members of the Jekyll Island club were not about to let this go on any further. Their plan was to introduce a bill intended to "stabilize" the economy and keep America away from inflation, bank runs and general instability, but this was a deception. The bill had the word Federal to make it sound like a branch of the government, and Reserve to give people the impression the funds were somehow backed up, which was not true. It laid out various branches around the country to give it an appearance of local control. In reality, it was a bill to enable the cartel to crush their competition and reclaim their monopoly and control of the monetary system. This bill would not be introduced or even supported by them; in fact, they would criticize it in public, all the while, being supportive of it in private.

Looking back, the Fed has never achieved its stated objectives because the objectives were false from the beginning. In the next one hundred years, The Fed presided over depressions, recessions, bailouts, financial crisis, wars, and instability, while stealing over 90% of the value of the dollar, sending much of our hard earned money to unknown banking partners and far off countries. It's truly amazing that America has survived the Fed's sheer weight and constant usurping power as we somehow maintained our greatness as a country, but how much greater we could have been!

What started out on Jekyll Island moved to become a dominant force in America. This history has been carefully hidden from the American public. Hollywood could make some great suspense dramas about the Fed but they wouldn't dare attack the shadow powers! If there were any widespread knowledge of these events of 1910, the government would be forced to admit the cover-up and redefine or eliminate the Federal Reserve System altogether. The angry public would demand it!

Franklin Roosevelt, who presided over the great depression, had this to say about the financial conspiracy in a letter to Colonel Edward Mandell House in 1933.

"The real truth of the matter is, as you and I know that a financial element in the large centers has owned the government of the U.S. since the days of Andrew Jackson". History depicts Andrew Jackson as the last truly honorable and incorruptible American president."

Col. House worked behind the scenes as a personal

advisor to Woodrow Wilson and FDR. He even had his own room in the White House during the Wilson years. He managed to arrange for the United States to
intervene in World War 1. Of course, House had direct contacts with the big banking interests of the time. Because his father made a fortune off the Confederate government during the Civil War, he had insider experience from the start. House is the one who selected Wilson for nomination to the Presidency. He selected Wilson's cabinet positions among other appointments. House wrote a fictional book in 1912 detailing future events in America. He described the depression and World War Two as if he knew what was going to happen. Although his presence was carefully hidden, he was a powerful force inside Washington for years and yet he has been discretely removed from the history books.
In 1912 Woodrow Wilson wrote about those who rule in the shadows;

"Since I entered politics, I have chiefly had men's views confided to me privately. Some of the biggest men in the United States in the field of commerce and manufacture are afraid of something. They know that there is a power somewhere so organized, so subtle, so watchful, so interlocked, so complete, so pervasive, that they better not speak above their breath when they speak in condemnation of it"

William Jennings Bryan had accepted the position of Secretary of State. He and Lindbergh had taken firm stands against the Federal Reserve Act. The bill had to pass Democrat Bryan before passage was possible. Wilson and the bankers tricked Bryan into supporting the bill after he was told there would be local control built in and presidential powers over appointments. He was also told the money would be issued and backed up by the U.S. Treasury with no inflationary powers built in. He was no match for the financiers who deliberately made the bill complicated and left open many doors for "reforms" in the future. He later quit his position in disgust over the Lusitania incident.

Many years later, economist John Kenneth Galbraith commented on the intentional complexity built into the banking system; "The study of money above all other fields in economics, is one in which complexity is used to disguise truth or evade truth, not to reveal it". Anyone listening to a Federal Reserve official speak can see how they use complicated formulas and terms to disguise their criminal activities. What they do is very simple; having a monopoly on the nation's monetary system, they maintain the right to create money out of nothing and draw interest on that same money, keeping the country in perpetual debt. The income tax (passed at about the same time as the Federal Reserve Act) being the method of cash flow to keep a steady stream of dollars going to the private banking cartel. If you write a check to the IRS, that check is cashed by the Federal Reserve System and the money goes to pay interest in the debt first, then maybe roads and bridges later.

Woodrow Wilson, the Democrat academic professor who had accepted the offer from the bankers to become president in return for his signature on their money bill wrote this letter of guilt after the fact;

"I am a most unhappy man. I have unwittingly ruined my country. A great industrial nation is controlled by its system of credit. Our system of credit is concentrated. The growth of the nation, therefore and all our activities are in the hands of a few men. We have come to be one of the worst ruled, one of the most completely controlled and dominated governments in

the civilized world-no longer a Government by conviction and vote of the majority, but a Government by the opinion and duress of a small group of dominant men".

Charles A. Lindbergh went on to start a progressive movement of sorts in Minnesota that eventually led to the Farmer Labor Party which he ran under for Governor. During the campaign, he was not allowed to speak at certain functions and in certain counties. His anti-war stance made it impossible to get elected to the Senate or Governor. His book pointed out the truth of America's involvement in WW1 which was for profit. Billions were made off of arms and military supplies. (Investigation of this fact led to the neutrality laws of the 1930s). The Lusitania passenger liner was intentionally run into German waters where it was torpedoed and sunk, swaying Americans to a pro-war stance. Millions of lives were lost in a war for no reason but for the gains of financiers, bankers, and the military complex. After Wilson said he would not "send our boys over there", he not only sent our boys over there to die, but set the stage for the American military industry to rake in huge profits, and billions more to be lost through inflation.
Lindbergh said;

"The plain truth is that neither of these great parties (Democrat/Republican) as at present led and manipulated by an 'invisible government,' is fit to manage the destinies of a great people, and this fact is well understood by all who have had the time and have used it to investigate".

It was evident that Lindbergh viewed both parties as corrupt and untrustworthy. Again, we find that Lindbergh agrees with Jefferson and many others that the general public must be informed and educated or they will be controlled. If the American people were well informed about monetary policy and the workings of government, the First World War and the depression could have been avoided. As Lindbergh pointed out,

"The remedy for our social evils does not so much consist in changing the system of government as it does in increasing the general intelligence of the people so that they may know how to govern. If they do not learn how to govern themselves intelligently, Socialism will be the result."

Going back to the book "The Economic Pinch" Lindbergh describes in detail the early days of the Federal Reserve. For example, in 1913 the bankers threatened an economic collapse unless the government gave them huge sums of money to prevent a "panic". Of course, they got the funding. In 2008, the same thing happened. George Bush got in front of the American people and threatened calamity, panic and total collapse unless the TARP funding went through Congress. Members of Congress were even threatened with martial law if the "emergency" cash did not go through. Again, the money was there for them.

This has happened countless times since the central bank emerged in 1913. Bailouts for railroads, banks, and other companies (purposefully driven into the ground) were always available through back room dealings. Lindbergh goes on to describe how branches of the government work with the banking interests to manipulate monetary policy for the betterment of the well-connected while the farmers, common workers and businessmen pay the freight. A huge system of credit was always extended to the crony capitalists while the farmers had to lobby for years just to get a paltry line of credit opened. Things continued on this way through the 1920s and the depression of the 1930s.

In 1934 Congressman Louis T. McFadden had this to say concerning the Federal Reserve System;

"Through the Fed the people are losing their rights guaranteed to them by the Constitution...the people of these United States are being greatly wronged...Every effort has been made by the Fed to conceal its powers- but the truth is- **the Fed has usurped the government***...the sack of these United States by the Fed is* **the greatest crime in history***...what King ever robbed his subject to such an extent as the Fed has robbed us?...it is a* **monstrous thing** *for this great nation of people to have its destinies presided over by a traitorous government board acting in secret concert with international usurer.*
When the Fed was passed, the people of these United States did not perceive that a world system was being set up here, a super state controlled by international bankers, and international industrialists acting together to enslave the world for their own pleasure".

McFadden was poisoned to death on October 3, 1936. He was the Chairman of the House Banking and Currency Committee from 1920-1931. It was the third attempt on his life. He was willing to speak out and paid the price.

So what does this all mean, and why would anyone care? Money, everything is based on money. We pay bills, buy groceries, purchase cars, boats and houses, even steal money. We spend it, we save it, we lose it. Politicians ask for "more funding" to finance roads, human services and wars. Telemarketers call you for it. Money is everywhere and in everything, all the time, every day of our lives. There is no escape from it, and an endless need of it.

Throughout history, the people who were able to "figure out" the financial system were the ones who became rich and ran the show. They either took the reign of power themselves or manipulated power from behind the scenes. Sometimes, sound money lasted for hundreds of years and served the common good by
simply functioning as a means of honest exchange, like in the Byzantine Empire or periods in Germany and here in the U.S. Fiat money however is the tool of tyrants, kings, and dictators. They have used it for centuries to control and manipulate the masses.

The Founding Fathers knew this well and sought to protect the common man from these elements. Finally, an experiment in self-government was given a chance, and it worked. Although Hamilton (and others) thought of the common people as "beasts that needed to be controlled" and wanted a substantial federal government and a central bank, their efforts were limited by Jefferson and others. Jefferson had faith in the common person and he was right.

Finally, we were free from big government and big money, and we prospered. Power was in the hands of the people!

Unfortunately, the banking centers have since returned the power to themselves. They have taken over the handling of money once again. They are able to print new funds into existence with the push of a button, thereby sidestepping the Constitution. They have caused depressions, recessions, wars, inflation, financial crisis, bailouts, housing crisis, high unemployment, and financial instability. The very thing they said would not happen happened. In addition, they channel and funnel money under, over and around our heads to politicians and government officials from the local level to the federal level. They also support a "shadow" government of secret agencies that get funded every year without voting or oversight of any kind. All of this is immoral and unconstitutional. We do not live in a Constitutional Republic any more.

Everything in society is run by money. The money however has become tainted. If this were a Monopoly game, and the banker guy was running downstairs making copies of those gold $500 dollar bills, the game would be rigged and he could pick the winners and losers, the same thing in real life! The stock market and its brokers, insurance companies, retirement plans, hardware stores, retail outlets, gas stations, and lemonade stands are all dealing with this "toxic" cash. Unless you spend it right away, it melts away like a Popsicle and loses its value over time. Legal tender laws force honest people to exchange goods and services with this "mafia money". When people deal with dishonest money, it makes the people dishonest. That is why some of us barter and trade and avoid dealing with money, because bartering is more out in the open, above board and honest. There is no attachment to taxes, inflation, and the long arm of government. All people still deserve and should expect honest or sound money, not funny money.

In the book; "A Game as Old as Empire" Steven Hiatt edits a collection of true stories dealing with the web of worldwide financial corruption. The Federal Reserve makes huge amounts of money available for the IMF to use around the world. The money is put to use, not to assist poverty stricken areas, but to further rob and pillage foreign lands and force the people to work their entire lives paying off massive loans as their countries are stripped of their resources. Here is a rundown of the contents…
   1. Economic Hit Men are hired to cheat countries out of

billions of dollars, "funneling money from the World Bank and foreign aid organizations to corporations and wealthy families. They use fraudulent financial records, rigged elections, payoffs, extortion, sex and murder".

2. Third World countries pay $375 billion per year in debt payments. It is a "web of control-financial, political, and military-that maintains the system and explains why it's so hard for Third World countries to escape".

3. Petrodollar deposits in international banks recycle money into new loans to developing countries.

4. Dirty money from drug trafficking, kickbacks, tax evasion, and money laundering totaling $500 billion per year flows from poor countries into offshore accounts.

5. 15 billion dollars was lost or stolen from the BCCI (Bank of Commerce and Credit International) before it was shut down. The bank funded such clients as Osama bin Laden and the CIA.

6. Atrocities in the Congo have been funded by Western corporations because they seek a cheap source of coltan, needed for making semiconductors which are then used to produce cheap cell phones and laptops.

7. Iraq will lose billions of its oil dollars to foreign companies in oil production sharing agreements.

8. Third World countries were supposed to receive billions in financial aid which would help the people progress. Instead, the rulers ran off with the money and forced the poor to work towards paying the debt.

In the Philippines, The Marcos regime was financed by the World Bank in the name of development and modernization. Instead they received martial law and no economic development.

9. The world's second largest financial institutions are called export credit agencies. They rely on billions of dollars in bribes to finance unneeded facilities and arm sales to strife torn countries.

10. Poor countries in Latin America and Africa are given

debt relief amounting to a small percentage of the total amount owed. The strings attached are so extensive, it actually makes matters worse than before the money is granted.

11. The global system of exploitation can be reformed with a system of global justice.

Obviously, the fiat-paper money system is taking assets from the American worker by force and funneling the money overseas to dubious financial centers. The poor remain destitute with no hope of getting better off just as the corrupt wealthy run away with the millions garnered from both the American taxpayer and the common peasants of the world. We are told every year that huge amounts of money are sent overseas for foreign aid when all along, it's nothing but foreign corruption.

The LIBOR scandal is one of the biggest financial swindles in history. Wikipedia says; "The Libor is an average interest rate calculated through submissions of interest rates by major banks in London. The scandal arose when it was discovered that banks were falsely inflating or deflating their rates so as to profit from trades, or to give the impression that they were more creditworthy than they were. Libor underpins approximately $350 trillion in derivatives. The banks are supposed to submit the actual interest rates they are paying, or would expect to pay, for borrowing from other banks. The Libor is supposed to be an overall assessment of the health of the financial system because if the banks being polled feel confident about the state of things, they report a low number and if the member banks feel a low degree of confidence in the financial system, they report a higher interest rate number. In June 2012, multiple criminal settlements by Barclays Bank revealed significant fraud and collusion by member banks connected to the rate submissions, leading to the scandal.

Because Libor is used in U.S. derivatives markets, an attempt to manipulate Libor is an attempt to manipulate U.S. derivatives markets, and thus a violation of American law. Since mortgages, student loans, financial derivatives, and other financial products often rely on Libor as a reference rate, the manipulation of submissions used to calculate those rates can have significant negative effects on consumers and financial markets worldwide." Just one more way bad money is used to ambush and attack the assets of the common person.

The gold standard was once a worldwide rock that kept us on solid ground and kept dishonesty to a minimum. Banks were limited on how much fractional reserve they could carry. Sometimes countries would go off the gold standard to prepare for war or some calamity, but at least the citizens knew about it, it was more out in the open. Fort Knox was once the guarded sanctuary of the countries gold supply, harboring the stacks of pure gold that backed up our money as per the Constitution. It has not been audited since the Eisenhower era. At this point, all the gold may well be gone, sold off and secretly transferred to the hidden vaults of private banks around the world. We now have a money system that "rides" by itself, backed with nothing. The dollar may be the world's reserve currency since 1971, the king of all money, but it floats on its own and is the recipe for one disaster after another. Through the corrupt Federal Reserve and the IMF, our toxic money is laundered and sent around the world for reasons and purposes we will never know, 16 trillion between 2007 and 2010. It can only lead to financial bubbles back home, and ultimately, a total collapse of the system.

It reminds me of "running through the sprinkler" as a child. There would always be one kid hiding behind the house next to the faucet where he had total control of the water flow. He would secretly watch through the bushes while turning the faucet on and off, or sometimes slowly increasing or decreasing pressure, watching the reaction of his friends at the other end of the supply line.

The Federal Reserve operates much the same way, twisting the money valve and watching how society reacts to it. The Fed has the incredible power to bring life and prosperity to the land or they can destroy it, turning it to dust. We must wrestle the control of money from them and reclaim this great power for ourselves.

The proper supply of money is much like the proper level of oil in a car's engine. Too much oil and the pressure increases, too little and the gears smoke and grind. In the money world, illegal profit can be made by adjusting the supply of money too high or too low. That is why we rarely have the right supply.

It has been said that the best way to rob a bank is to own one. The following is a letter I sent to the local high school...

I think it important in today's global world that high school students become aware of the power and influence of the Federal Reserve System, the International Monetary Fund (IMF) and other world organizations. Through manipulation of the monetary system they are able to supercede the U.S. Constitution and make the Congress and President virtually irrelevant. We are supposed to live in a Republic where the elected leaders work and defend "we the people". It is obvious politicians are working for someone else other than the people; they sell out to special interests leaving the public with very little representation, and few choices at the voting booth.

There is no point in learning economics unless students are made aware of this long standing problem. The Fed is a private banking cartel, a hybrid of big financial powers and government insiders. It is partly owned by foreign interests and works together with corrupted officials here to bring us an over $14 trillion deficit, interest payments on our own money, and the almost complete devaluation of the dollar.

Now they push for a world currency along with the decline of Middle America through intentional manufactured financial crisis and endless wars. There is no transparency and a refusal to be audited on secret transactions (that any American would protest). Over the years they have worked with international corporations to manipulate teachers colleges, the education system and the media to disguise who they are and what they are doing.

It's finally time for students to learn the truth. The sleeping giant of America is awake and suspicious. Through the efforts of the Tea Party and other patriotic organizations, the secrets and cover-ups of the Federal Reserve System are being exposed.

It is very disappointing and disheartening when high school students learn not more than a passing overview of the Fed. They remain clueless and unaware of its actual mission and its unconstitutional workings. I submit this is no accident. The ruling elites and money powers have seen fit to produce a world where people

are more interested in reality TV, sports, movies and other useless forms of entertainment. The minimal political interest we have is a pendulum swinging
between the right and the left, when in fact both sides work for the same masters. Students must resort to the internet, talk radio, and other alternative news sources for good information. They cannot rely on libraries, public schools or politicians. The education system is supposed to be the center of learning, the teaching of general knowledge. Instead it is the center of superficial information, and a mask on reality. Can you imagine the excitement in school and around the community if the fire of truth was lit for us!

Most people have no clue about the Federal Reserve; they may have a branch nearby and know nothing about its functions and connections. Central banking was frowned upon by early leaders like Thomas Jefferson who said it is more of a threat to liberty than a standing army. Most don't realize we are on a fiat money system and our savings are subject to devaluation. I say a real study in economics is not complete without a thorough investigation of the Federal Reserve System. We have the right and deserve to have a hard, sound monetary system. We need to shed the current regime which encourages fraud and criminal activity leading to crisis, wars, and poverty. The criminals who silently manipulate humanity from behind the scenes should be exposed for what they are so we can set a course for a better, brighter future.

Needless to say, the letter went unanswered.

Facebook can be used to share political positions with others around the world. Here is an example of one of my postings;

Ronald Dixon; The main problem is that we are not paid for our work with real money, we are given Federal Reserve Notes which, if not spent immediately, are in turn inflated and devalued. That is why they can steal from our retirement funds and savings and investments. The authors of the Constitution knew this would happen and they addressed this problem in article 1 section 10. It stipulates nothing but gold and silver coin is to be used. It was that way until 1933 when FDR forcefully confiscated all gold coins. The Federal Reserve is unconstitutional in its very existence. This is not a Democrat or Republican problem, it's a total lack of intelligence on the part of the American people. The public schools are keeping monetary issues like this in the dark.

From there others put comments in, some agreeing, some absolutely in disagreement. The point is that we have open conversation, unlike the past where things were limited between people, especially miles apart.
 Here is a parody of what might happen if the American people remain unaware of the true nature of money. Given the high level of economic ignorance in this country, it would not be surprising if...

Seven Democrat senators and three Republicans are devising a bill called the Money Normalcy Act. Under the proposed law, everyone in the country would have access or have in their home a money printing machine. Anytime cash is needed to pay bills or go shopping, the device would be available to use without limit. This would bring fairness to all people, at all times and phase out banks, credit cards and loan companies. It would also serve to finally obtain equality among all Americans. It is expected to have the support of all Democrats and established Republicans. The only opposition will come from the Libertarian Party who says it would bankrupt the country and there would be no reason for anyone to work. Supporters of the bill call the Libertarians fear mongers, hateful of human equality, fairness and progress.

The financial element has the American people so deceived that the "Money Normalcy Act" would probably pass into law with no questions asked.

The following is a question I sent in to a Republican debate in 2011 for the candidates to answer. They never used it but it would have been the right type of question to ask...

The Federal Reserve is coming into the spotlight lately as an institution having more power than most people realize. How would you insure that the Fed provide sound money so the everyday worker can be rewarded with real money and not inflatable paper?

On the page 63 is an image of Franklin Roosevelt's gold order of 1933 to be "posted in a conspicuous place".
I suppose people didn't realize the extent of the situation. There was not much of a fuss as the gold coins were simply handed in to the Federal Reserve in return for paper bills. Citizens thought they were doing the right thing to help the country. FDR was a trusted man who was elected to high office four times in a row. What the people were really doing was trading their constitutional rights for worthless pieces of paper in the windows of the local bank. The lesson here is that each generation needs

to fight the revolution again. We must be vigilant. If we let our guard down, just for a moment, the money powers will gladly step in and take our rights away in a flash.

There was no reason for the depression to take place. It was a carefully planned, methodical looting of the American people that started as far back as the Woodrow Wilson era. When the government went bankrupt in the early 1930s, a repayment plan to the bankers had to be worked out. First the actual gold money was confiscated and then the Social Security plan was instituted to force everyone to pay back the bankers debt. As soon as the money is collected, it is spent. There is not nor has there ever been a private lock box for each individual. Workers of today are forced to pay directly to retired citizens in what amounts to be a massive pyramid scheme, another reason why we are always under the threat of financial calamity.

The public schools should teach children that abundance is a good thing and that we should all strive to be wealthy. Instead, the upper class is demonized and prosperity is frowned upon as children go through the left-leaning school system. Children should be taught all about the Federal Reserve System from day one, which is in fact a private company controlling our nations monetary supply. We should be taught how to own gold and silver from an early age and how to be thrifty and save money for retirement, and then we can eliminate the costly social security system and even the IRS forever. There are many more honest ways to finance government than a wealth robbing income, medicare and social security tax, especially if we get government back down to manageable levels. A managed government system encourages fraud, waste and poverty while a free and private economy encourages wealth, dignity and prosperity for all.

POSTMASTER: PLEASE POST IN A CONSPICUOUS PLACE.—JAMES A. FARLEY, Postmaster General

UNDER EXECUTIVE ORDER OF THE PRESIDENT

Issued April 5, 1933

all persons are required to deliver

ON OR BEFORE MAY 1, 1933

all **GOLD COIN, GOLD BULLION, AND GOLD CERTIFICATES** now owned by them to a Federal Reserve Bank, branch or agency, or to any member bank of the Federal Reserve System.

Executive Order

FORBIDDING THE HOARDING OF GOLD COIN, GOLD BULLION AND GOLD CERTIFICATES

[body of executive order]

FRANKLIN D. ROOSEVELT

For Further Information Consult Your Local Bank

GOLD CERTIFICATES may be identified by the words "GOLD CERTIFICATE" appearing thereon. The serial number and the Treasury seal on the face of a GOLD CERTIFICATE are printed in YELLOW. Be careful not to confuse GOLD CERTIFICATES with other issues which are redeemable in gold but which are not GOLD CERTIFICATES. Federal Reserve Notes and United States Notes are "redeemable in gold" but are not "GOLD CERTIFICATES" and are not required to be surrendered.

Special attention is directed to the exceptions allowed under Section 2 of the Executive Order

---

CRIMINAL PENALTIES FOR VIOLATION OF EXECUTIVE ORDER
$10,000 fine or 10 years imprisonment, or both, as provided in Section 9 of the order

Secretary of the Treasury

Yes, gold coins were confiscated in 1933 by Franklin Roosevelt. There was a penalty of jail time and fines for not cooperating. Again, the USA was bankrupt and the Federal Reserve collected the gold from the American people as payment. The social security system was put into effect to essentially make additional payments to the Fed for a perpetual debt that can never be paid off. The depression was a terrible affliction imposed on the good people of this country for no reason other than to degrade and control the masses while enriching international bankers and their government connections. The 30's should have been a time of prosperity and human advancement. Instead it was a long period of misery and strife. In 1975, Ron Paul's Gold Commission helped to make the ownership of gold coins legal once again for the common citizen.

According to the Federal Reserve website of Minneapolis, 95% of the value of the 1910 dollar was gone as of 2009. In defense they claim money has "relative value" based on the moment of time it's in. Relative value however does not help the people on fixed incomes who lose purchasing power as the years go on. As the Fed pumps more liquidity into the system, our lifestyles decline and it dawns on us that we don't have as much as we used to. It seems like we work twice as long to get the same result. As a child I was told to get a good job and I would be able to have a nice home and a lake cabin. As it turned out, it takes three jobs just to have one home and no lake cabin. This is the hidden effect of a central bank's power. The money we make from work quite literally is spent all over the world in the form of bailouts and handouts. It goes to enrich the lucky few who happen to know how the game is rigged.

The Dodd/Frank banking reform bill of 2010 actually expands the powers of the Fed by making them consumer watchdogs and giving them the power to break up large companies. President Obama went on to sign the bill that actually preserves and protects the money powers. Meanwhile Ron Paul's popular "Audit the Fed" attachment received minimum attention even though it exposed the Fed's money laundering activities to the tune of $16 trillion.

Again, we can see the problem with "fiat' money. If human beings are given the opportunity to use it, they will use it and eventually *some* will abuse it. That is human nature. That is why the founding fathers outlawed its use in the Constitution.

One of the biggest scams is the partnership between government agencies, bankers and large corrupt companies. What they do is secretly run a business into the ground intentionally only to ask the willing government for a bail out. Then the government and the failed business split the ill-gotten money. This has been done especially with banks and savings and loans, but also with car companies, railroads and other big business. The FDIC is always right there to use taxpayer money for bail outs. Car companies like General Motors and Chrysler, freight train companies, and public unions. The list goes on. The point is that the Federal Reserve is always there to dole out our hard earned cash to all sorts of places, people, and things without us knowing about it. Every time they print money or bail out a company, it slowly eats away at our assets and our savings. I stand on the side of all honest people when I say we must have *monetary reform* and an overhaul of the two party system. We can't reelect these same people over and over and expect different results!

The interest in Presidential debates is proof the American people are drinking the same old Kool-Aid again. The two parties will have little effect on this country as long as the Fed continues to be the glass ceiling. The Fed chairman still has the power to push the

magic money button and increase the funds of central banks and corporations worldwide without going through Congress. It is digital theft of the highest order. 70% of Americans do not even have $500 in cash on hand. We are in financial slavery and don't even know it.
The two parties follow the marching orders of the Fed and promote their hand-picked candidates. Coke and Pepsi are promoted the same way even though other companies make better products. We buy what is advertised. A vote for either party is completely wasted because the direction of the country will not change with either one of them in power. The evidence is the general downward trend of our prosperity and liberty the last 50 years, we have less and less no matter who is elected (selected).

It could be called the fourth branch of government, the Federal Reserve that is. It is a hybrid banking-government organ that has tremendous power over us all as it spends/loans/grants trillions of dollars without any congressional oversight, debate, or discussion from congress. The great secret of money manipulation has been kept in the closet for a hundred years. High schools make sure there is never any serious discussion of how money really works. It is glossed over and the truth is carefully hidden.
  Ron Paul, a champion of freedom and liberty has succeeded in passing a bill called Audit the Fed. Although partially intact, it did force some information to be released to the public. As mentioned before, a stunning 16.1 trillion dollars had been released by the Fed from 2007-2010! Again, there was no oversight or debate, the money was simply spent. How can this happen under our noses? What can we do about it? Ron Paul's book "End The Fed" explains the situation we are in and how we got here. Some people would say our

money is produced by the government. The Bureau of Printing and Engraving may produce the physical money, but its value is determined by Federal Reserve practices. The endless line of credit the Fed extends to so many interests has to stop!

The Fed is supposed to preserve the value of our money through its independent policies; instead it debases the money to suit the needs and conveniences of a deficit spending government.

Obviously, Fanny Mae, Freddy Mac, the Federal Reserve and big bankers colluded together with the FDIC to cause the financial collapse of 2007. It was a scheme hatched in the 1980s which paid the financial crooks big dividends. Programs like the "Community Reinvestment Act" enticed people to take loans out on homes they could not afford. It was a program designed to "help the poor and minorities". The loans were then "packaged" and resold to cover up the crime like dirt rolled up in a rug. Years later, when the loans came due and there was no money, the money was then extracted from the working taxpayer. Millions of hard working people saw the value of their homes, savings and assets reduced significantly. The elaborate money grab took place with no one going to prison. In fact, there is a lot of laughing and celebration of an embezzlement well done!

Efforts are being made to develop an algorithm which has the capability to trace all financial transactions to their source. This means the financiers behind the 2007 financial collapse can finally be identified. We are set to uncover the world's biggest financial scandal. Is there a conspiracy to shut down this knowledge? Time will tell.

<u>Fractional Reserve Banking</u> allows banks to literally loan out money they don't have on hand. If ordinary people knew the nature of the game, it would end quickly. This method has been used by our first central banks which

loaned out huge sums of money to the public, creating a booming economy, only to draw back the money supply creating a downturn which enabled them to seize property through foreclosure and bankruptcy. Profits were then kept by the central bank and its affiliates. This engineered boom/bust cycle is the same process by which today's Federal Reserve operates, only on a much larger scale. The great depression is an example of intentional engineered bust cycle. The United States experienced massive growth in the 70 year period without any Central Bank starting in 1840. As soon as the Central Bank returned to life in 1913, we have been under the threat of war and economic calamity. The great financial empire operates outside of government oversight. This empire absorbs its profit from the American people tax free. The following is a list of the owners of the Federal Reserve;

The Rothschilds of London and Berlin; Lazard Brothers of Paris; Israel Moses Seif of Italy; Kuhn, Loeb and Warburg of Germany; and the Lehman Brothers, Goldman Sachs and Rockefeller families of New York.

Only 4 percent of all money is in the form of cash, the rest is simply a computer entry which makes it simple to reach into your pocket and steal money. Individuals go through a bank screening process before any "loan approval". This gives the *appearance* of banks loaning real money when in reality they are creating money out of the clear blue sky. There is no risk to the bank what so ever.

The abuse of fiat money is not only the crime of the century, but also the tool used to enslave humanity through the ages. Paper money is the blood of tyrants. Jesus chased the money changers out of the temple for good reason. It is a crime leading to wars, inflation and economic turmoil causing the destruction of whole countries. It is the tool of governments to manipulate and control the unknowing masses. The crime rarely leads to the perpetrators getting caught or even recognized. It is the thief living among us that comes on to us like a friend but robs us of our freedom, wealth and liberty. The elite money men make sure there is barely a mention of the monetary system in the schools and in the media to keep us ignorant and uniformed. Those who learn the financial ins and outs can then manipulate the money system. They are sociopath, mentally unstable, power hungry, and immoral. They are the inferiors who rule over us. The Constitution was written under the assumption that people would be moral. In an immoral world, the document will not work. That is why the government is in the business of blurring the lines of right and wrong.

~ Sound Money and Gold~

There is something truly emotional about gold. The yellowish metal reflects light and easily melts into brilliant coins and jewelry. We search the shipwrecks in deep ocean waters, and hammer down inside the earth, chiseling in an ongoing, maddening frenzy to obtain the mineral. It has enticed fathers to leave their families and travel west to Colorado, California and Alaska. It has been the fate of nations and been a major force in the direction of human history. Just what are the advantages to owning gold?

1. A great way to turn your paper money into a hard asset. The government cannot wave a magic wand and devalue gold like it can with paper. It is like real estate, tangible and three dimensional. If you work for a reward, may that reward be in gold so no one can take it from you. You can lose great sums of money in stocks, mutual funds, in the bank, and even

under the mattress in the form of inflation. Gold gets you off the grid and holds your wealth permanently.
2. Identity thieves can steal money from your bank account, credit card, social security number, or even a cash machine, but they cannot touch real gold in your possession.
3. Gold is easily recognized, and can be bought and sold anywhere in the world.
4. It has out-performed most everything in the stock market for the last 20 years, so even though there is no guarantee of profit, its track record is beyond compare. It always does well in an economic collapse.
5. A great way to pass along wealth to your family.
6. If you like shopping, spending money, or have a spending compulsion, why not buy gold? You can't lose! It's fun to search for and find various gold and silver coins in catalogs and internet sites. The best part is you are buying something of real value, real money, not clothes, trinkets, or do dads that eventually lose value and end up in a second hand store.
7. Most of all, when you own gold, you are holding the most sought after metal in human history. The emotional charge you get from its shining brilliance brings on a feeling of well-being and good luck. The Bible says money is the root of all evil. I interpret that to mean "the misuse of fiat money" is the root of all evil. After all, Jesus chased those (Federal Reserve) money changers out of the temple in a fit of rage.

The Bible says the streets in heaven will be paved in gold. That tells me gold is the blood of the gods.

It is important for America to return to gold and silver coinage. A few states have legalized it. Paper money is a lot like a perishable food, it has to be eaten (spent) quickly before it spoils. If you choose to save it or invest it, inflation will eventually spoil its value. Gold is immune from the effects of inflation; it is one of the few things we have left to preserve wealth.

Judy Shelton is a former professor of economics, an author and contributor to the Atlas Economic Research Foundation and the Wall Street Journal. Her book "A Guide to Sound Money" was presented to members of Congress for their consideration. The guide lays out the importance of sound money in history and its value today. The Constitution allows for the coining of money through the Treasury, not the general printing of it by the money powers. There is a difference. The return to sound money would protect our savings and investments from the tool of inflation which secretly robs us of our wealth. It also stops the abuse of political power. Sound money is the single most important issue of our time, and all time.

The economist Ludwig von Mises (1881-1973) has been kept deliberately obscure. His life, teachings and theories have been ignored and kept in the dark. He had great influence on the development of the Austrian School of Economics. Libertarians like Ron Paul and Peter Schiff subscribe to this philosophy. The Austrian school accepts that the consumer decides what is to be produced and in what quantity. Attempts by a government to determine the means of production cannot work because exact calculations on what is to be produced are impossible.
Von Mises proved that socialism in all of its forms simply cannot work.
He was born in what is now the Ukraine, near Austria. His parents were wealthy with connections to Austrian nobility.

At the age of twelve, he could speak four languages. He was eventually influenced by Carl Menger, Max Weber and Eugen von Bohm-Bawerk. He taught at Vienna University from 1913-1934. During this time he was an economic advisor to individuals connected to the Austrian government. Von Mises was a hard worker, careful and organized, precise and deliberate in his work and analysis.

He later went to Switzerland and fled to New York after Hitler took over Germany. He was an unpaid professor at New York University from 1945-1969. After the war, Europe had to be rebuilt and much of what Von Mises believed came into practice. He was directly involved with the reconstruction of Europe. Since the governments had been defeated and were weak and out of power, the open market was all that was left to rebuild and replenish the conquered and bewildered nations. One of the greatest economic booms in all of history took place at that time, producing abundant evidence that the free market system not only works, but is far superior to any other system. Europe had rebuilt, retooled and was reborn out of the ashes of WW2.

Austrian economics, free society, free trade, liberty, limited government, non-aggression, non-interventionism, self- governance, self-ownership, libertarianism and spontaneous order are all related catch phrases of this free market approach.

"Human Action" is the title of one of his great works. He distinguishes between free and government controlled markets. Business cycles are caused by government interference. Without a market economy, it is impossible to organize and lay out an economy over complicated systems throughout the country. Demand cannot be known without prices; therefore planned economies cannot and do not work as seen in the collapse of the Soviet Union. After the country fell, a notable socialist type economist Robert Heilbroner admitted von Mises was right all along. The consumer is the ultimate decision maker, not a government agency. It is best to allow freedom of the people, not government, to naturally dictate the flow of the economy.

Ayn Rand and Adam Smith should be mentioned at this time. Rand was a friend of von Mises and a great novelist dealing with issues of human liberty and free market economics. "Atlas Shrugged" and the "Fountainhead" are classic books and films of human struggles and individual victories. In 1776, Adam Smith of course set the world abuzz with his work called "Wealth of Nations". In it he laid out the foundation of free trade and economic expansion, showing how the natural "selfishness" of humanity is the one thing that somehow brings us all together for the general good. He was influential in the way nations began allowing free trade since both sides of an individual trade were benefiting.

Economist Milton Friedman was also a great champion of freedom and the free markets. He and many other organizations and individuals including the Atlas Foundation have given us a world of good facts and information. We need that today to convince people from all walks of life that we desperately need to reclaim freedom, liberty, and a solid money policy. Its time we resist the tides of big government and totalitarianism that are creeping upon us. Like butterflies, we have been wasting time chasing paper airplane money when we should have had real gold all along, like the constitution stipulates. The working poor don't need another minimum wage increase; they need to get paid in real money, silver and gold. That in itself would bring them out of poverty and prevent the bankers from stealing their wealth. Any study in the history of money debasement will show you that as the value of money is tightened, poverty increases and the morality of the country declines. We can see this happening in the United States the last 40 years, since we left the gold standard.

I envision a return to real money. Legitimate business would be poised to do much better than right now. They would be inspired to create new and better products, hire more people, train them better and reward them with actual gold and silver. This would create a chain reaction to sell more product and services at ever cheaper rates while their employees would reap the great benefits of their paychecks. The purchasing power of the money would be at a high level which would bring about increased spending, improving the already fast moving economy. All people rich and poor would have great opportunities and motivation to drive forward and enrich their lives. Crime would go down since being honest and working hard would actually pay off nice dividends. Problems like domestic abuse and alcoholism rising from economic insecurity would be eradicated and minimized. People and their families would be happier, more prosperous and secure because the money they earn would have a valid store of wealth. It's all possible if we as a society demand control of the money supply. We must take it back from the private bankers. We can then set the value of the dollar, outlaw inflation, and look forward to a healthy, wealthy nation once again.

So what do we do now?
Realize that We the People have the Constitutional right to sound money. The government has the obligation to protect us from dishonest funny money. We have the
right to be rewarded for our hard work with the real thing, money that cannot be dissolved or inflated. The first thing is to bring about awareness. Tell friends and co-workers, tell the media, write posts on the internet.

Above all, do your own research, read, and read some more. The next thing is to vote and support leaders and politicians who are aware of this and are willing to eradicate bad law and stand behind the Constitution.

Are you still unconvinced? Is this some conspiracy theory? You may be surprised to learn that typical Democrats and Republicans are the biggest conspiracy theorists. The media is constantly whipping up new charades, false claims, phony polls, and ridiculous stories to get the public excited and mislead us down the road of gossip and useless news. Meanwhile, those of us who are beyond the circus of two party politics are quietly digging into the real hard core information concerning the new world order. This is not a theory, this is conspiracy fact. The actual criminals hide behind a smokescreen set forth by the media. The average person has no contact with them until we pull the money strings. They finally revealed themselves during the 2011 audit of the Federal Reserve. Many Fed associates, banking officials and politicians were against the audit and these are the people who have been called out and reared their heads to the public. Yes, the conspiracy is real and it must be stopped. I look for a time when all people understand the value of sound money and that money should be a store of value for the individual and not a means of inflation and manipulation by an outside force.

It is important to tell the school board, teachers and superintendents of your thoughts on the subject. It is supposed to be their job to teach basic knowledge and not "hide" things from the public. Teachers themselves are unaware of this history and information. They may be surprised to hear from you and may not even know what you are talking about. They are also the victims of the system. The idea is to create an explosion of information.

Once we have this flow on the move, a revolution will be in the making. Lies will be exposed and the truth will be heard!

In conclusion, political reforms are important, but little is going to change for the better until monetary reform is complete. The two parties shuffle themselves in and out of office year after year and their actions are basically ineffective because we have a super authority on top bringing new money into creation which completely bypasses the democratic process.

There is much discussion of politics in the media and in academic institutions. Degrees are awarded in political science, the study being complex and filled with complex possibilities. However, I submit that when a central bank exists, the system is *automatically* socialistic in nature because the wealth is redistributed by the printing of money. The problem is that wealth is transferred from the poor and middle class and given to the privileged few at the top! I feel it's impossible to have a constitutional republic if that includes a central bank. A central bank (like the Federal Reserve) is legally able to release new money into the system without the consent of the people or its representatives. With every release comes a devaluation of the existing money which amounts to legalized theft. I look forward to a world without paper fiat money, a world where each and every individual retains the value of what they have worked for. A government cannot bring equality by debasing the money. Redistribution is a failed policy. The way to reward people with an honest day's work is having honest money to begin with. Only then, can a great society exist.

"I have discovered the secret to the philosopher's stone, which is to make gold out of paper"

~John Law 1707

Chapter Three: Right, Wrong or Left?

*"defending freedom means defending
those you disagree with"*

There are some shocking moments that happen from time to time when that inner light bulb goes on. Moments that challenge your view of the world and knock out the foundation you thought was so stable.

I was riding home on the seventh grade bus one nice day as the warm breeze swirled in through the little square windows. I watched the trees go by and felt the hard bumps of the stiff suspension. Somehow my friend and I got on the subject of God. He said "I don't believe in God." It was a shock! A statement so plain and easily spoken, how could he say such a thing? How could he not believe? He's such a nice kid! He went on to explain how he was raised to be an atheist. From that time on, every time I rode my bike past his house, I thought: That's where the atheists live! But I accepted it and the world went on somehow, and I survived.

My view of the political world was very limited as I grew up. School avoided the subject and at home I was taught that Republicans were for the rich and Democrats for the poor. That's where it began and that's where it ended. The only discussion was which Democrat to vote for. In ninth grade I was finally taught the difference between a

Liberal and Conservative, and the teacher thought those should be the names of the parties themselves.

It finally happened in college in political science class. The instructor simply said Reagan will win this year's election because he's promising to dramatically cut the size of the administration, instead of raising taxes. This will put more money in the hands of the people, where it belongs. Right then I was hooked! Of course! Make the government smaller and we will be better off, we can keep more of our own money! That was 1980 and Reagan won by a landslide. Now I thought I knew everything... but no.

~The Page Turner~

I once knew an intellectual named Terry Thomas who could make history come alive with endless discussion and quests into the nature of reality and the logic of the country's founding. He always had a paperback in his hand, his finger- the bookmark. He could explain the causes of WW1 during a commercial break in a football game. I couldn't help but get a minor in history just being around the guy. I and a few friends would sit around for hours and mostly listen to his ramblings. He would talk of how the common person did not know too much of reality and history because of the inculcating function of the public school system. He was very much a patriot however, believing in the ideals and philosophy of the American Revolution. He shocked us with his thoughts on the Civil War. How Lincoln centralized power and brought on the conflict but having nothing to do with slavery. Some of the greatest names in history that we take for granted were actually the bad guys, and some of the most obscure leaders were the good guys. He said, "America is the land of golden opportunity but should be roundly criticized."

He talked of how the church once ran everything and now we have sort of an institutional tyranny quietly easing us into totalitarianism. He was indeed, a Libertarian. This is heavy stuff for a group of guys only interested in being in a rock and roll band! But his discussions would get us discussing amongst ourselves. Soon we were off on our own theories and philosophies of life. The important thing is that we were thinking, and thinking is the key.

He emphasized the importance of not letting the good things go unnoticed. Many are the armchair philosophers who spread doubt, fear, and negativity from their perched recliners, political wizards who never see the glass half full, it's always half empty. They need to know there is not a spook around every corner and a dark cloud drifting overhead. We have food to eat, a place to sleep, shoes to wear, cars to drive, and lives to be lived in spite of our downfalls and the hard times we go through. There is always some ray of hope or crack in the edifice which allows light to come in. The blind somehow see, the deaf find a way to hear, and the lonely always have hope. Always reach for whatever good there is and expand upon it.

Many times when young people break off from the church or school and form a new political reality they drift into some form of socialism. It seems like a natural thing to do. After all, it's the big businesses and powerful politicians that are to blame. A system that protects and defends the common man is more suited to what freedom is all about, right? It might be Progressive, liberal, left wing, Democrat, or Democrat Socialist, or some other such label. The problem with such ideologies is that they all lead to one thing and that is a power structure having one or a few people at the top and the rest milling around at the bottom. This leads to a large percentage of the wealth accumulated to a small percentage of people. When this happens, the common people are controlled and have no incentive to work and be productive. This has been the problem with the Soviet Union or Russia for hundreds of years. To me, it's the biggest waste of human talent and initiative in world history. Lives of millions have been wasted, plundered and stolen. Millions have been outright killed. The ingenuity and creative powers of generations of people have been lost to a Communist cesspool of human tragedy, robbing the world of great inventors, thinkers, creators, artists, and hardworking citizens. If you want a productive society, people have to have incentive to work and make money, to be able to keep the fruits of their labor for the benefit of themselves and their family. Getting up every morning and working for someone else or some socialist ideal is not going to inspire anyone to produce! The fountainhead of life is wealth. Wealth is the natural effect of hard work. Hard work is performed by humans who see a vision for themselves first and society second.

The traditional rank and file Democrat is a hardworking, church going, tax paying citizen who may or may not belong to a union, but supports unions none the less. The family may be poor or live in the suburbs at the middle class level of society. They take a vacation once a year as money and time allow and basically obey the laws and have some funds for retirement. They will rely on social security and Medicare as they grow old. They will pass their home to the wife or husband who will then pass it to the children. They tend to vote Democrat because they fear large companies will take over the country otherwise. They support public schools and gladly vote for yes for any district referendums. They are suspicious of any Republican because they represent "the rich."

Democrats believe we humans can handle only so much freedom and then big brother must step in and manage the rest. Regulation, laws, and taxation are thought to be a necessary function of an ordered, civilized society. The Democrats are always the defender of the poor and the destitute. There is never a shortage of misery, poverty and hopelessness for them to point to and make their case of ever expanding and far reaching government. They claim big companies and rich people only care about themselves and their money, and they in turn support politicians who support them.

The truth of the matter is this; if the rich spend too much time worrying about helping the poor, they have less time to do what they do best and that is make money and run a business. It is not only important, but necessary in a prosperous society to have individuals and corporations *laser focused* on their daily tasks. Everybody should hone their skills and dedicate themselves wholeheartedly to what they are doing. We need to give full attention to our activities and not be distracted by the world around us. *This in fact makes the world a better place and reduces poverty.*

Even after heavy taxation, American companies and workers still manage to donate billions of dollars per year. The totals would be much higher in a free market economy. Anyone tempted to support ideas of socialism and big government should look at the lessons of history. The freer the people, the better off the people are.

Overtaxing the wealthy has been the downfall of many nations and empires through history; the Athenian democracy, the Roman Empire, and in Spain when the wealthy Moors were driven from the land. It is tempting, but not rational to look at the poor and the rich and try to artificially "equalize" them. It is one thing to criticize the improper and illegal gain of wealth but quite another to complain about entrepreneurs gaining wealth honestly.

James J. Hill wisely summed it up in 1909;

"the effect upon industry, prosperity and national character of a constantly mounting tax rate is just as certain as the effect of drawing checks upon a bank to an annually larger and larger percentage of deposits made. In this way, insidiously and without realization by the general public, often under the specious names of improvement and reform, capital is dissipated, discouraged and quietly abstracted for industry. In this way the volume of employment is greatly lessened, because there is less capital for payrolls. In this way high prices and high wages and high taxes may all work together for the impoverishment of a nation by exactly the same process that works impoverishment of its soil. The countries in which such forms of taxation are carried out furthest are precisely those in which employment is scarce and precarious, and labor finds it necessary to lean more and more heavily each year upon the weakening arm of state and public charity. No state need ever borrow again if it is wisely and honestly governed."

Today's politicians should take a good look at Hill's statement, read it forwards and backwards, and apply it in their own surroundings, if they have any honest bone in their body.

In World War 2, the United States raced to develop the atomic bomb before the Germans. A secret place was chosen in Los Alamos, Nevada. Every single obstacle to human distraction was removed to allow the scientists to work full time on the bomb. Full power was given to the individuals there to dedicate their entire focus to the assignment. They weren't bogged down with taxes, regulation, and thoughts of community diversity. They were allowed full freedom to work, discover and finally complete the assignment in record time, a rare thing in governmental history.

Analysis of the great advancements of the industrial revolution tells us it was done in an environment of open markets and unbridled freewheeling individualism.

The government stood out of the way. Just think if individuals across America were lifted out of the burden of high regulation, taxes and governmental oversight? The great things we could accomplish!

If you have any doubts about the power of capitalism, take a close look at West Germany after WW2 and compare it to East Germany in the same time frame. West Germany was in ruins when the word got out there would be no real central government to hinder the reconstruction. A new currency was established in 1948 which made for sound money. This enabled an economic miracle to take place.

A free people worked and cooperated with each other to rebuild the country at a rapid pace and went on to enjoy a high standard of living in the 1950s and 60s. Contrast that with East Germany where a heavy handed central power stifled growth and created a disenchanted populace with a low standard of living. Their greatest accomplishment was a wall to keep people in. We must be vigilant in America because socialism can creep back to us slowly. At one time, not too long ago, a one income family could support a house in the suburbs, two cars and a lake home. Nowadays it takes two incomes to have half as much!

Once big government gets out of the way, lean, efficient government, private charities, and church organizations, (who are dedicated and focused themselves) can then step in and manage the caseload of the truly needy in society, saving the country trillions of dollars each year.

The current system is bogged down with heavy administration costs and inefficient bureaucracy that are bankrupting this country. If individuals and businesses succumb to collective thinking and behave like "part of the whole" permission is then given to government to expand beyond its proper role and function. It becomes too large and actually creates more of what it was meaning to prevent in the first place, and that is misery, poverty and hopelessness.

The greatest of all rights is that of the individual. Free individuals create the best of all possible worlds, not a perfect world but a place where the extremes and the severity of problems is reduced and the goodness of humanity is maximized.

<u>Libertarianism</u> calls for freedom. Freedom is a proven concept in this country. Our inventions and advancements have pushed civilization to new levels of prosperity and brought the very poor to a new level where they have real opportunity. The argument that the ever increasing complexity of civilization calls for bigger and more expansive government is fallacious thinking. The concept of freedom always has the same definition no matter what the situation; it is the same mechanism that works in the simplest societies all the way to the complicated, complex world we live in today. That means we should be free to pursue our dreams with a bare minimum of regulation and resistance. When distractions are taken away, individuals are free to focus their energies and use tunnel vision to pursue their goals. Leadership and coordination with other individuals then produce truly great things, things that would be impossible in a big government situation.

Democratic voters have their suspicious arrows aimed at the wrong people. It is not "the rich" who are taking too much of the pie. In a free society there is no pie because wealth is unlimited. It is not logical to rob Peter to pay Paul. Besides, how often does the government collect money from the rich and spend it on themselves?

It is proper to give all people the opportunity to move upward or downward as they so choose. Inequality is a sign of a healthy economy because with freedom, we end up at different levels for many different reasons. Artificially stacking people in the same boat just to achieve equality is ridiculous.

Libertarians point out a very serious problem. There exists an element which is above and beyond the Congress and the President. President Obama has called the Congress "ceremonial" in function. The right/left two party system is pure theatre specifically designed to keep us entertained and distracted. Instead of attacking each other, we need to identify the real culprits who exist beyond our normal range of sight. Ron Paul, Jesse Ventura, Alex Jones and others have identified these people. If one follows the money, they are revealed. If one threatens their source of funding by audit, they become agitated. The Federal Reserve System is a group of international bankers who run the country through the monetary system. They have unlimited wealth and power. They and other global organizations create war, and the boom and bust cycles of the managed economies of the world. Let us not argue amongst ourselves, we need to work together and focus on the real enemy. No government or elite class can stop an idea whose time has come. The idea now is to take back the country from those who conspire against us. Not by violence, not by raising a hand against anyone, never by force, but by the conviction of our ideas.

<u>The contemporary Liberal</u> is much more complex than the traditional rank and file Democrat. They have taken

on new concepts and beliefs and are more active in specialized groups and movements. Some personal freedoms are emphasized more often. They demand a new type of politician who caters to their individual needs and wants. They are organized and take full advantage of lobbying and influencing special interest groups. They are outspoken and active. They may be artists who ask for more funding or want a new museum. Environmentalists who demand more money for climate research or work to close off parts of the nation to industry and oil drilling to protect an endangered species. They may become extreme in protests and destruction of property. Abortion rights advocates, pro-union demonstrations, anti-smoking campaigns, light rail and mass transportation, and the unending drive to make government ever bigger and more intrusive on the lives of individuals. They believe, like Alexander Hamilton, the common people cannot watch out for themselves, they need an all-encompassing central government to control and run things. Government must be there to assist, manage and organize every facet of society or we will naturally flow into anarchy and chaos because somehow we are not up to the task.

As Terry Thomas pointed out, if human beings cannot be trusted, then why are human beings running the government? If we are basically evil, greedy, selfish, nasty and stupid, then why are we put in positions of power and control? Apparently politicians are something other than human!

There is a definite difference between the traditional and the contemporary Democrat, differences that the old guard is largely unaware of, and would be embarrassed by. One thing is for sure, the Democratic Party has perpetuated a great fraud on the American people. They claim to represent and defend the working poor, the "little guy", but they actually keep us in the dark and

limit our lives in many ways. They want us educated enough to stay out of trouble and earn a living and pay taxes, but wait...
We are not told about the Federal Reserve in school. We are not taught monetary functions and how credit and finance work. We are not warned about the corruption of government and banking, and the powers of the insider class. Instead, we the people are taught to go to work and keep quiet, and if there is no job we get assistance. If things seem wrong or out of place, blame the other party.

<u>The Republican Party</u> claims to be for economic freedom and liberty but they play an even more deceptive game. They are really the flip side of the same coin that pretend to fight for us in the artificial war between the two sides.
The typical Republican believes in a limited government along with a belief in a strong military presence. They are generally against heavy tax burdens on individuals and corporations, but hold views against personal freedoms like prostitution and drug legalization. The *old style* Conservative more closely resembles a Libertarian. The newer Conservative allows more big government in certain situations. Most evangelical Christians fall into this category and tend to be pro-life.

  What I see today is a Republican Party supporting the military plantation and the Democratic Party supporting the welfare plantation, both being a heavy burden on the American taxpayer. Libertarians support both economic and personal freedom. I submit the Libertarian Party holds the traditional Constitutional beliefs that not only built this country, but are the answer to taking back the country in the future.

What I see today is not so much a schism between conservative Republicans and liberal Democrats. What I see now is a growing gap between government workers and non-government workers, two factions of society growing farther and farther apart. This is the new war zone developing. Local, state and federal employees want their benefits, vacations, time off, early retirement and lax working conditions. They will fight, demand and coax anybody in a leadership position to not only protect their nest egg, but increase it in size. This is a natural reaction to protect themselves and their families but it comes with a price tag. It is at the cost of their neighbors and friends in the private sector. Government workers assume their money mostly comes from the taxation of the "rich." They have no qualms claiming additional funding for their pet projects and personal wage and benefit packages. What they don't understand is the money and funding comes at the expense of the common (private sector) worker. Many studies confirm the average government worker is paid better than their private sector counterpart. The public sector teacher, road worker, librarian, and middle manager are far more likely to negotiate a pay raise than the average worker in the private world. The money comes from complicated formulas that keep the taxpayer at arm's length from the state workers. Many times the taxpayer has no clue of this hidden process. Those who are supposed to protect the taxpayer find themselves in an ambiguous position, a conflict of interests. They bargain for public employees having been paid off or bribed by unions and money laundering schemes. It gives the government worker a tremendous advantage over the private employee.

For many years, this system has managed to survive under cover. The vast wealth of America has provided a sort of shield protecting the corruption of government. But now the game is over. It is obvious the country is broke. The nation has run out of money, we cannot print any more without dire consequences. Assets, home values, and retirement funds of the private worker have been drained to support big government and international bailouts of banks and countries. Everyone agrees the middle class is diminishing. The Democrats wrongly accuse "the rich" for stealing and looting the wealth of the average person. The real truth is that money is being extracted from the private worker to fund the average government worker. There is no mechanism to "tax the rich." If the rich are taxed, they simply increase the charge for their products or services; they pass along the increase to the consumer. For example, the cigarette lawsuit forced cigarette companies to pay many millions in damages. The money collected was simply spent by the state governments who received it. The price of cigarettes increased to make up for the loss. It was simply a shift of money from the smokers to the government. Another way business avoids taxation is to move to a tax friendly state or, as we have seen, move operations out of the country altogether. This causes job loss and unemployment.

The hidden problem, the invisible, unseen method used by elitists now and throughout history is the manipulation of the money itself. Yes, the rich and privileged are running away with our money but not in the way we think they are.

The accumulation of wealth is a great thing only if it is done honestly. Today we have many honest businesses that support their communities and provide safe places to work and prosper. The problem is when big business *conspires* behind the scenes with government to forge unholy alliances and make deals without proper legislative means and processes. The Federal Reserve provides the cover and stealth necessary to launder the funds and keep things invisible and hidden from the

public. The Republicans are made to appear the villains when in fact it's a combination of the corrupt two party system that is bought out and controlled by corrupted corporations. The answer is to break the bonds of these unholy alliances and restore the free market economy. Free markets and sound money will force all companies to compete on a level competitive playing field. We need to eliminate corporate/state fascism and bring back true free enterprise. It is the only proven way to naturally balance power for the benefit of all people. We have to vote for and elect people from outside the system. The Libertarian Party, Tea Party, and other political organizations provide the wisdom and knowledge necessary to take back the country for the common man.
It is time for the average government worker to realize their wealth and assets are on the back of their fellow private sector workers!

It has been said that politics is announcing what has already been put into place. The back room deals, the pay offs, and construction overbidding bring us to what we have today; beautiful results masking billions of wasted taxpayer dollars. The bottom line is that elements of free enterprise build what we have, but how much governmental chaos and disorder do we have to go through to get to the ultimate conclusion?
Towering skyscrapers, landscaped veneers, winding tree lined approaches, rolling golf courses, yachts skimming the harbors, Lear jets tracing across the skies, and long bridges spanning rocky cliffs. These are signs of a healthy, wealthy economy, the symbols of human achievement; results of hard work and ingenuity, the things that raise the level and quality of life for everyone, rich and poor, Democrat, Republican, everyone. Even great socialist thinkers and theorists finally had to admit that, yes, because of capitalism; the poor were indeed getting better off!

The wealthy should not be ignored or despised; they are the flower that blossoms when the plant is healthy and well fed. They are the sign of a good economy. Instead of seeking to confiscate their fortunes and money, we should be striving to be at their level. We should be taught in school to value wealth and teach how it works. Wealth should not be just tolerated, it should be celebrated. Youth spend too much time in useless pursuits and roads leading to self-gratification. Taxation should be removed for those under 20. Let them work and feel the gains and the power of reward. All too often they seek the quick buck in drug dealing, stealing and burglary. Working at a normal job should yield honest, tax free money.

Libertarianism is apart from the other two parties. It involves small, but effective government, government that revolves around local and states' rights. We need to defend our borders, not police the world. We need a central court system, not a justice system that allows hardened criminals to go free while putting drug dealers and prostitutes in jail for victimless offences. We need to unleash the power of individual people working and coordinating themselves in groups having leaders that produce and grow the economy; we need a free choice education system that will produce these leaders, inventors and technologists that will lead the way to the future. We need an education system away from the tentacles of government. We need to go back to the original playbook that builds lives and futures leading to wealth and prosperity. This is the playbook of liberty and freedom.

Pollution is an interesting example. The cleanest parts of town are always private business parks and boulevards. Corporate headquarters have sharp cut hedges, mowed grass and a lack of litter. Any public facility has a tendency to lack upkeep because it has no real owner.

Compare public parking ramps to private. I once worked at the JC Penney ramp in Anchorage, Alaska. Every night we would pick up all cigarette butts and trash. Every spring a total wash down and re-striping took place. The public ramp down the block was overrun with blowing litter, junk and the stairwells served as a hangout for teenagers and drug dealings. Evidence that private trumps public.

The private Pennsylvania turnpike was for years a model of clean, well maintained service for public thoroughfare. Once the superhighway was sold to the government, the quality of the road went down and the tolls went up.

Poor parts of town are riddled with graffiti, junk, trash and litter on every corner. Public housing apartments are sloppy and falling apart from lack of basic maintenance. This happens because there is no ownership, and the people are totally dependent on welfare checks and freebies from the government. This disrupts not only the surrounding environment, but also the family life of the inhabitants. Public property and crime go hand in hand. Private property stimulates upkeep, cleanliness, and good family life. Any rental unit will have less attention given to it than a private residence because there is not a vested interest in the property. Private property brings more prosperity to society and less pollution and waste.

Factories and industry are more likely to take care of their surroundings if they actually own the property. Many times, a manufacturer leases land from the government which makes them more likely to pollute the area because it's not their own property. National parks are scenes of overuse and land mismanagement. I would like to see groups like the Audubon society buy these areas, limit public usage and go on a user fee basis. It's not a matter of some people being evil and others good.

It's a matter of allowing all human beings to put themselves in a position of ownership, which reduces the chances of pollution, and increases the chances of a better, more productive life.

The mass media will always criticize Libertarians for being pro-drug and anti-government. The truth is that we Libertarians believe in a small, but effective government, a government that protects its people, instead of policing the planet with a worldwide military force. A government that puts criminals behind bars instead of filling the prisons with drug dealers and prostitutes while allowing rapists, murderers and child molesters free for lack of space. A government with a sound money standard that guarantees people actually get what they work for and keep it without fear of inflation or confiscation.

The drug world is an interesting phenomenon. The American people could end the problem tomorrow if we would simply end the use of recreational drugs! Since we insist on using marijuana and cocaine, we must take responsibility for supporting big government, the drug cartel, the murders, the violence and the drug pushing on our children. We could run the drug dealers out of town tomorrow if we cut off the demand, simple as that. If you use illegal drugs, you are adding fuel to the fire.

Efforts should be made by the people to demand the end of this costly drug war. We are filling the prisons with poor wayfaring youth who need help, not incarceration. In addition, there are actual good uses for marijuana. It is not addicting and destructive like its legal counterparts, cigarettes and alcohol. It can assist those with terminal illnesses, eye problems, and other medical needs. It is a more benign, natural help to the human body versus potentially dangerous and addicting prescription medications. Keeping it illegal is a full time interest of the pharmaceutical industry for obvious reasons.

The Libertarian position is as follows: as long as there is a demand, the supply will continue one way or another. Why should taxpayers be liable for billions of dollars going towards a failed drug war? There also is a growing body of evidence that shows law enforcement perpetuates the trade and flow of illegal drugs. For example, the CIA is known to have made billions off the international opium trade since the 50s and is connected to the Mexican cartels.

Interviews from drug kingpins in prison reveal interesting insights into the economics of illegal drugs. Many young people start using drugs because they sell them first. Lured by fast easy money, they become involved in the inside world of substance dealing and pushing. Along the way they try out and use their own inventory and become hooked and dependent on what they are selling. Decriminalizing these drugs would take away the incredible profits and slow down the experimentation that gets the youth of America initially started down the wrong road.

There is mounting evidence that our own government feeds off the enormous profits of illegal drug use. Narcotics units, police departments, prison workers, judicial systems and many other branches of government have large and ever growing budgets to handle the "drug war". It is a big industry. Indeed, the CIA among other units of government actually run drugs and assists cartels in doing their dirty work. The media plays its part by showing high profile arrests and symbolic drug crackdowns which keep the image of big government legitimate in the eyes of the public, while at the same time the Mexican border is left intentionally porous to allow the flow of drugs to go on without end, injecting

America with decay and contamination that also extends back into Mexico, making matters worse there.

The truth is that all drugs should be legal and the government minimized to give maximum freedom and liberty back to the people, and the people should take back their lives and become useful, productive and free members of society once again. The wide world of drugs both legal and illegal is a tool of the ruling powers to keep America internally corrupted. Americans are becoming mentally weak and unable to defend our own rights, and live as a free people. Instead, we are entertained, drugged up and rapidly becoming wards of the state, which leads to totalitarianism.

The Libertarians call for an end to the madness. All drugs should be decriminalized and or made legal based upon the decisions of each state. Prohibition is a complete failure and only strengthens drug cartels and increases government corruption making the matter much worse than it has to be.

The American people need to become better citizens, and better stewards if liberty, taking an interest in themselves and the community around them. Adults need to set an example and stop abusing drugs and alcohol. Let's get away from self-gratification and start thinking about others.

<u>Schools and Parents</u> need to teach the value of money and the healthy drive to obtain it, instead of condemning the "rich". Wealth is a good thing and leads to intelligence, morality and a step away from poverty, drugs and a welfare lifestyle. Instead, the government nurses people along like children, fostering generations of dependency.

If you ever serve on a jury, make it known you are aware that any person can be pronounced innocent on the grounds that you view a law as unjust. You have the right to nullify any case on those grounds.

In 1950, a typical family paid only 2% of their budget for taxes, by 2010, its 25% or more. We are spinning our wheels trying to make ends meet. We must have two wage earners to maintain the same pace as one wage earner years ago. So much for the lake home and vacations, it's a thing of the past. Again, this is due to the scandalous inflation of the dollar.

Foreign Aid is another waste of money. Billions are sent around the world with little or no improvement in the recipient's situation. In fact, to keep the money here and improve our own economy would be more beneficial to the world at large because free trade would be improved and increased. For years, money has been laundered from the Federal Reserve to the IMF which ends up as loans to poor countries. The people themselves never see the money as it goes directly to corporations which set up industries with the sole purpose of extracting resources from the land and export all profits, leaving nothing for the poor inhabitants. That is the true reason for poverty. It's not that the countries are poor; it's that they are being systematically pillaged of their land and resources.

Freedom of Speech is essential with no restrictions or censorship, also allowing dissenting opinion of the government itself. TV, radio, print media, and the internet should not be censored, but should be a place of ideas and debate.

Gun Ownership is an important right of law abiding citizens. Prohibition of such things like alcohol, drugs and guns does not work and goes against the Bill of Rights.
Banning guns only makes it easier for criminals with guns to perpetuate their crimes.

Health Care was affordable just a few years ago. Now, the government has intervened through Medicare, Medicaid, the FDA, and the Affordable Care Act. It is responsible for 50% of all costs. Insurance companies have colluded with government to intentionally cause an inflation of prices. This increase encourages the public to support and move forward legislation to socialize all care into a single payer system. A socialized system would discourage investment in new technology and scare away future doctors, and cause a massive increase in government bureaucracy, fraud, waste and death panels. What we need is a return to simple free market health care, deregulate the industry, limit lawsuits, and simplify it back to a user friendly system. Allow competition to return quality health care to America at a reasonable price for all.

<u>Immigration</u> is a major problem. 12 million illegal individuals make their home here, pay no taxes, use our welfare system and send whatever money they can back to Mexico. Mexicans are taught in school that the southern United States is actually their own territory that was stolen from them in the past and it's up to them to re-conquer it.

The fact is that Americans were originally invited to the area by Mexico to work the land and fend off cattle rustlers and natives. We later conquered the Mexican army and treaties were officially signed that made the land part of the United States. Today, because of corruption and poverty in Mexico, there are millions who wish to cross over to a better life. In years past, immigrants were funneled through Ellis Island. Many times people were turned away if they had an illness, a criminal record, or had no relatives to stay with. If they were allowed in, they had to learn English and assimilate into the culture, even changing their names. The system made for a smooth transition into society and exhibited productive American citizens. Today we have politically correct politicians and establishments catering to the

illegal flow of immigrants. What they get in return is votes, power, and authority at the cost of confusion, criminal activity and loss of jobs for the American people. Both political parties are guilty of allowing the flood of illegal immigration. Our leaders appear to be working along with international powers to "water down" middle class America and melt us into the rest of the world, thereby confiscating our wealth and assets.
The solution is a return to strong Constitutional law enforcement and requirements for any and all people who wish to immigrate here and become Americans.

At this moment the Patriot Act and the rise of the police state is crushing the privacy rights of the American citizen. The war on terror is being used as a pretext to systematically strip us of our Constitutional rights. A close look at the events of September 11, 2001 is now in order. New questions need to be asked and answered. Either the multibillion dollar security institutions of America completely failed to do their job or factions within our own government allowed or encouraged the attack upon the innocent workers at the twin towers. New investigations should be launched before our own government grows too big and conquers us from within.
Taxes are eating away at the pockets of working Americans. 250 billion is spent each year just in the military. The government at all levels is bloated and scandalous with fraud. We need to scale back the number of bases and serviceman worldwide. Many rich countries are on military welfare. The Constitution specifies protection from foreign enemies, not a worldwide police force dedicated to make war and create profit for international bankers and industries. We need to privatize services of government and cut taxes not only for common people, but for businesses that create the jobs and opportunity.

Endless are the examples of government corruption from the local level to the high echelons of the invisible ruling class. The maintenance man at city hall might be taking the county truck on personal errands. The clerk or administrator might be skimming money off of overcharged bills. Maybe the state patrol office has too many catered lunches per year. The post office buys too many football tickets for their employees. Private companies are overcharging the county for services and materials thereby bloating the budget for the taxpayer to pay. Maybe the roads are intentionally paved poorly so they can repave in a couple years. Does it seem that public employees get a lot of pension money, early retirement and paid days off? How often do doctors double bill Medicare for the same incident? Then we have the Fed printing billions of dollars behind the backs of the American people and bailing out corrupt banks and lending institutions after years of fraudulent practices and scams. OK, how many lawyers and judges accept bribes and payoffs every day? How many poor people abuse food stamps and welfare benefits? What about the military? Too many tanks, bombs and wars going on! Who pays for all this? We pay; the working middle class. We pay the big bill and it reduces the span, scope and context of our lives. We are then limited to what we can do.

  In spite of all this, we do have shelter, clothes to wear and food to eat. We have a high standard of living with cheap good and services. The free market still provides us with the latest gadgets, stuff and entertainment. It is still the land of opportunity, although not golden anymore. The country is slanted downhill, and we are slowly stumbling in the wrong direction. We need a constitutional renaissance, a peaceful revolution to reclaim our basic freedoms and liberties once again. My mission is not to paint the world black and condemn the world and everything in it, for we are a good people doing good things for the most part. We are not perfect as individuals and when honest people end up in dishonest situations, unfortunate things can happen. However, I have total faith in humanity if we can realign ourselves with what brought us here to begin with, that would be individual freedom with no political stipulations.

The middle class is tired and worn out. We have been the backbone and the engine for this country for a long time. We work hard and keep our homes maintained, and our families strong. All we ask in return is a small, reasonable size government responsive to our basic needs. The situation we face is out of hand and out of control. We must elect leaders who understand our plight and work to bring us back to the original playbook that has served us so well in the past, The Constitution.

The very things we despise in life; crime, poverty and war are caused by a uniformed populace, our naivety allows it to happen. We are so buried in the sand we invite the bad guys to run the show. Jefferson pointed out many times that a free people must be informed and educated. It's not a matter of voting Democrat or Republican; it's a matter of becoming aware and knowledgeable of history and current events and acting on that personal platform every day. When it comes time to vote, a healthy dose of suspicion for any candidate who wants our trust is a must.

A Libertarian based country would allow all people to prosper and live better, more productive lives. It has been said that big government is necessary to guide, control and take care of the country. I contend that government cannot be allowed to regulate and police itself! We the people must be empowered to keep it at bay and under control.

If not, we will be ruled and controlled by a lesser force.

A case in point is Sandy Springs, Georgia. The town was once a bastion of debt, corruption, high pensions, and crippled infrastructure. Thanks to 100% outsourcing of government services, taxes are down, the roads are smooth, new parks are under construction, government fees and wages have been reigned in, and the quality of life has drastically improved. Officials are re-elected by a 90% margin of victory. It's too bad municipalities across the country have to go broke before they finally adopt Libertarian measures!

Here is an email I sent to a person running for county office...
"It was good to see you at Irondale. I am a Ron Paul delegate and I can see how the establishment is moving mountains to prevent any real change and pushing Romney on America which will do little to stop our countries decline. Meanwhile youth are attending Ron Paul rallies by the thousands as the media ignores it.
I think the property tax should be eliminated as they are trying to do in North Dakota. The basis of this country is private ownership of property and self. We are not a free people if we pay rent to the county for life. We should also be moving towards gold and silver money. One of the biggest injustices is how we work hard all week, pay taxes and what is left over is then taken by stealth through the inflation tax. Working people and business have the right to constitutional sound money. The corrupt monetary system is at the root of every financial problem we face. There would be plenty of prosperity and wealth to go around if we tackled this one hidden problem. The wealth of America should stay here unless we voluntarily send it overseas. Right now the Federal Reserve thinks they can take our hard earned money and just give it away around the world by the trillions. In

addition, the military is out of control, not only is there a plan to continue war indefinitely, but the wars and the enemies are manufactured from the start. This drains the country of even more money and actually makes it less safe for its citizens. No wonder why Ron Paul has more support from the military than all other candidates combined. You have my vote if you are serious about taking a stand for real change, change that would be controversial and difficult, but proper and right".

The Ron Paul (Libertarian) delegates were able to win a total of 6 states in the Republican primary of 2012. That made him eligible for nomination at the convention and a speaking position. Unfortunately, neither of those happened. The GOP party stripped many of the delegates from power, changed the rules and ignored Ron Paul and his duly elected delegates completely. The evidence was overwhelming that the establishment will not allow grass roots influence of any kind and they took further measures to prevent it in the future.

The lesson is that efforts can be made to change or reform one of the two parties, but more often than not, the reformers butt their heads against a glass ceiling, unless the proposals are more totalitarian in nature. The mega government/media/political/banking elements have a virtual lock on the curriculum and agenda of the two party system. It is like a huge snake that moves slowly and silently. Efforts to radically change its course will be met with road blocks and dead ends. Alternative political movements are the only way to create real change.

George Washington advised us to meet on the battlefield of ideas. It is never wise to use force or violence to achieve anything. We must appeal to the human being's sense of reason alone and persuade with rational thought rather than any type of force, be it mental or physical. Humanity will never advance under the threat of a gun or indoctrination. Humanity will only move forward under the light of freedom and individualism. Libertarians have been accused of being isolationists because the foreign policy stresses nonintervention. On the contrary, a free people would associate, cooperate and integrate much better in an open market setting than they do now in a military style show of force that the Pentagon distributes around the world. It is actually *militarism* that isolates us from others.

The two party system is rigged to the point where voting for either side is destructive because it gives the system assurances their actions are approved of. The two sides always compromise on what amounts to a decline in our quality of life since whatever they do costs money and expands government. The entire game is rigged from birth to death to keep us acting and reacting only within certain parameters of thought. Think twice before casting a toxic vote for one of these parties, it is dangerous to give them your stamp of approval.

Yes, we all need a certain amount of conditioning, preparation and vocational training for life but that comes from a strong family and community, not from elitists in ivory towers. In addition, we need organization, coordination and leadership, but that comes from our free associations, not from forced governmental agendas.

Unfortunately, political emotions run high in the pendulum of two party politics. A sharp divide is created by and amplified by the compliant media. Many times Americans are swept away in one of two false viewpoints created by the duopoly. For example, in 2008 when the price of gasoline spiked to $4.00 per gallon, the Democrats blamed it on the gas guzzling habits of people driving SUVs and the increasing worldwide demand for fossil fuels which also caused global warming. The Republicans blamed it on environmental activism and not enough drilling. The truth is that Goldman Sachs bank had been working for years on freeing up billions of dollars from pension funds and retirement accounts to "invest" in commodities. Once this flood of new money went towards the oil index futures, the price at the pump jumped and started the great recession. The real cause of the problem was hidden behind the bickering of the two parties and the media who ran cover for the power brokers.

In conclusion, the two party system is in fact one organization operating against the American people. It has a bad track record, as the corruption increases over time. There is slight opposition between the parties but they always compromise in the end and stick together as an opposing force against real change. They will raise their sabers in unison when threatened by a third party.

Certain policies are not determined by elected officials. There is an underlying power grid that determines the course of local, national and global policy. They believe in servitude and a one world order. I believe in one world greatness which is the result of freedom and liberty.

"I know no safe depository of the ultimate powers of the society but the people themselves; and if we think them not enlightened enough, the remedy is not to take it from them, but to inform their discretion by education"

~Thomas Jefferson

Chapter Four: The Education Plantation

"a school should be a place to discuss, debate, and ponder life in the process of discovering the world and who we are as individuals"

When I was young, I walked to school on pleasant fall and spring days. I slowly made my way past rows of neat suburban homes, one after the other, with clean well-kept yards and closed garage doors. Each house resembled the other except for the roof lines, type of siding or breed of dog. So it seemed to me that my fellow students were the same as those houses, little variances here and there, but basically we were alike, cut out of the same mold, equal patterns, identical in most respects. We were like those rows of houses, just enough of a difference to tell us apart and not much more.

Nevertheless I felt something was out of place. Some of us were subtlety different than the rest, apart from the flow, out in left field and aloof from it all, out of touch but we didn't know exactly why. Not so much in isolation but far enough outside of the flow to fall through the cracks and exist in sort of a semi-functional reality. I was in the middle, sometimes joining the crowd and other times hanging out alone. The main group of kids roamed together like a herd of buffalo. Anyone "out of the ordinary" was chastised and scoffed at. Even the teachers were biased, keeping things on an "even keel." Therefore, anyone displaying odd behavior was labeled "weird", made fun of or ignored, and "corrected" by the dutiful instructors. I watched as bullies pushed around the weaker kids and the "normal" elite group would make sure they stood apart from the oddballs. An artificial environment of behavior was created, stratifying the students into a stream of conformity and non-conformity. That may explain why adult problems such as drug addiction, emotional imbalance and disease could be traced back to early school difficulties brought on by this conformity system. Instead of individualism being promoted and urged, the opposite occurs. This went on throughout grade school and beyond. Part of this scenario is just kids being kids, but much of it was the way students and teachers reacted to the built in behavior and socialization programs.

The 1960s saw a decrease in local and parental control favoring more state and federal control over the school districts. With this new power came even more emphasis on a mandated curriculum favoring behavior modification, and loss of individual thought and critical thinking among the students. We were taught to exist in herds and learn what it is to be "normal". Psychiatry was stamping its ideas even more so on the education system. This made for an obedient populace and a nation of ill-informed adults.

Private schools have served to keep the onslaught of public education somewhat in check but even those systems are regulated by the government. Home schooling has become more and more popular in the last 20 years as a result of the failings in public school. I do not want to minimize the efforts of teachers because they were dedicated and caring, doing the very best they could. They were simply caught up in a governmental system that no one really understood, no one but the

self-styled elitists behind the scenes who orchestrated the system.
Sometimes I got off the school bus as the engine roared and moved away in a cloud of smoke. The sounds of children faded away in the distance and I was left with a sense of perplexing wonder of what it all meant. The answers were not to come for many years.

The first thing to do is take education out of the hands of government, and get rid of "compulsory" schooling. Allow parents to make their own decisions about education. That will bring the parents back into the mix and back to the table where they belong. The problem today is that a wedge has formed between parent and child, and the almighty school administrators make the major decisions. The very idea of the local community making decisions and determining school subjects is frowned upon. Even those who can afford a good private school are still forced to pay for the public. The claimed neutrality of the system is a misnomer because the values of collectivism and big government are the overriding themes throughout the school years. What else would you expect from a system run by the government? It's a self-protected cartel.
 Public schooling has become a self-serving monopoly. The very purpose is socialization and the inculcation of values. According to my report card from the 60s, it says "the purpose of education is behavior modification". That alone should be enough proof for any skeptics.
We have schools across the country that are "drop out factories" producing teens who end up on drugs and go to prison where it costs society billions more for years of room and board and health care. It would be cheaper overall to simply pay for them to attend private school and not drop out. It's the unions in the public schools that do not allow bad teachers to be fired and

administrative costs to be cut. In New York, "rubber rooms" are full of bad teachers who are not allowed in the classroom but sit there all day and collect their pay and benefits, reading magazines, waiting for their hearings and living off the work of the taxpayer. Clearly, it's all about the teachers, not the students. Attempts in Washington D.C. to correct the failing schools have been met with resistance. Michelle Rhee has instituted reforms that cut out much of the bureaucracy and reworked teacher's salaries. Still, the union is resistant to change and disallowed an important vote.

There are alternative schools across the country in the worst parts of town that are very successful working with poor and disadvantaged students. The answer for the ills of the country is to force all public schools to compete in the real world or shut down and allow better schools to take their place. A school having a fierce competitor down the block would be the best medicine. They would be forced to streamline, fire bad teachers and provide a better product.

School Unions have gone from being a basic protector of workers to a massive interest group funneling billions of dollars to politicians and their crony friends. Greed, big money and corruption are the rule of the day from top to bottom. Meanwhile the country is teetering over a cliff. The time has come to rethink where we came from and where we are going.

Government is not allowed in the doors of our churches, but we allow it to have total dominion over our schools starting at age five. Why is there a wall of separation between religious faith and government but not between government and education? We have learned through the centuries to distrust government because of its track record, the corruption, totalitarianism, and tyranny. Why do we stand aside and allow it to creep so close to our personal lives?

I firmly believe in local and parent controlled education, financed by the parents, their charities, their churches, or any other means besides the state. Once the state "pays" for the service, they control what is taught and what is not taught, the parents become stooges with no real control.

Observers from America went to Prussia back in the 1840s to study their government schools. Our entire education system was then lifted from this early model, the same model that kept the German people so obedient to authority and led to the mass murders of Hitler. It's the same thing today. In the words of Terry Thomas, "what they want is a shaped, engineered, planned society where everyone thinks, acts and behaves like everyone else". So what we are dealing with is not only a union cartel, but a socialist, unconstitutional institution that is totalitarian in nature. Former teacher John Tayor Gatto wrote "The whole system was built on the premise that isolation from first-hand information and fragmentation of the abstract information presented by the teachers would result in obedient and subordinate graduates, properly respectful of arbitrary orders." but "According to our own DNA and fingerprints, everybody is a unique individual" and school should support that reality.

Albert Einstein commented that the thirst for knowledge and curiosity is squelched by the forced set of material on the student, which makes them less curious and even bored (paraphrased). Labor unions were in support of public schools because it took children out of the labor force and there was less competition.

Charlotte Iserbyt, a government whistleblower points out that Wilhelm Wundt, the father of experimental psychology, who established the first experimental laboratory in Leipzig, had a tremendous influence on the school system as it adopted his idea that psychology was indeed a true science and it ought to be applied in the field of education.

The Dight institute for Human Genetics at the University of Minnesota was kept open until the late 1960s. Charles Dight was a medical professor at Hamline University before it merged with the U of M in 1907. He was a supporter of Adolph Hitler's eugenics program having brought the movement to Minnesota and believed it could merge with socialism to eradicate "defective" individuals from society. His letter to Hitler in 1933 praised his attempts to "stamp out inferiority".

Horace Mann supported the common school movement that made all education standard coming from a single agenda. Political disputes and arguments were not to be tolerated in the classroom for it would introduce dissention in society. This entire movement is faulty from the beginning. The country was founded on dissention and the more people (especially students) are involved in differences of opinion, the greater is the ultimate strength of the nation. Every day that goes by there is a great loss of emotional interest in the classroom because debates and arguments are effectively banned in school, what a tragedy! William H. Seawell from the University of Virginia has said that "each child belongs to the state."

Around 1910, philanthropy was the order of the day with robber barons Carnegie and Rockefeller. Andrew Carnegie set up public libraries and Rockefeller gave to colleges and universities. This money was not for general education as most believed; rather it was to be used for the makings of a planned society, helping to create a nation of obedient, uniformed citizens. John Dewey, the father of progressive education had connections with the

Germans just as Henry Ford had connections with Hitler.

Many centuries before, rulers, kings and tyrants yielded the sword and threatened personal injury or property damage to those who rebelled against them. Reality itself and the guidelines for living were set forth in religious dogma and written in the holy books. Anyone who had a mind to go against the official rules were chastised, called heretics and maybe put to death. The Christian doctrine of original sin was the foundation that society lived and functioned under both in Europe and America. All things were filtered through and approved by the priests and church officials. Natural disasters, political structures, philosophy and the very parameters of life were all handled in some way by the doctrine of original sin. The church ruled over the masses and made it difficult to progress without free thinkers and advance scientific thought.

Charles Darwin and the concept of evolution began to take shape in the 19th century. Eventually it merged with humanism and psychology to challenge and finally replace the doctrine of original sin as the dominant viewpoint and foundation of the education system. Christianity remained as a remnant from the past, being an important spiritual and moral code for millions but lacking the dominating power of its glory years.

The importance of the first amendment cannot be understated. "Congress shall make no law respecting an establishment of religion or prohibiting the free exercise thereof." The problem is that secular humanism has encroached itself as the official state religion. Humanism teaches we are primal beings without a soul that need to be manipulated and socialized into proper obedient members of society. The entire concept of God and spiritualism has been removed and replaced with another theory or explanation of human behavior. Within this concept lies psychiatric terminology that explains all human activity, good and bad. The written texts and manuals of the prominent psychologists and college professors serve the same function as the scriptures of the Bible did in the past. Thomas Scasz has thoroughly discussed this transformation.

Both psychology and religion explain all human behavior and both have been backed up by law. Both are given official stamps of approval by "science" or "God". Both however are in fact *unscientific* and have led millions of non-believers or deviants to harassment and even death. The thousands of so called witches that were burned at the stake compare with the thousands who have endured shock treatments and medication abuse in modern times. Many millions of unlucky citizens, who lived under Nazi, Chinese, Japanese or Soviet rule, were turned into human experiments and then murdered. For the rest of us, the human race has and is enduring the oppression of the various dogmas that spring up from time to time, including here in America.

The theory of "mental illness" is the latest in a series of oddball attempts to explain every behavior. It was preceded by such things as Craniology or the study of bumps on the head. Eugenics is another movement that had some roots in America before Hitler raised it to a new level.

The point is that the public school system has a basis in religion. There is nothing wrong with a free school having a basis in humanism as long as the people attend freely and at their own expense. The same goes for religious schools. What we need and what Americans desire is a free and open private market education system that functions apart from the government. History has shown again and again that we cannot trust the government, especially in an important area as education. Let us eliminate compulsory attendance and allow a natural development to take place. We will find that Americans will be more literate and able to think critically and freely in a free school system. This open system will develop the leaders we need and the scientific advancements that are necessary for our future. New schools will study the Constitution and the importance of sound money. We must transform ourselves from a docile, socialized, and subdued people to a critical thinking, individualistic, freedom minded and highly educated citizenry. It can be done.

Take a good look at society now. The illiteracy rate is high, and some graduates have a hard time reading their own diploma. We are in a collective television and cell phone trance, stoned faced "American Idol" watchers.
I don't blame the teachers totally, unless they blindly follow the school's curriculum. They can also be victims of the system. There are many fine instructors that do their best within the corrupt system. The real problem is the inflexible hard-nosed administration. We have a bloated school bureaucracy that will think nothing of closing down schools for a day to attend rallies, protesting their own benefit packages. (Wisconsin 2011).
It's a sad state of affairs. At some point, we have to take a good hard look at the system and make some major modifications. The other option is to do nothing and let the two party system manage the decline of this great country.
  The public school maintains and supports a statist situation. There is never any discussion or talk of real change. It is a self-protection mechanism. Each new generation of children is taught to obey and respect the state.
  Historically, whole nations would fight each other as they tried to force religious beliefs on their neighbors and the neighbors would force theirs on someone else. Finally, the concept of separation of church and state

was developed. We are long overdue to adopt the separation of school and state. Today's schools are more like jobs corps centers. The simple job of educating youth has been turned into a circus of highly paid administrators in expensive buildings. The actual classroom has become a minor part of the equation. The school unions band together to create a billion dollar a year monstrosity that has a never ending appetite for increased funding. The student is a passenger on this jumbo ship of failure. The whole school year is laid out in advance with numerous vacations, half days and time off for the administrators, leaving the students with wasted down time.

The very idea of taxation to pay for schools should make everyone suspicious. Since the districts have a never ending "flow' of funding, it is easy to hide the money from the public and it creates a huge advantage over any private school. Once in a while we hear of a bad superintendent being "paid off" to leave the district. These payoffs could be as much as $200,000 or more. If this is going on, what else is going on behind the scenes? Meanwhile, students come and go to school every day completely oblivious to the money laundering that goes on at the district level. This criminal manipulation of taxpayer money is reason enough to dump the school system as it is.

A decline in student performance can be traced to the time when unionization first took hold during the 1960s. The unions insulated the growing school bureaucracy to the point where inefficiency became the norm and it became ever more difficult to fire bad teachers and streamline school personal at all levels.

In my experience, school life was like a red carpet laid out before us and we simply had to walk down the line without ever being able to criticize the march onward. If someone asked why, they were ignored. As a student and a parent I was never asked to fill out a survey to rate the school or to rate a teacher or principal. They are a protected class. I was never asked to rate the curriculum or to suggest a new textbook or subject matter. The very idea is regarded as dangerous to the establishment. The only ones making these decisions are elite university heads who think they know better than the average parent. Parental analysis should be a basic practice in education. We should be *encouraged* to suggest and criticize, not *discouraged*.

I learned all the stories. Paul Reveres Ride, George Washington and the Cherry Tree, Betsy Ross knitting the flag, Lincoln and his axe, the major wars and why they were fought, slavery and woman's suffrage. I memorized the national holidays and dates of great events.

I was given an official spyglass to look into, along with the other kids. Looking through the glass I saw a kaleidoscope of painted events set forth specifically for us to believe in and reinforce our reverence for the nation. With my hand over my heart, I uttered the pledge of allegiance with my fellow classmates. Little did I know a veil was carefully laid in front of me, a veil so invisible and subtle that one would never know its there. It served as a backdrop between fable and fact, truth and falsehood. Eventually I learned how to peel back the veneer revealing the fascinations, excitements, disappointments, horrors and discoveries of a hidden world that functions above and below us, like finding a new planet in the solar system. History suddenly became three dimensional, alive and moving. Things started to connect and make sense. It was no longer a poster or date on the calendar. It was now a living creature, an animal that upended my thoughts and brought on a new fascination of what is. I've been looking through the secret window, peeking over the fence to see just what our leaders are up to. The events of yesterday are pieces to a large and expanding mosaic of time.

I envision a high school class where kids do not slump over in boredom but clamor to get in and can't wait for class to start. They discuss the meaning of sound money vs. fiat money, or the evolution of mankind vs. creationism, or maybe liberalism vs. conservatism, and third party politics. Maybe the Civil War was not fought over slavery but economics and northern aggression. I see students in lively debates and arguments going on the whole period and extending out in the halls well after the bell rings, controversial subjects being the rule, not the exception.

That is what is missing in today's education, a reason to be there. Instead of presenting students with a "safe" and sanitized overview of dates, times, and places, why not make it come alive with opinion and opposing viewpoints? History as we are given today is served up to the students as a dry, neutral blend of conformity and non- dissention. When you study history however, it *requires a viewpoint* to discern what happened and why it happened. For example, the South interprets the Civil War much differently than the North. In order to get a good grasp of history, we must realize it is a fluid study; there is no ultimate right and wrong or statement of fact on many historical accounts. We should debate the issues and not just blindly accept some instructor's opinion or take for granted the interpretation of a textbook.

There is a definite line of thought that flows out of the public school mouthpiece. Teachers are taught what to say as fact and what subjects to avoid. Educators do not want to go against the board or make parents angry.

However, in order to discuss the real meaning of history we must take sides, form opinions and work towards some form of consensus. We may then form valid conclusions only after lively debates which include our feelings on the subject and wide interpretations of a particular event. If this type of atmosphere is impossible or frowned upon by the public schools, I submit we need to dismantle compulsory state schooling and move towards community based learning where local parents decide what and how to teach, not blindly relying on the Department of Education. An opinion based school would make for more attentive students, less distraction and a greater interest in not only history but all subjects.

Over 200 million people were killed by their own governments in the twentieth century. That makes it painfully clear that the biggest threat we face is our own power structure. It follows that education should not be in the hands of government, but in the hands of the parents and local communities for obvious reasons.

The argument for open market education is very neatly struck down by the education establishment. They always make the case that many poor people would be without educational opportunities. The financial structure would be in disarray, leaving children out in the cold. Secondly, millions of disabled individuals would not be allowed in private school situations because of the great expense associated with their disabilities. Finally, without a common format and curriculum there would be cultural chaos and irregular social structures evolving which would weaken the fabric of the country.

To answer these objections, one must realize the debate itself would never seriously occur in the school setting. How then would we ever find out if it would work or not? There is tremendous resistance in the educational world to even bring up the subject of separation of school and state.

I liken it to being a slave on a plantation. Never was the subject of freedom discussed among the slaves or the owners. The power structure was maintained at all costs, any talk of freedom was heretical and therefore banned. The same thing occurs in the realm of education. School officials would never entertain the idea of free market education because it cuts into their lifestyle, their income, and their internal reality. They have gone through a lifetime of inculcation and socialization themselves to the point where they could not possibly consider any alternative. This alone should be enough evidence that we live in a shaped and planned society, and not a truly free society.

History tells us that before public schooling, there were charity schools and scholarships set up by the wealthy to insure the education of all people. The psychiatric community is going well out of their way to make sure there is enough mental illness to cover almost everyone on the planet except them. This gives the education establishment more reasons to demand a monopoly on our lives. It's for our own good you see. After all, how would a free market school keep up with all the medications and allowances for the disabled?

The truth is that there is never a general problem that exists where a free people don't come up with a solution for. The truth is that a free market education system would supply the needs of the disabled better than government. Instead of three figure incomes going to high up district employees that have no contact with students, all the money would flow to the needs of the children, thereby guaranteeing full attention and outcome to the student. What scares the establishment most is the idea of a truly free America where people have their own thoughts and feelings about reality. The concept of individualism is carefully hidden from us. That is why we need to pry the power out of the hands of the state and demand educational freedom. Their idea is to control and manipulate reality for the "good" of the common whole. Liberty is what the country was originally founded on. Freedom is what built America. History tells us that freedom is what made life better for the poor and gave everyone opportunity. Freedom brings out the leaders and advance thinkers who go on to improve our standard of living. The best way to improve the lives of the people is to leave people alone and not be tempted to interfere with the natural order of things. Unfortunately, there are too many liberal mined do gooders who self-appoint themselves into positions of oversight and control. They make the illogical argument that humans cannot govern themselves, therefore the elite professors (being human themselves) must step forward and do the job. Interestingly enough, one of the first subjects they eliminated out of the schools is logic class. That way, no student could figure out the obvious fraud of the institution they belong to.

As in the monetary system, what we need in America is a parallel school system, one which would compete directly with the failing existing system. What would happen is predictable. The very good public schools would streamline themselves and offer a good product for the consumer. Other schools would refuse to change and sink into a financial collapse wherein a new private and more efficient system would emerge for that particular neighborhood. This transformation would also transform the attitude of the entire community. People would feel pressure to get involved and get off the sidelines. More community involvement would enhance the entire education experience. Old timeworn institutions like teachers unions would no longer stand in the way of budget balancing and ever increasing property taxes.

The American public schools have survived as a sort of

hybrid between a controlled institution with a stated purpose and a somewhat successful popular place for us to learn, read and write and experience the unique way of being American. Many of us have cherished memories of teachers, schoolmates, sports, extra-curricular activities and good times in school. I do not want to understate and undervalue the importance of those memories and experiences that make us all American. Schools have been part of the family and part of the neighborhood. Many good people and good ideas have come out of public schooling, but we are enriched *in spite of* the system, not *because* of it.

We have managed to carry on the American dream with a monkey on our back. Once we achieve total educational freedom, we can do much more. The system needs to be roundly criticized and examined for its many shortcomings. Drastic improvements are needed soon before the American dream is gone for good.

In a world view, the free market would bring likeminded people together under the concept of liberty. Free trade and open market activity would replace war and strife caused by big government, big banking and various forms of socialism. So it goes with education, total educational freedom means parents and students decide what to study and how to implement those studies. An employee of the school is answerable to the parents, not the state. Many kids simply are not interested in school. The reason is obvious; they and their parents have no control over the curriculum. The big decisions are made by the hidden elitists who occupy the hallowed university buildings and psychiatric corridors. We need to wrestle control away from these self-styled mega managers and bring education back to main street. Then you will find kids lining up at the schools front door.

Gerrit Smith, an early critic of public schooling said that

"it is justice and not charity which people need at the hands of government. Let government restore them to their land, and what other rights they have been robbed of, and they will then be able to pay for themselves- to pay the school masters, as well as their parsons." Education has been cleverly removed from the responsibility of the family to the realm of government. This must change. Libertarian Herbert Spencer spelled out the rights of children and the rights of family. The state has no right to come between a child and their personal educational wants and needs. If the child attends a private school, this school should not be regulated by the state and the students in it should not be charged for the public school. All schools should be in direct competition with each other. Standing in the way of this logical reasoning is the vast conspiracy to engineer society according to the theories and will of those in ivory towers. What we have is a battleground of freedom vs. collectivism which is nothing more than a fight against tyranny.

Like the monetary system, the first thing to do is introduce competition. Remove the compulsory attendance laws and allow open rivalries between schools and let them fight for the students. This would be the quickest and easiest way to improve education overnight. Instead we have a dinosaur school system, resistant to change and not open to new ideas. The school unions continue the leaching of money from taxpayers while solidifying the unchanging, unresponsive administrative blob that slows down the country. If families cannot be trusted to educate their own children in their own way, there is no point to pretending we have liberty and freedom at all.

Every so often the Federal government comes up with an educational scheme to realign public schooling. In 2013, "Common Core" was introduced. It is a new way to

rehash old attempts to regulate society. Hidden amongst the deliberately confusing technical jargon there are new methods to regulate behavior and influence character,
such things as mood meters, data mining, facial expression technology, MRI scans, sensors, and a tracking system to follow a person through life, from birth to workforce. Children will be grouped into three separate divisions depending on how they can serve the state best. Once private school records will now be shared to all government departments. Cash strapped states are being bribed to accept large amounts of money if they sign on to this costly program. Meanwhile administrators in a Georgia public school district were caught "improving" student test scores so they would be eligible for bonuses. How long are the American people going to stand by and tolerate this corrupt system?

In 2013, Ron Paul announced the release of his home school teaching materials, which are free up to the 5th grade. Students are sure to get a well-rounded education in economics and political theory, not to mention logic and rhetoric. Hopefully, families will take advantage of this program and others to fight back against the system.

At the dawn of civilization Greece and Rome allowed anyone to start a school and set their own curriculum. In America, we have gone from the one room schoolhouse to larger schools where seats were bolted to the floor facing forward. Then came state run schools, federally run schools, and now schools where the United Nations, world government and big corporations set the curriculum. *What on Earth are we doing?* We have strayed a long way from the teaching of basic knowledge to adopting a human engineered program that does not educate, but indoctrinates! No wonder there is so much allocation of money and time dedicated to children since they are the biggest resource in a totalitarian world.

We Americans must stop the flow of educational power to the top and bring it back to local control. Then we will have a nation of literate, hardworking, functional citizens creating a free and prosperous society which in turn will minimize despair and poverty.

"true education is closely associated with change, the agent of revolution, always fitting us for higher change, an instrument for making us something other than what we are"

~ Herbert Spencer

Chapter Five: Conspiracy Fast Track

*"all that we see and hear is the object
of someone's creation"*

There is a concern in the education establishment and in the media that too many American citizens are becoming conspiracy theorists. The public library has numerous books debunking conspiracies while having few actual conspiracy selections. The complaint is that we are now splintered on our view of history when only a few years ago, we were basically unified on our view of the past.

This speaks volumes on how far "the wool" has been pulled over our eyes! In a free society, why would there be a "unified" view of history? Free people would discover and contemplate various aspects of the past and come up with different conclusions based on a wide variety of historical accounts. It certainly would not be agreed upon by all.

The internet has given humanity a new tool to explore the past and we are discovering things the public schools have tried to hide for years.

The Federal Reserve System is a major example. Although the schools claim there is a study of the Fed., there is never any critical analysis of its history and beginnings. There is never a real study of what sound money is and how we could live perfectly well without a central bank.

Many conspiracies point to a wholesale collapse of the economy with martial law and boots in the streets etc. This may never actually happen because of the way we are being eased into totalitarianism by the deceptive mechanism of incrementalism. A student of conspiracy should stand back and take in the big picture. How did the country look 30 years ago vs. today? The average family was much better off and living a higher standard of living in the 1960s. A total collapse is not being allowed to happen because then the game would be over. Instead the nature of the game is a slow, agonizing decline at a glacial pace. The ultimate goal is still a worldwide organized control grid run by government/corporate powers.

The truth is that the American people have always been suspicious of politics and politicians. The conspiratorial Democrats accuse Republicans of secretly working with oil companies to raise gas prices, start wars in the Middle East for resources and even call them racist for being "against" the little people. Meanwhile, the Republicans talk about the "liberal media" and how the Democratic Party is actually socialist and leading us into totalitarianism. Both parties have called the other Nazis and all sorts of derogatory names. This illustrates how conspiratorial the American people already are, but are wholly unaware of the treasonous class in the shadows.

Now that we have gone online, the world is changing fast. Today, we are no longer bound by the reality that plays out on television or newspapers. We are free to wander the great information highway and decide for ourselves what is fact and what is fiction. We are now focusing our sights on another element that runs the country, the one that has been so cleverly hidden in the background for decades. The country has been on autopilot for years and stays on its course no matter who we elect in office. Thankfully now we are turning from attacking each other to discovering our real enemy and that is the NEW WORLD ORDER.

Our friendly libraries should have entire sections on conspiracies, alternate histories and a full selection of DVDs available for checking out. Instead, there is next to nothing. Libraries are supposed to serve the public while backing the 1st amendment. Instead, they are streamlining information that protects the corrupt government and hides the identity of the real power brokers.

~Drawing Back the Veil~

ABORTION...A topic heavily debated and talked about.
Forty six million abortions take place every year around the globe. Surgically removed fetuses have gone into trash cans still alive and have been rescued by nurses who heard their cries. The rescued babies have grown up to talk about the experience and stand against the practice. The new world order, which includes heads of state, bankers and other elitists have come out publically in favor of worldwide abortion and the promotion of homosexuality to reduce and limit human population. Margaret Sanger, the founder of Planned Parenthood, was a eugenicist who believed in a master race. She also believed in the "unfit' nature of the black people. The organization had direct ties to Nazi Germany. Many people have reasonable arguments for a women's right to choose, but they should do some research on the very institutions they support. Many times these institutions have their origins in something quite sinister, and the same ideologues who founded them still exist behind the scenes.

AGENDA 21…The United Nations blueprint for depopulation and total human control. In 1992, at the Earth Summit in Rio de Janeiro, President Bush signed on to one of the most oppressive plans of human control ever conceived; The United Nations Agenda 21/Sustainable Development Program. It cleverly works from the bottom up, starting in local city halls and at the county level to promote such things as sustainable development, smart growth, and high density urban living. It aims to corral all of humanity into workable segments of people living in interactive, environmentally friendly gathering places. All plots of land and water will be categorized and indexed. All land use will be regulated and private property eliminated. The "needs" of the community will take precedence over the individual. It seeks to lower the standard of living for those in America, to slow us down and regulate our energy use. Bill Clinton's Council on Sustainable Development is the implementation tool where all Federal agencies must comply with Agenda 21. All costs paid by taxpayers through such things as bonds. We are encouraged to bypass home ownership in favor of renting in small functional developments. Those who still own their own homes and retain private property are being forced out by high property taxation and new regulations.

Arrest and harassment of individuals is occurring across the nation. Martha Boneta in Virginia was fined $5000 for not getting a proper permit to have a birthday party on her property and two more fines for advertising a pumpkin carving and having a small shop to sell produce and crafts. The county board upheld the zoning administrator in her appeal. Earlier she had been told to not cut grass on 20 acres of her property because it was hallowed ground from the Civil War, this lasted two years before the county admitted a mistake. Although her party never took place the harassment continued. Environmentalists refer to some people as penny-loafers when they "misuse" their own property.

Family farms are being forced out of business by corporate farming and others living in outlying areas are in danger of losing their land. All land is subject to restructure and rezoning to comply with the new environmentalism sweeping across America.

Private property, which used to be a hallmark of our country, will be a thing of the past. Homes and land will be unaffordable or confiscated to force people into the city. Light rail is being built across the country, in spite of many objections, to accommodate the new wave of people to metropolitan life.

The housing crisis of 2007 was the result of a two-pronged attack on the American people. First, buyers were provoked into purchasing homes they could not afford, causing a massive sweep of foreclosures across the country and a massive transfer of wealth from the middle class to the government and the bankers. Secondly, this power play set the stage for further implementation of Agenda 21. Keep in mind the elimination of private property is the ultimate end game. Local groups are being infiltrated, politicians are being selected and unregulated immigration is being encouraged to lower living standards and increase multi-nationalism, watering down the language and dividing up the country into easily manipulated units.

New codes and regulations are forced upon us, limiting our lives and taking away the freedoms that made this a great nation. Every homeowner or land owner is subject to fines or jail time if they choose to disobey or fight against the system. The government has positioned itself to target anyone that speaks out or stands against Agenda 21. Everyone is a potential suspect or threat. People are being told what they can do and cannot do on their own property. Smart water meters are being installed to regulate water use and spy on the public. New laws are on the way to force the installation of energy efficient appliances with the idea of "saving money" and "saving the earth". Utility companies then request a rate increase because they are "losing money" from the decline in power usage!

The history of humanity records a lesson we all should learn. Anytime a group of self-styled elitists try to manipulate and control the rest of the masses, it turns into chaos and confusion. The success of America came directly from the blossoming of natural rights. These rights include the ownership of private property. When people own their own land and property, they are more productive and more willing to organize and cooperate with others. This creates a better society and a smoother running country than what any state controlled situation can offer. For some reason, we always have people in our midst who think they know how to run things better than anyone else. Individuals have to stand up and raise a standard against them. When society puts freedom first, it makes for the best of all possible worlds.

<u>AIRLINE CRASHES</u>...Operation Northwoods, developed by the Chiefs of Staff in 1962, outlined ways to harass our own airplanes, blow up our own ships and blame the events on Cuba. Since then there have been a rash of suspicious crashes that point towards intentional mayhem including Sept. 11, 2001. In "The Medussa File", Craig Roberts explains some of these incidents;

On Sept. 1, 1983 a Boeing 747 Jumbo Jet with 269 passengers was shot down by the Soviets as it made its way to Korea. It had strayed way off course and travelled for a long time over Soviet land and air space. The Soviets quickly got to the crash scene and discovered practically no bodies. US Congressman Larry McDonald was a missing passenger. He was involved with an investigation of the world banking cartel and the Federal Reserve and was a dedicated anti-communist. He had discovered a web of links between individuals from both Moscow and New York who supported the cartel. Was the plane misdirected to get rid of McDonald? A Tokyo radar site had tracked the plane to an island where it actually landed, contradicting the earlier story of an ocean crash. Another story states that the bodies were cremated.

Pan Am flight 103 went down in Lockerbie, Scotland on Dec. 21, 1988. It was odd that so many FBI agents arrived on the scene so quickly, in less than two hours after the crash. The town is a full 350 miles from London. Americans were there, "fiddling" with the bodies and identifying them with small white labels, and they were searching for something. Unmarked helicopters were circling the area for days. They finally found a small microchip that they said was traceable back to a Swiss timer which was sold to Libya. The bombing was then blamed on Khadaffi, the leader of Libya.

  Back on July 3, 1988 the US ship Vincennes mistakenly shot down an Iranian A-300 Airbus with 290 passengers aboard. According to Iranian law, they believed in an eye for an eye. The Iranian government soon set up a contract to down an American airliner. The timer was set on flight 103 to go off in the air over the Atlantic but the plane was delayed two hours explaining why it exploded over Lockerbie. It appears elements of the US government knew about the exploding device and did nothing to stop the incident. High ranking officials were pulled from the plane. As it turns out, there was a massive drug smuggling ring coming through Lebanon.

A bag of drugs was on flight 103. Major Charles McKee and CIA chief Mathew Gannon threatened to reveal the extent of the illegal drug trade once they got back to the states. Every bad guy knew they would be traveling on flight 103. The bombing was arranged by government insiders to cover-up the drug trade. The bombs were assembled and delivered by the revenge minded Iranians and the whole thing was blamed on a wild eyed nut case from Libya.

December 12, 1985. Arrow Air DC-8 explodes in the sky soon after liftoff in Gander, Newfoundland. It was bringing back 248 US soldiers from duty overseas. Strange boxes survived the crash and firemen received symptoms resembling nuclear fallout disease. The entire crash site was quickly bulldozed and many items simply buried at dump sites. HAWK missile parts or human remains of the forces that failed a covert hostage rescue attempt may have been aboard the plane. The official version is that the airplane iced up during take-off and crashed but witnesses report seeing the aircraft flame up and explode in midair and carbon monoxide was found in the soldiers lungs meaning there was an explosion before the crash.

July 17, 1996, Long Island NY, TWA flight 800 explodes in midair after takeoff, hundreds of witnesses see a reddish-orange glow and hear a loud explosion before it breaks into two pieces and falls to the ocean. Other witnesses saw a streak of light shoot towards the plane moments before the explosion, like a hand held missile. These witnesses were intimidated to change their story. A few hundred "Stinger" missiles were left over from the Afghan –Soviet war and some were in the hands of terrorists, meaning the government may have tried to cover this information up. Another theory is friendly fire from a military exercise that night. The thing that rings true is that the government won't talk about it and the media tells a different tale.

ALIENS... There is a possibility that we are being visited now or in the past. There is also a chance that we came from somewhere else to begin with. It's possible that we will go to another planet and become aliens ourselves. That being said, what can be demonstrated for sure is that the government has created an alien hoax. They have gone to great lengths to make it appear like they are covering up knowledge of aliens, when all the while, they are the aliens. For example, lighted projections have illuminated the sky above Phoenix to make it appear like some giant spacecraft is hovering overhead. False accounts of space landings and space craft have been concocted by our own air force and aerospace affiliates to get the public worried and distracted by UFOs. This is one of the tools to distract the public as discussed in the Report from Iron Mountain in the 1960s. The alien phenomenon is nothing but a huge manufactured distraction. A light show is being put on by our own government.

Aliens are an example of a reverse conspiracy. They make it look like they are conspiring to hide the aliens when all along they are conspiring to make us think there is a conspiracy! The use of holograms and other devices make it convincing. The aliens are us.

Project Bluebeam is an elaborate government plan to electronically transfer godlike images in the sky to fool millions of people. Telepathic waves would be sent through the air to "communicate" with those who look and listen. How dumb they must think we are!

AMERICA FOR SALE ...It is no secret that foreign countries have been "investing" in this country. The

Japanese have purchased golf courses in Hawaii; land and businesses have been sold to the British the Chinese. The Federal government has unlocked our national parks and allowed the United Nations to begin a slow takeover. President Clinton was instrumental in large portions of Utah going to the Feds. The percentage of Federal land increases by the year.

In 1992, George Bush's executive order gave permission to sell American infrastructure to private concerns. By 2013, many states and cities have put their property up for sale or lease simply to make up for budget shortfalls. Gov. Ed Rendell of Pennsylvania and Mayor Richard Daley of Chicago are two such examples. Ed Rendell attempted but failed to sell the entire Pennsylvania turnpike to foreign interests and Mr. Daley sold the rights to parking meters for over a billion dollars on a 75 year lease to Morgan Stanley and its foreign affiliates. The parking fees immediately went up and parades were canceled because "rental" had to be paid to use the streets.

The culprits in these buyout schemes are sometimes the SWF entities. Sovereign Wealth Funds are nationally owned investment entities connected to central banks and have massive purchasing power. To keep a low profile, they usually buy minority stocks. The reality is they are very powerful organs of deceit and may very well be responsible for the next financial collapse. The parking meters in Chicago were purchased by well-known companies who immediately sold most of the shares to Abu Dhabi securities in the United Arab Emirates.

ANCIENT HISTORY...Geologists and Archeologists have, for the most part given us a wealth of unbiased information about the formation of the earth and the development of its natural and human history. Many great thinkers have presented information at the risk of their own lives including Copernicus and Galileo. Today, we don't lock up people for their new discoveries, but many points of view are ostracized and ignored. Fossils have been discovered at the "wrong" ground levels that cast doubt on the mainline theories of evolution and cultural movement. Scientists have been fired or reprimanded for publishing these findings. Charlton Heston's film, "The Mysterious Origins of Man" takes a close look at this forbidden knowledge. The Bible speaks of strange flying machines in the first chapter of Ezekiel and other books describe miracles that could be the result of some alien force that may have visited this planet. The Bible itself is incomplete, there are many texts not included and many that could have been lost or changed along the way. It remains as a valuable view into a culture long lost.

Throughout the world there are mysteries in the ground and in the ocean that seem to point to a greater civilization that may have occupied the planet thousands of years ago. In the Caribbean Sea there are ancient stone walls and pillars. In South America what appear to be ancient landing strips are visible only from above. In Africa, the pyramids make modern engineers wonder how they were constructed. Primitive batteries have been found in Egypt. This all makes us wonder how we got here and why we came to the Earth. Was Mars our original home? It looks like there was water there at one time. What about the universe? A new theory speculates that what we see as stars is nothing but a mirage or a hologram projected in space for us to look into. Maybe this is the only awareness we will ever have, one flashing life. Maybe we are eternal in one form or another. All options should remain on the table and new ideas should be encouraged. Although we seem to desire an explanation, explanations can be limiting to human growth. We need a new attitude that anything is possible and what is possible may be beyond our comprehension...for now.

ARCHEOLOGY...As we have seen with the 'global warming' phenomena, science can sometimes be an agenda driven movement rather than a pure study. Christian observers have noticed the field of archeology to be exactly that. In the wild drive to "prove" evolution and discredit the creation theory we find dinosaur remains and other fossils telling a fabricated story. Many of the dinosaur bones as seen in museums are made of plaster. Two or three actual bones are dug up and scientists guess as to where the others should go and how they are shaped. Then a false line of descent stems from the false initial conclusions. The truth is that many of the historical time ages and eras are assumptions and conjectures based on little actual evidence. The idea here is to manipulate data to fit the needs and conveniences of the evolutionists as they continue their quest to "prove" we descended from the apes. Meanwhile the Christian scientists manipulate the same data to push their own theories regarding creation. The documentary by Charlton Heston concerning forbidden Archeology shows that modern human footprints have showed up in the same strata as the dinosaurs, which blows a hole in all the traditional theories.

My suggestion to the scientific community is please just stick to the facts and quit promoting your own personal considerations. Remain neutral and just state the facts without personal bias and religious overtones. After all, we may have come from aliens all along.

The problem is that many research organizations are 'agenda driven' rather than truth driven.

ARMAGEDDON...The Great War that ends the earth as

we know it. The Lord returns to claim his domain and cast the Devil and all the sinners to hell. Most religions have a form of this foreboding story.

For centuries, we have been told by Biblical prophets that the earth is full of sin and must be destroyed. The belief in this story is dependent upon it never actually happening. The threat of it happening is what brings order and sanity to the people, or at least it used to. Human beings need a sense of arrangement, and faith supplies that need. Threats of this nature were created originally to control others, be it conquest or tax collection. In today's world, faith is more of a tool for mental survival and there will always be those who feel an intervention coming soon, the world coming to a violent end as the Lord takes his people to heaven.

I can only refer to Luke 17:21 when Jesus was asked about the location of heaven; "Heaven cometh not by observation, but the kingdom of God is within you."

BILDERBERG GROUP...The media shined the spotlight on talk show host Oprah Winfrey whenever she met with top film makers, artists, spiritual leaders, authors, and dog trainers. Meanwhile, the Bilderberg group has been gathering every year since their first meeting in the Netherlands in 1954. The world's top bankers, corporate leaders, media moguls, charities, financiers, military leaders, policy groups, heads of state, intelligence agencies and every other important person on the map are always there. Kissinger, Rockefeller, Clinton, Gates, Theile, Bernanke are just a few of the hundreds of big names. Yet, the media is silent and will scarcely discuss the topic. For years, we were told the group simply didn't exist.

Now we know the invited members meet to discuss their plans for future global events and major market directions.

The official Bilderberg website says the group is secret because they want their members to feel free to discuss current events off the record and without media scrutiny.

The truth is that major decisions are made about many things including wars and the economic rise and fall of nations, for example, the formation of the European Union and the Iraq War. Traditional media like newspapers and TV stations have been monopolized by the Bilderberg's to keep a tight watch on what is to be processed as information to the masses. It is a Federal law that US leaders do not meet in secret, yet they do.

The masses of people are being targeted with food and vaccine additives to thin out the population. It is a dicey ballgame to control 8 billion of us. Before enough of us find out the truth, the hope of the Bilderberg Group is that there will be less of us to deal with.

CHEMTRAILS...Chemtrails are particulates released from aircraft to affect the atmosphere or drift downward through the air to the ground. CONTRAILS are the natural release of water vapor that turn to ice in the sky. Chemtrails can hang in the air for hours and are usually composed of three chemicals, aluminum oxide, barium, and strontium.

Sometimes the intention is to treat the air so it will support electromagnetic waves to make weapon systems work better. Other times molds, fungus, and bacteria are used to spray upon an unsuspecting population for experimental purposes. Eyewitnesses have seen ash like clouds floating around in the air after aircraft placed webs of chemtrails in grid-like patterns in the sky. The term geo-engineering refers to artificially changing the earth's climate or placing chemicals in the sky to reflect the sun back into space to decrease the effect of global warming. Depopulation, weapons and communications agendas are also in play. Public secrecy is of course utmost in importance.

As far back as 1953, zinc cadium sulfide was sprayed over the City of Winnipeg to find out how many people would come down with sore throats and ringing ears in an effort to predict future cancer rates from the treatment.

A gel substance was dropped on Oakville, Washington in 1994. People came down with the flu and animals died. A police chief became ill when he handled the material. It turns out the substance contained human blood cells and experimental warfare bacteria. FEMA officials later came to town and intimidated people who had been on the show "Unsolved Mysteries" talking about the incident.

In 1997 William Wallace of Kettle Falls, Washington was plowing his fields when Navy airplanes crisscrossed the sky spraying his remote farm with a fine mist. He later became sick and lost not only his cat but his job also. He took his story to a Spokane news station which did a 2 part story. He was sprayed again probably as a warning.

Is the government secretly spraying to study the effects of biological weapons? Are they trying to give us diseases to lower population? Are they manipulating the climate? Just what are they doing and how long will it take for us to wake up?

CHILDRENS RIGHTS...Children have the basic right to food, shelter, health, education, protection from harm, and recreation. The biggest threat to child protection oddly enough is the government itself.

Progressives and members of academia are working to wrestle control of children from the parents. The family unit is a major obstacle in their plan to regulate and manage society. Children are encouraged to "report" their parent's bad behavior to school authorities or law enforcement. This would include if the adults own firearms, are involved with protests or radical political or church groups, are depressed or use alcohol or drugs, and many other "suspicious" activities. Children may take their own parents to court for having too many rules. They can even divorce their parents.

Ironically children are not encouraged to be individuals in school and their behavior and thoughts are heavily regulated, but at home they are urged to rebel against their own household. This is just another sign of "Big Brothers" growing influence in society.

<u>COMPUTER CHIPS</u>...In her book "Spychips" Katherine Albrecht discusses the new technology of implanting RFID chips into the flesh of people to track them and monitor their purchasing habits and whereabouts. Some tracking chips are located on the packaging of food products and actual cash we all handle. Chips can be turned on and off by authorities to disable the lives and livelihoods of the citizens. This goes hand in hand with national ID cards.

<u>CIGARETTE LAWSUITS</u>...A clever way for the government to grab a few extra million. Cigarette company spokesman were brought to court and paraded in front of congress. They were forced to testify about the health hazards of smoking. A lawsuit was filed and won by the states. Little money was awarded to the millions of smokers who supposedly suffered, instead the millions were sent to each individual state for use in "prevention programs". The bulk of the money never went to those programs, instead, it went to the "general fund" and was then spent to cover state debt. The cigarette companies raised the price of their product to cover the loss in court, and again, the public paid the price. Be kind to smokers, they pay big taxes!

CLIMATE CHANGE...Throughout history, people have felt responsible for volcanic eruptions and violent storms. Somehow they offended the Gods. Commoners have been made to feel "guilty" about a flood or earthquake. When Greek ships were ravaged during a storm they laid blame on themselves or their enemy because some deity was driven to bring their wrath upon them. The truth is that we generally have no effect on weather patterns, global temperature, and climate change. It is a manufactured crisis put out by world governmental powers to make a lot of money, make us feel guilty and control our behavior. (See chapter 8).

Wind power is actually a type of solar energy. As the sun heats up air, the air rises causing a vacuum of moving air. Common sense would tell us that the more heat, the more wind, which means global warming would increase wind driven power. Yet, we are told global warming is a bad thing. There are many ways to attack this theory. Suffice it to say that the man-made climate theory is a way to maintain cash flow to researchers, force America to use less fuel, and exert control over the people.

Let us concentrate on obvious problems like food toxins, and water and air pollution, problems that are identifiable and require simple solutions. The weather has a mind of its own and the Earth will do what it's going to do regardless of what we do.

CLUB OF ROME...Founded in Rome Italy 1968, their slogan reads; "a group of world citizens, sharing a common concern for the future of humanity." Originally, they were composed of academics and industrialists who were taking a look at the future of the world. The Committee of 300 is closely related to the Club and directs economic trends and affairs of Europe. Its 1972 report says its mission is to "to act as a global catalyst for change through the identification and analysis of the crucial problems facing humanity and the communication of such problems to the most important public and private decision makers as well as to the general public." They were responsible for inspiring the brutal one child policy in China.

A 1991 publication claimed that "divided nations require a common enemy to unite them, either real or made up" Items that fit the bill are global warming, overpopulation, famine, and water shortages. The conclusion being that the real enemy is *man himself*. The club is nothing more than a collectivist think tank wanting to promote global governance.

CONSPIRACY HYSTERIA...A book on conspiracies would not be complete without a mention of false hysteria. Throughout history innocent human beings have been victimized as whipping boys and scapegoats for the ills of society. Elaborate and false conspiracy theories have developed, confusing and tricking people into believing a lie, the idea being to deflect blame or explain away evil in the world. Gossiping housewives across the fence and high level propaganda hurt the innocent.

Blood libel, a very old conspiracy, is term used to explain how the Jews have terrorized other religious groups and is totally untrue. The Protocol of the Elders of Zion is supposedly a written transcript laying out their plan to take over the world's finances and control the human population. These false conspiracies of the Jewish people were accepted not only by Hitler, but also Henry Ford who had his picture in Adolph's office. Although corrupt financiers and bankers were the cause of WW1, and some of them happened to be Jewish, it does not follow that all Jews are evil and must be exterminated. The mass killings of the Jews in Germany during WW2 are a prime example of how hatred and innuendo can get wildly out of hand.

The inquisitions of Europe rooted out heretics who were jailed or tortured. The Salem witch trials placed blame on so called demon possessed people which led to several hangings. Even in the psychiatric field, hundreds of people were "diagnosed" in the 1980s as having suppressed memories of child abuse when in fact it never happened. Many parents were falsely accused of Satanic ritual abuse to their children. Finally reason prevailed and all but a very small percentage were found to be innocent.

The Sandy Hook school shooting on Dec. 12, 2012 claimed 26 lives. Here we have an example of the sloppy media getting facts wrong in early reporting of the event leading to false conspiracy claims and theories. Gun control groups and proposed legislation quickly followed as they tried to exploit the tragedy.

President William McKinley was fatally shot on Sept. 6, 1901 at the Pan American exposition in Buffalo NY. Leon Czolgosz, a wild eyed anarchist said he killed the President for the good of the working class. Violence is never the answer and it only serves to disqualify the study of conspiracy and gives patriots a bad name.

There are real cover-ups rampant in the world but alongside that is conspiratorial hysteria which can lead to great harm and disruption of people's lives. The smoke, mirrors and shadows that lurk in our midst must be analyzed and explained before we pass judgment. The power elites in the world are more than willing to spin a story and create lies to confuse us and lead us down the wrong road. It is tempting but illogical to connect every dot to with other dot. That is where conspiracy hysteria can cast a shadow on the genuine study of history.

CONSTITUTIONAL REPUBLIC...I wish we still lived under this system but unfortunately it has been hijacked from us. Some of us think this is a democracy but it was originally set up as a republic. In a democracy the so called mob rules if it achieves 51%. Therefore, we elect representatives to run the country and to vote in our best interests. Although we retain a certain element of it, most politicians are paid for and bought out by corporations, banks and other special interest groups. Individuals and major parties structures have been taken over long ago which leads me to the myth of the "two party system".

The two parties are set up the same way as professional wrestling. They determine what issue is going to be discussed and then go on stage in front of a willing media, presenting a staged match between the two warring sides. Some of the participants actually believe the game is real until an outside force threatens the event. At that point they form a cartel and move to fend off the invader. The Green Party and the Libertarian Party have felt this combined onslaught for many years as both major parties combine forces to block them or any third party from having any real effect on an election or issue. Therefore I say that we do not live in a constitutional republic when the political system is so much manipulated. I would say it resembles more of a corporate state fascist government. The oath of office to obey the Constitution is forgotten a minute after speaking it.

COUNCIL ON FOREIGN RELATIONS...Incorporated in 1921, one of the founding members of this notorious group was none other than Colonel House, the man who assisted President Wilson in setting up the Federal Reserve and getting the United States into WW1. Other founding members include J.P. Morgan, John D.

Rockefeller, Paul Warburg, Otto Kahn, and Jacob Schiff, also members of the Federal Reserve club. Morgan eventually gave up influence to The Rockefellers, who believe in one world governance.

The CFR has been promoting the New World Order for a long time through the manipulation of media, education, grants, and political control. Most big name politicians are members. They represent the power elite and their intention is to water down the sovereignty of the country and dilute the Constitution. Felix Frankfurter, Supreme Court Justice (1939-1962), said: "The real rulers in Washington are invisible and exercise power from behind the scenes." Almost 4000 members strong, the CFR establishment has been running our international affairs for 60 years. In addition, they have set up the two party system so that each side is nearly identical. That way "the American people can 'throw the rascals out' at any election without leading to any profound or extensive shifts in policy" so said Carol Quigley in 1966. This group works closely with the Trilateral Commission and the Bilderbergers to exert globalist policy. There may or may not be an outright conspiracy between these organizations, but there is an unwritten flow among them to subvert the Constitution and limit the freedoms of the people of the United States. They defiantly work together in that vein.

DRONES...The (UCAV) full size unmanned combat air vehicles are for offensive attacks in foreign lands and surveillance domestically on Americans. It is said that a new type of spy drone resembles a small bird or even a mosquito. These aerial vehicles are equipped to attack from the air being remotely controlled by humans in a safe position. Drones have killed suspected terrorists and even American citizens without trial raising Constitutional questions.

Samir Khan and Anwar al-Awlaki were killed Set. 30, 2011 in Yemen and al-Awlaki's 16 year old son Abdulrahman died from another strike on Oct. 14, 2011, all US citizens. If someone gives the word to kill, the drone can be maneuvered into position and do the job. Since there is no judge and jury present, the killing can be at the pure discretion of the person giving the orders.

Although no weapons are currently allowed in domestic drones, 30,000 have been ordered by the end of the decade to be launched into the skies of America, all in the name of public safety.

<u>DRUGS and the CIA</u>...There is a long history of the CIA tolerating the drug trade and also taking profits from drug sales to fund covert operations. There is also evidence of this agency intentionally facilitating the use of drugs around the world and in America. Criminal activities have been supported as arrests and indictments have been prevented.

During the Vietnam War, the CIA used their own Air America Company to run supplies and ship opium to its next checkpoint to be made into heroin which grew to become a terrible addiction for the US troops. Opium grew all over the region but it wasn't until the CIA came to the scene that big money could be made from the finished product. 100,000 Hmong were killed and many still live in fear because of the intervention of the CIA and their large scale operation (which also included food and supplies). Time has now shown that the United States had no business being there at all. The war that killed so many was a farce.

The Iran Contra affair began in 1985. President Reagan illegally supplied weapons to Iran which was an enemy of the United States in hopes of securing the release of hostages held in Lebanon. The profits of the sale went directly to the Contra "freedom fighters" in Nicaragua.

Oliver North of the Marine Corps facilitated the exchange and moved to create money for the Contra freedom fighters. Suspicion exists that North used drug money in the process. It later came out in the Kerry Report that members of the State Department were involved with drug trafficking that gave profits to the Contras. The CIA backed Contras distributed crack cocaine into Los Angeles. Gary Webb exposed the process in a series of articles published in 1996 in the San Jose Mercury news. The CIA was heavily involved with money laundering through the now defunct BCCI World Bank.

The CIA also used the BCCI bank to launder profits from heroin trafficking in the Pakistan-Afghanistan region which funded the Afghan War against the Soviets. This increased the flow of narcotics to America and Europe.

Bill Clinton, George H.W. Bush, George W. Bush, Jeb Bush and Dan Harmon are suspected in being connected to the Mena Intermountain Airport, Arkansas. It may have been used as a CIA cocaine drop point in the latter part of the 1980s. An investigator named Russell Welch opened a letter containing anthrax spores. His doctor's office was subsequently raided and the test results stolen.

Vicente Zambada Niebla, the son of Ismael Zambada García, a top Mexican drug lord, said after his arrest that he was given permission to smuggle drugs to America if he gave up information about rival cartels.

Dictator Manuel Noriega of Panama was given permission to continue drug trafficking for many years if he funded the Contra groups in Nicaragua. CIA director George H. Bush supplied Noriega with hundreds of thousands of dollars for his work. Later, when the scam was made public, the United States invaded Panama and captured Noriega.

Before 1993, the CIA allowed Venezuela to ship one ton of nearly pure cocaine to Miami International Airport as a way of gathering information on drug cartels. It ended up on the streets.

These are just a few examples of the way a government agency will exist behind the scenes and run covert operations not approved by Congress and the people.

How many lives have been destroyed by the very drugs the CIA has profited from?

EDGEWOOD ARSENAL...In 1947, the OSS intelligence agency was dismantled and the CIA was born. German scientists were scooped up by the Soviet Union and the United States after WW2, helping both nations build space programs. A top secret facility, hidden in the forests of Maryland was used to experiment on military "volunteers." Surrounded by security fences and guards, this Army research laboratory became something more than just a developing and testing ground for chemical agents.

In 1922, Edgewood concentrated on the study of chemical weapons. After WW2, new information came in from the infamous Japanese Unit 731. Nerve agents and mind control was the next level of interest.

Volunteers were invited to the complex to test new uniforms or advanced ammunition systems. They were never told about being human guinea pigs. They came for the weekend and received doses of experimental drugs in rooms with bolted down furniture. Careful observations and data were recorded.

According to a Veterans Affairs pamphlet, "between 1950 and 1975, about 6,720 soldiers took part in experiments involving exposures to 254 different chemicals."

In 1974-75, Congressional hearings resulted in disclosures and compensation given to some families of subjects who died. Many veterans suffer from chronic debilitating illnesses and were never informed of what they were given which included barbiturates, nerve gas, tear gas, tranquilizers, narcotics and hallucinogens. A class action lawsuit has been filed against the Defense Department and the Dept. of Veterans Affairs.

The Soviet Union was conducting the very same tests on their own people during this time. Does that give us the right to experiment on our people? The propaganda we hear every day is that we are a free people, and military personal take an oath to defend the Constitution and fight to protect liberty. How can this be true if our own government has routinely preformed trials and testing on our own soldiers without their knowledge? What good is the oath? We are no better than the very tyrants we claim to fight against.

FAITH...In all of its forms, some benign, some dangerous. The idea that we don't know everything produces a yearning in people to explain things and package their anxiety's and fears in grids of faith. The problem is when faith turns to subversion, subordination and coercion as it sometimes goes from a place of refuge to an oppressive force of totalitarianism. Like many things, faith can be good and it can be bad.

FEMA CAMPS...When the economic situation gets bad enough, Homeland Security may require martial law and the use of national emergency centers or FEMA camps to deal with civil unrest. HR 645 submitted Jan. of 2009 authorizes and legalizes the use of these camps. Built on military bases, these facilities would be able to keep large numbers of people imprisoned for long periods of time. This would be in combination with security cameras, fusion centers and military police for the rest of the country. Readiness Exercise 1984 calls for the suspension of the Constitution, declaration of martial law and the placement of military commanders in charge of state and local governments. Plans have already been drawn up to section the country into military quadrants.

FLUORIDE... Grand Rapids, Michigan was the first to add fluoride to its water supply back in 1945. Now, over 72% of the US population has fluoride in the drinking water. Germany, Sweden, Holland, and the Soviet Union have stopped the practice of fluorinating their water.

In the 1930s, the aluminum industry was looking to add fluoride to public water supplies rather than having to dump the waste somewhere else. Gerald Cox first came up with the suggestion from Francis Frary, chief scientist for ALCOA in 1939. Frary was concerned about his workers exposure to fluoride. The Mellon Institute in Pennsylvania, a defender of asbestos, backs up the suggestion to defend the aluminum industry. Fluoride is one of the leading air pollutants causing bone disease in humans and animals and was the cause of countless lawsuits. The Atomic Energy Commission had documents reworded to hide the fact of fluorides toxicity to go ahead with the building of the atomic bomb.

Edward Bernays, the father of propaganda and public relations, went on to sell the public to the "safety" and goodness of fluoride for tooth care even though it is an industrial waste product and a neurotoxin that lowers IQ in children. It's no wonder communities across the nation are working to get fluoride out of the water supply.

FOREIGN AID...How often do we hear about money and aid going to foreign nations? How poverty stricken Africans and poor suffering souls living under some evil regime need our help? It catches our attention and makes the President look good as he dishes out help and assistance. Many times the funds never reach whom it is intended. The plain truth is that our government assists large corporations to plunder and steal resources from poor countries around the world.

Through the IMF, economic "hit men" offer foreign leaders high interest loans. When they are unable to pay back the money, the natural resources are taken over. If they refuse the loan initially, CIA Jackals form a coup and overthrow the existing leader. If the Jackals fail, then our military moves in and forces the issue. This has been done in Iran, Iraq, Afghanistan, Ecuador, and many others since 1953. This is how the ruling class keeps its thumb over the rest of the world and keeps people living in poverty and unclean conditions. John Perkins explains it all in his book "Confessions of an Economic Hit Man".

GAY RIGHTS...People that choose an alternative lifestyle should have the same rights as anyone else. Throughout history, homosexuals have been persecuted, tortured, beaten, burned and locked up. Even in later years, they have been discriminated against in many ways, forcing many to recoil into a life of depression, drug abuse and loneliness. It has been said that the homosexual lifestyle is more dangerous than smoking cigarettes. The life expectancy is shorter and there are more emotional problems and diseases. Explanations for the behavior have ranged from being under the influence of evil spirits, to mental illness, to genetics at birth and free choice.

The Defense of Marriage Act was signed by President Bill Clinton in 1996 as a way to protect the definition of marriage as only between members of the opposite sex. Since then, many politicians on both sides of the aisle have changed their positions and now oppose DOMA and support same sex marriage including Clinton and

Obama. Gay partners have been unable to collect insurance, Social Security, and tax return benefits because of this ban on gay marriage. Society will eventually render some decision on the matter as far as the definition and legal rights of marriage. In the meantime, there is a bigger concern.

The lingering problem is with organized Gay activists who are pushing for something more than just basic human and civil rights. There is a movement to force all Pastors and Priests to preform same sex marriages against their will. Also, to teach and discuss homosexual issues to grade school age children in all public, private, and home schools by law. Furthermore, there is a "Gay Bill of Rights" in the making to force employers to hire gay, lesbian and transsexual individuals while make it difficult to fire them. This and similar laws should not be tolerated in a free society. The idea of the Separation of Church and State is not only to protect freedom of religion but also to halt any ideal or religious view from taking over the state!
 There is something deeper to all of this. Many prominent, influential elitists are calling for and supporting the breakdown of the traditional family and to encourage the loosening of society's morals. The tight knit family unit is under direct attack through education, movies, media and political action throughout the country. The overlords know what it takes to control individuals and that is to corrode and undermine the one thing we have that is difficult to break, and that is the family. Any way to go after the family is being encouraged including the promotion of homosexuality, welfare, single family households, drugs and even crime. Gays and lesbians have a legitimate right to demand basic freedoms, but their movement is being hijacked by others with a more sinister endgame.

For example, in February of 2013 the State of Massachusetts passed a law protecting the transgender status of children. Children are allowed to proclaim membership of the opposite sex at school and enter either bathroom and change what gender they want to be at home and at school, of course the parents had no input.

The United Nations and the academia of the world are pushing for a decline in worldwide population. To do this, they need the masses to become confused in a world that dims the lines of traditional thought and promotes moral relativism. Fortunately, attempts to reign in the masses this way are always doomed to fail but they can create a lot of havoc and destruction. As Rush Limbaugh said;

"the destiny of human beings in not to be controlled."

Through centuries of trial and error, society has come to accept the notion that a biological family with one man and one woman is the very best arrangement for raising children. Although it should be legal for two people of the same sex to join in a partnership and enjoy their basic rights, they cannot abridge the basic freedoms of other people to associate with and form organizations based on the nuclear family if they so choose. It is the right of private organizations and people of faith, to set rules on who can and who can't be a part of their membership, like any other private affiliation.

There is never going to be a utopian environment where all people are equal and happy. The very nature of inequality and freedom sets the stage where individuals have an *opportunity* to gain personal fulfillment. This is the ultimate state of being, to have that opportunity.

GEORGIA GUIDESTONES...In northeastern Georgia we have the American version of Stonehenge, five giant slabs of granite rising above the ground topping out at 16 feet supporting a 25,000 pound capstone. This mysterious monument gives us "instructions" on how the planet ought to be run in the future. It also predicts the movements of the sun and stars. Eight languages lay out the guidelines for the future of humanity.

No one knows who really paid for this and who is responsible for this expensive endeavor. A man named Robert Christian came to Elberton Granite Company in 1979 with the surprising instructions of how to build this structure. He said that a small group of anonymous people were paying for the project and their names would be kept secret forever. An astronomer had to be brought on site to determine the complex cuts and directions of the massive stones to make a perfect clock, calendar and compass.

The question is who really paid for this monument and why was it built. What power has the unlimited financial resources to fund such a project and tell a free people how to think and act?

Here are the inscriptions...

"LET THESE BE GUIDESTONES
TO AN AGE OF REASON"

1. Maintain humanity under 500,000,000 in perpetual balance with nature.
2. Guide reproduction wisely-improving fitness and diversity.
3. Unite humanity with a living new language.
4. Rule passion-faith-tradition- and all things with tempered reason.
5. Protect people and nations with fair laws and just courts.
6. Let all nations rule internally resolving external disputes in a world court.

7. Avoid petty laws and useless officials.
8. Balance personal rights with social duties.
9. Prize truth-beauty-love-seeking harmony with the infinite.
10. Be not a cancer on the earth-leave room for nature-leave room for nature.

This has all the earmarks of a totalitarian rule or at the very least well intentioned individuals doing nothing more than paving the way to an upside down utopian existence.

<u>GMO</u>... Genetically modified organisms. Much of the food we eat is genetically modified including corn and soybeans. Since the introduction of GMOs in 1996, illnesses that were once rare are now epidemic including cancer, heart disease and autism. The genes of one species are forced into the DNA of another for experimentation purposes. It creates crops that fend off insects but also have side effects on human digestive systems. The resulting gene sequence is foreign and not existing anywhere in nature. Our immune system then attacks the unrecognizable new sequence. The FDA was forced to release internal documents showing of their knowledge of the potential damage these foods may cause. Michael Taylor of Monsanto was in charge of policy at the FDA and allowed the food to go to the public as is with no testing. The Bt toxin that is present in the food then stays in the human body permanently and is even transferred to a fetus. The GMO food creates "leaking" digestive walls which then cause food allergies, which are on the rise. The GMO crops sprayed with "Roundup" are becoming less nutritious and causing birth defects in humans and farm animals. The Agricultural Department has chosen to ignore the evidence. Mothers are encouraged not to eat GMO food

because the bad genetics can get passed own to the next generation.

It is not surprising that the global elites themselves avoid GMO food at all costs. GMO crops are supposed to increase yield and bring a bounty of food to feed the world. The fact is that yield decreases and the crop is inferior and the use of herbicides actually increases. The goal of Monsanto is to replace all natural seed with GMO seed and create a market that serves only the chemical producers. That explains why the globalists are harboring and hiding natural seeds for their own use. The United Nations has a stranglehold over the colleges and universities to keep any criticism of GMO technology to a minimum and punish those who speak out against it. The effects of GMO food are reversible, and people around the world are demanding ordinary food again.

<u>GOVERNMENT ADMINISTRATION</u>...Every so often there is an investigative story that exposes government corruption as if it were the exception rather than the rule. The truth is that waste and fraud occur on a daily basis in all levels of government, from the street sweepers to the military and everything in between. Most departments are bloated with unnecessary over-paid employees and costly retired former employees who come back to work as double-dipping "consultants". Things do get done because there are many honest hard working government people, but they are caught up in an inefficient publicly run wasteland. The American people should not tolerate this, we should demand a more private society where fat is trimmed out of the system and government is severely reduced in size. Government should be lean and mean, serving the public rather than leaching from it.

This is true at the local city hall, the county, the state,

the metro councils, to the federal level and beyond. You need look no further than your local municipal building to find waste and corruption. Between the good deeds of the good deed doers, there is a secret web of money laundering. A county worker may get a free asphalt driveway or the city hall janitor drives the maintenance truck home on weekends. Maybe doctors at the county hospital are double billing Medicare patients to double dip into our pockets.

All of these things add up to unseen corruption, and a massive waste of taxpayer money. The United Nations agenda 21 has infiltrated small localities around the country pushing its green philosophy without us knowing about it, and it costs a great deal of money and slows down our economy in the process.

Instead of following the process of the Constitution, many laws are passed administratively where the voter has no say in the matter. The EPA for example passes new regulations frequently without any debate, forcing business and homes to "upgrade" equipment and abide by new standards. Taxes on electricity, new emission standards for coal fire and cement plants, and many other new regulations take their toll on the economy and employment. There is a list a mile long of various governmental agencies. Each one will take care of their own budget first which of course includes wages and benefits. After they give generously to themselves, they will go on costly departmental missions to help change the world to fit their own idea of what society ought to be, further trampling individual rights in the process.

GOVERNMENT CONTRACTS... Many times when the Federal government or a state pass a law for a proposed bridge or highway project; they already have an idea of what company is going to get the job, and what corporation will sell the materials. With this knowledge,

board members, Senators, Mayors and all the 'connected' class have inside information. They are able to buy stocks low and sell high to make millions of dollars even before any
work is started on the project. The state of California has gone bankrupt from insider corruption among other things. Public works projects have been laced with cronyism. The same occurs in all states. It's not how hard you work in America; it's who you know and what title you have.

In November of 2011, on the show 60 Minutes, House speaker Nancy Pelosi was asked about the hefty amount of money she made from insider trading, (buying initial public stock offerings). She shrugged it off saying it was legal. After the airing of the show, it didn't take long for Congress to introduce 'the stock act' which would prohibit Congressional insider trading. Of course, they all stood in line to support the bill but only after making millions before that time.
  In 2011-2012 the Obama administration pushed for a stimulus bill supposedly to help get jobs for out of work Americans. $535 million went to building Solyndra, a solar energy company promising to add jobs in the clean energy sector. Instead, plants have been shut down and jobs lost. Where did all the money go? Obama has talked about American jobs yet tax money goes to Sweden for its green industry. 60 billion dollars was used to prop up General Motors and Chrysler Corp. Failing companies making inferior products. They should have been allowed to fail or consolidate into the auto industry; instead the move was nothing more than a massive union bailout.

<u>GUN CONTROL</u>...The second amendment clearly gives us the right to keep and bear arms for the following

reasons; organizing a militia system, law enforcement, a deterrence to tyrannical government, repelling invasion, and suppressing insurrection. After a series of illegal shootings in 2012-2013, President Obama gave 23 executive orders to curtail the use and ownership of guns including forcing doctors to question their patients about their gun ownership status. This is clearly a violation of Constitutional division of powers. Instead of trying for a repeal of the second amendment, the Obama administration tried to use executive privilege. They also intend to create a national gun owners registry to keep tabs on every gun owner. Such a registry would eventually lead to disarming the country and confiscating all firearms from the American people, a step that England and Australia have already taken.

David Clarke is the Sherriff of Milwaukee, Wisconsin.
He has made the public statement that all citizens have the responsibility to defend themselves because the police cannot always get to the scene of a crime fast enough. He also reassured the public that he would not be a part of any confiscation plan. He and others like him will be working to protect our Constitutional rights and fight against the globalists who wish to destroy the country as we know it.

HAARP...Going north to Gakona, Alaska, there is an interesting facility which stands for "high frequency active auroral research program". They claim to study the Earth's ionosphere for navigation and communications research for the military and civilian populations. The weather is not supposed to be affected in any way.

Weather modification has been used for many years. Cloud seeding has been used by farmers and by the military in Vietnam when an intentional flood was created to slow down the Viet Cong. There is no question the government has looked into this area very seriously.

Weather can be used as a weapon of war, creating storms and producing a field of energy that can stop incoming missile attacks while carving holes in the atmosphere which would allow deadly radiation to the enemy's landscape. It can also thwart enemy communications.

Droughts can be ravaged upon unsuspecting countries, forcing them to sell land and resources. It can even be political in nature, using weather to "prove" the theory of climate change or global warming. In addition, storms could be created or modified around coastal areas to produce widespread damage, calling on government for response and money. Theoretically, HAARP can cause earthquakes and volcanos. Underground bases and submarines can be located. The radio signals can be used for mind control over vast populations. In the new era of genetically engineered crops, large chemical companies could theoretically modify the weather so only their brand of seed can grow in certain areas.

The transmitters at HAARP are supposedly strong enough to heat layers of the atmosphere which can alter warm and cold fronts, causing radical changes in climate and weather patterns. Waves of heat are steer-able and can be directed around the globe, even altering the flow of jet streams.

<u>HEALTH INSURANCE</u>...One of the great scams is the cost of health coverage. In the early 1990's JC Penney placed ads in the newspaper asking for part time workers. The job featured a good wage and *full health care coverage*. At the time, health insurance was a bargain.

A person could get great medical care at low cost. In 1988, $15 a month covered a young person with catastrophic coverage. Since the industry was for profit, new advancements came year after year for the benefit of the consumer. Apparently this was not good enough for the industry. Certain groups kept pushing for a single payer socialized system. Behind the scenes, insurance companies, pharmaceuticals, and the rest of the health care plantation made a pact with the devil. President Obama's health care act of 2009 was written by the health care industry and their lawyers to deliberately undermine their own industry and monopolize health care.

A monopoly cannot occur in a free market, only when the government picks winners and losers. Each company scrambled to be the favored provider. The government *and* the health care industry intentionally drove up prices over a 15 year period, making it impossible for some to pay and a making it a huge burden for others. The costs continue to rise.

The Sherman Anti-Trust Act of 1890 written to limit cartels and monopolies has exempted the insurance companies since the McCarran-Ferguson Act of 1944. In other words, health insurance companies are free to price fix and form cartels to monopolize the system. The government has stood on the sidelines accepting bribes and campaign contributions to keep their mouths shut as billions are raked in to these giant companies and their associated industries in the health care field; the areas of pharmaceutical, psychological, and medical education and practice. They are all tied together in a giant state sponsored monopoly which is costing the public trillions per year in unnecessary expenditure. The very poor are free to use the emergency rooms as their personal free clinics which add to the costs.

The system was broken by 2008 and then along came "The Affordable Health Care Act" or Obamacare. There were a few Representatives like Louisiana Governor

It was Bobby Jindal who wanted to end the anti-trust exemption but it was thrown out in committee before the bill was voted on. Why? Because President Obama, after using threats and bribes to pass his bill, accepted bribes himself to keep the insurance exemption the law of the land. He wanted the glory of passing the landmark bill and also to keep contributions flowing to the Democratic Party. The result is that we still do not have a truly free market approach to health care and the actual cost will soar for the American people. Nothing was solved. Instead, an estimated 70% of us will not be able to pay our own final health care and nursing home costs. Any money saved and assets accumulated will be eaten up to pay the exorbitant fees. Many people realize it too late and make a mad dash to give away assets at the last minute to qualify for Medicaid. Others hide their money in trusts or under the mattress. There is anxiety and stress in our last days instead of relaxation and financial independence. It becomes a race to poverty, where feelings of guilt and fear replace what should be prideful transfer of wealth to our loved ones.

Meanwhile, teaming up with public education and psychiatry, America is the home of the medicated. The diagnosing of learning disorders and mental illnesses make a fertile field for profit. The industry flourished to the point where many Americans are now hooked on dangerous legal drugs for a lifetime, and sharing the prescriptions with each other. Regulation has increased on organic foods and natural vitamins to stifle competition.

The Hemlock Society and other right to die organizations are fighting for the basic human right to pass away and avoid lengthy illnesses, unneeded suffering and expense. The problem is that the long drawn out process of dying is a so profitable to the industry that we as a society are willing to put our loved ones through the final horrors of death to just to keep the money flowing and nurse our own conscience.

Marijuana, a cheap cure all and replacement for expensive medications, remains mostly illegal. Prices on drugs and medical tests are skyrocketing. The costs for simple doctor visit or a pair of crutches is beyond comprehension. The public has been fooled into thinking that the health care system is "out of hand" and the government must "do something about it". In reality, the system has been intentionally run into the ground by both the government and the industry itself. Thus we have a massive double down conspiracy. While most people stood against national health care, there were enough public outcries to finally sneak legislation through with some well-placed bribes and threats. Although Obama promised his health care act would produce no new taxes, the Supreme Court ruled that it is a tax.

Very similar to the banker written Federal Reserve Act, national health care became law in part because the public was told the old system was broken and "something had to be done." Obamacare then passed through Congress during a Christmas and was signed into law. The entire law should be repealed and we should return to open competition which will adjust prices back to where they should be. We should be free to go across state lines for health insurance, much like auto insurance. With socialized medicine, the future of medicine is dim. Quality of care will be reduced and the system will be gummed up in costly bureaucracy, litigation and rationing. In addition, it will take over a large section of the economy, and we cannot allow the government to encroach that far into our lives. This is all part of the new world community and their quest for total control.

HOLOGRAM UNIVERSE...What could be a greater secret than to find out the entire universe is nothing but a projected hologram? We may be living within a vast illusion designed by unknown powers.

Modern science has been looking into this possibility for decades. Could we live in a parallel universe or multi-dimensional existence? These are questions that can be answered if we can somehow get beyond the drive to control each other and realize we all live on a spaceship hurling through time and space. There are places to go and places to see in this universe we live in.

What we see may simply be a mirrored image or projection of something taking place on a distant surface.

Plato told the story of the shadowy figures prancing around on a cave wall that somehow connect to a greater reality beyond the cave. The quantum mechanics theory and the string theory combine with the study of black holes and thermodynamics to postulate the idea of a hologram.

There may be an alternative surface where a distant process of reality is ongoing with a mere reflection of that process influencing what we perceive in this plane. The shadows they cast are the thoughts and images we take for granted, as we live out our lives.

ILLUMINATI... One of the great all time conspiracy theories is the effect of free masonry, the Illuminati, the Knights Templar, and other pagan systems on world leadership.

The Alta Vendita was written by an Italian secret society called Carbonari in the 1820's, which had associations to the Illuminati. The goal of the movement was to infiltrate and change the Catholic Church to a more liberal and progressive stance more along the lines of the French Revolutionaries. The change was to take place over many decades and finally overtake the leadership and the Pope in its influence. There is no question the movement was sponsored by non-Christians who believed the Church was antiquated and needed modernization.

The earth has seen its share of symbolism and deity worship in seats of power. Going all the way back to the sun gods of Egypt, to the plurality of Greek and Roman gods, to Islam, Hinduism, Christianity and everything in between, we have seen it all. We have experienced the total effect of mankind's imagination on the way we have enslaved ourselves and tried to order our lives around these beliefs. We have used graven images to stabilize society and explain the unknown and also to ransack the ignorant and control their lives.

The Jews have long been the victims of a false view that they control the banks and the world money system. They are blamed for every bad thing that happens when in reality they are a resilient and hardworking people who deserve respect and freedom.

It is no secret that those in world command are obsessed with pagan ideology, masonry and idolatry. Anyone in power who worships these little Gods and kneels down in front of owl statues should be ashamed. They certainly have risen to the level of their own incompetence. The secret meetings, strange handshakes, hidden codes, languages and all other rituals they partake in is proof to me of their own self-deceit. This is childish behavior on display. On one hand they dominate and control our lives and then somehow seek to justify this insidious behavior with the worship of carved animals and coded messages.

It is not worthwhile to spend any time on the Illuminati or any other pagan conspiracy. Leaders who conjure up spirits from plastic skulls and worship cardboard goddesses should not be taken seriously. These things are not based on reality to begin with even though they have a web of influence that spans centuries. I regard it all as misplaced fantasy. Washington DC is laced with masonic imagery and symbolism. The streets are laid out in perfect geometric designs and many of the buildings bear masonic carvings and rosaries, but why? If idolatry is taken too seriously the damage to society has been and can be severe. Those who conspire against humanity are attracted to these secret oaths and hidden ecstasies when they should be driven towards science, astronomy and other more worthy endeavors. If we would all concentrate on science, and put our minds together, we could better the world and make it fit for all to enjoy and experience. Every single person born into this world has the right to freedom, dignity and liberty, let us dispense with the ancient symbolism and reinvent the gods.

<u>IMF, WORLD BANK, AND ECAs</u>...The wealth of the world is wrongly held by financiers who have ties to the IMF, World Bank, Federal Reserve and the giant banks. The money from honest working people is embezzled and laundered around the planet. The wars keep the world unstable which makes it easy for corporations to move in and extract money and resources from the poor countries.

It's a matter of blind luck as to where people are born if they are to be poor or well off. Here we have a chance, while in poverty stricken countries; there is little or no chance. Most leaders and politicians are at least remotely connected to this elaborate scam that goes on year after year.

Export Credit Agencies hold at least 25% of all debt of developing countries which totals $430 billion per year. They may be public or government insured private companies. They hold a country hostage by lending them money under the condition that they only purchase goods and services from certain corporations. This arrangement raises the unemployment of the host country and destroys local businesses. In addition, the outside corporations will come in and ruin the land and pollute the waters of the host country.

New Guinea 1984, The BHP tailings dam burst and allowed 80,000 tons of pollution per day to spill down the Tedi and Fly rivers, damaging breeding grounds for the ocean fish used as a livelihood by the local fisherman. Thirty thousand villagers demanded compensation but BHP refused and even tried to make it illegal to claim damages. There was an out of court settlement. The size and scope of ECAs are just another way that tax money is used to fund and operate massive financial organizations without the knowledge of the typical American citizen who foots the bill.

After WW2, a monetary system was needed to mend the destruction and set up new rules for the nations to abide by. In 1944, 730 delegates met at the Mount Washington Hotel in New Hampshire to deliberate the new system. The International Monetary Fund (IMF) and the World Bank Group was created. The US dollar was set us as the reserve currency backed in gold. In 1971 President Nixon took us off gold convertibility once and for all, thereby ending the Bretton Woods agreement. The money turned into a free floating disaster and opened the floodgates of debasement and contamination. The IMF and World Bank then operated without the binding power of the gold standard. Corruption, money laundering and financial disaster was set in motion. The original intention was to have these groups temporarily assist nations short of money, but that mission has been turned into a scandalous operation which has the effect of keeping poor people poor and third world nations starving, not allowing any prosperity. In essence, we have our boot on the poor nations of the world and will not release them. Some believe the Civil War ended human bondage and slavery, but it is alive and well today.

According to inside economists, the IMF, World Bank, and the US Treasury encourage corruption by lending money to tainted foreign leaders who intentionally loot the cash and allow the people of the country to go with little or no assistance. There is evidence that President Clinton fixed the Russian elections to get Boris Yeltsin elected because he would be a willing counterpart to promote grand larceny against the Russian people.

There is a link between these organizations and the United Nations as they all work together keeping nations poor which reduces energy usage, satisfying the extreme environmentalists. They also sterilize the population with laced vaccinations. South Africa wanted to produce their own aids vaccines but the giant drug companies would not allow it until public pressure made them back off.

India and China refused the "bad medicine" of the IMF and have experienced profound growth rates. This goes to show that we must work to minimize the importance of so called world organizations. The best way to promote prosperity is for these international groups to back off and allow the nations of the world to make their own decisions and keep the dirty money out of circulation.

IMMIGRATION...It should be obvious that both political parties and all administrations of the last 4 decades have purposefully allowed illegal immigration. The southern border has remained porous to allow multiculturalism, diversity, and cheap labor. Our leaders want the United States to lose its identity and absorb itself into the rest of the world community. This is a grave mistake. The unique culture of America that has revolutionized the planet for the better is under direct attack. The illegals have brought strife to the country. They not only take jobs but demand benefits. It is costly to our heritage and sovereignty. Legal immigration and the proper assimilation into society has added strength to the country.

The Mexican government at one time distributed 200,000 survival kits for those planning to sneak over the border. There are so many Mexican citizens that cannot be absorbed into their own system that they are encouraged to go to the U.S. Mexican soap operas have advertisements from Washington to come across and take advantage of the benefits that are listed and linked on the White House web page! Mexican schools teach how the southern United States is really stolen territory.

If the United States remains intact, the world will have an example to follow. If it blends into the rest of the world, there will be no shining beacon on the hill and the world will become a watered down, crime infested temple of socialism.

IRON MOUNTAIN REPORT...Published in 1967, this report is the work of a 15 person panel set up by the Kennedy administration to study what the country should do in times of peace. It was supposed to have been secret, but one member leaked it to the public. Leonard Lewin admitted in 1972 that the book was really written by him and was a spoof. Whether this was a hoax or not, it brings up some very interesting theories of how the government might operate behind the scenes.

The report concludes that peace is not an option in today's world. We need to be in a constant state of war as part of the overall economy and have a fictitious enemy. Blood games, sports and alternative foes should be a part of everyday entertainment to divert collective aggression. Alien life forms should be created to scare the public and colossal environmental theories and threats dealing with uncontrollable pollution, a giant space program as a way to pour money into for years to come, also a worldwide police force. In order to control population, ways to limit births and adding drugs and poisons to the food supply.

　Looking at today's world, the Report from Iron Mountain, whether real or fictional, was a prophetic piece of work. In the modern world, we are fighting a fictitious enemy (the terrorists) with no end to war in sight. We build massive sports stadiums at public expense and pay the players millions of dollars to go out and get banged up just for entertainment value. Reports of alien beings, flying saucers and UFOs are filling our spare time with diversion. The media promotes environmental disasters like the Ozone effect and global warming to somehow get us to use less fuel and energy. Finally, the police state and the surveillance revolution threaten to take even more liberty away. The Report from Iron Mountain should be taken seriously, hoax or not.

LOTTERY... One of the shadiest scams of all is the government lottery. Tax payer money is used to advertise and entice people to spend what's left of their hard earned money on decorative pull tabs where the chances of winning big are extremely low. Ads are run on television and billboards. Gas stations and grocery stores hit you in the face with various games and flashy cards. The compliant media broadcasts winners and tells people they can be the next millionaire. When someone wins, they lose half their winnings to taxes and the state walks off with even more. As more people get addicted, the government spends more tax money on gambling addiction programs.

　It's one thing that people support big government by force and quite another that we foolishly give them even

more money through the lottery. It's a sad state of affairs. Very little of the money goes to a "good cause" and most of it is eaten up in more government bureaucracy to run the lottery system and the "general fund".
  When an audit was done in Minnesota, the head lottery chief committed suicide out of embarrassment of what the study might show. Although I support the idea of legal gambling and gaming, it should remain in the private sector only. State run lotteries are a disgrace.

MAFIA... For many years, the criminal underground operated without the knowledge of ordinary citizens. We were told crime sprees were the result of detached groups and individuals working on their own. There was officially no mafia or organized crime syndicate. The truth is that organized crime is hundreds of years old with organizations and structures operating more efficiently than some countries. They have worked for the government and government has worked for them. Sometimes they are the government. I would say the United States of America is now run and operated by professional criminals at the highest level and it has been for some time. The Mafia is real and near to us.

MEDIA... The mechanism that deceives the masses and keeps us in the dark is the media, in all of its forms, TV, newspapers, radio, and the like. Average people may think they are getting an objective view, seeing two sides of a story; the problem is the two sides of the story are carefully marshaled and monitored to make it appear controversial when in fact the real truth is hidden from view.
  In the last 20 years, conglomerates of media have developed as the big companies get bigger by combining and buying out the smaller ones, thereby concentrating

knowledge. Now we have mega corporations fueling data to us. Usually, the information is of poor quality and filled with celebrity gossip and war coverage that has no depth or investigation behind it. Mass media is reluctant to get to the root of problems and only tell us the final chapter, like in the case of the Enron and banking scandals.

Radio stations have been fused together across the country creating the same problem as TV, same with newspapers. Unfortunately, political coverage is just as bad in that those running for office are picked and chosen by the mass media and others not to their liking are ignored.

Advertising has turned into a monopoly and new movie releases are thrust upon the audiences, making their run through the theatres, cable and DVD release. Massive profits keep making the big companies even bigger and the real information we get from the world is ever more limited in scope. The internet is an exception as alternative viewpoints are available. That is why there is a push to regulate the online experience and take over the internet.

The political world is an example of this deceit. The major job of the media is to promote selected candidates hand-picked by corporate power brokers. The two major parties pretend to oppose each other while keeping any third party at arm's length from the public. The media takes sides and sets up arbitrary discussions and debates which excite the viewers in a false contest where the desired outcome happens no matter who wins or loses. The media can then fill the rest of our lives with sports, trivial cable shows and a myriad of entertainment meant to steer our minds from what is actually happening in the bowels of government. There are many good and worthy things in media that are useful to us but as long as they are owned and run by mega-corporations, they will never fully serve their true function and that is telling us the straight truth. MSNBC is 80% owned by General Electric, which supplies arms and weapons to the US government. Yet, the agenda of the channel is to take a position against war. Just a few giants own all the major media which means they determine what we see and what we hear. Comcast and AOL Time Warner serve 40% of all cable households. The First Amendment is supposed to provide an uninhibited marketplace of ideas, not a corporate run stream of half-truth and deception.

Americans more and more rely on alternate information from the internet and whatever written and spoken tidbits we can come up with. The good news is we are becoming more aware and more interested in deeper meanings. The media is being exposed.

Amber Lyon, an Emmy award winning investigative journalist has blown the whistle on her former network CNN. The government actually pays CNN not to run stories and also run stories favorable to the government agenda. This is nothing more than propaganda to manipulate the public. One of her stories in Bahrain would not be aired because it went against the "story line".

Bahrain is a US backed country that was caught terrorizing their people, not a good thing to have on CNN. Amber and her crew were eventually dismissed.

In another example of media half-truth, a speech by Iranian leader Mahmoud Ahmadinejad was edited to hide his sentiments on peace because the Pentagon no doubt wants a new war with Iran, and they want to portray him as the "evil dictator."

<u>MK-ULTRA</u>...In 1973, CIA director Richard Helms ordered all MK-ULTRA files destroyed. The only knowledge we have left is the sworn testimony of its

participants. In 1977, The Freedom of Information Act produced some 20,000 documents relating to the project.

This CIA mind control endeavor ran from 1953-1973. Starting in 1953, the CIA and its Nazi German assistants began experimenting on innocent subjects. Up to 7000 servicemen went through the process. Many of the drugs used like LSD and Marijuana ended up on the streets as part of the hippie culture of the 60s. The CIA may have shaped the culture as much as the Beatles and the British rock invasion. In fact the government may have been involved with the deaths of some of the big names in rock music like Jim Morrison, Jimi Hendrix, Janis Joplin, Brian Jones and other assassins like Sirhan Sirhan who shot Robert Kennedy. John Lennon was watched and viewed as a threat to America.

MK is German for mind control. The idea was to search for and find the best ways to take over a person's independence and use the individual for preforming covert actions like spying and assassination and then alter brain functions and adjust their mental state. Some of the tools used were LSD, hypnosis, sensory deprivation, isolation, verbal and sexual abuse, and torture. Colleges, Universities, hospitals, pharmaceutical companies, and prisons took part in this covert experimentation of unwilling subjects in order to further information on how to manipulate foreign leaders and interrogate Soviet spies and maybe how to murder our own people. There are internet sites that list hundreds of suspicious government deaths. Unwitting subjects have successfully sued the CIA for over $7,000,000 in damages.

Government mind control and abuse stories branch out far beyond the CIA. Well known are the Atomic Veterans who were the victims of nuclear radiation experiments from 1945-1962. Up to 250,000 veterans were intentionally exposed with no special protection. The idea was to find out what would happen if we were attacked. Military personal served as the willing guinea pigs for the Pentagon.

The VA continues to deny claims even with a high rate of leukemia and brain tumors. Agent Orange, which cleared away vegetation in Vietnam, is another chemical that caused many veterans to suffer. $180,000,000 was paid out in an out of court settlement. Another cover-up was the Gulf War Syndrome which affected 20,000 veterans and killed 7000.

Individuals like Candy Jones and Cathy O'Brien have spoken out about their own experiences which included a secret personality for Jones and child abuse for O'Brien. Ted Kaczynski, known as the "Unabomber" had volunteered for a psychological study at Harvard around 1960. The chief researcher was Dr. Henry Murray, a veteran who furnished the CIA with information. Who knows whether Kaczynski developed into a human time bomb?

One of the main tactics in "brainwashing" was removing any potential guilt felt by the subject that they would someday be judged by a higher power. This allowed the subjects to be programmed into killers who had no remorse.

There are also examples of mass mind control. One involved the Peoples Temple in Jonestown, Guyana. Charismatic leader Jim Jones led his followers to a remote area and used drugs and mass hypnosis to achieve his control. Congressman Leo Ryan was killed there during his investigation. The official story is that 914 people died from poison laced "Kool-Aid" when the evidence shows they died from other causes. Some were strangled and others were shot. 80% of the bodies had needle marks and no autopsies were allowed to be done. Ryan may have stumbled on a large-scale CIA experiment. His aide had received information that the MK-ULTRA experiments did not end in 1973.

MONEY...What better way to control us than to control the money we use? Millions of hard working people have their money abducted through pure stealth, a slow leak in their wallets and bank accounts. Covered more in chapter 3, the monetary system of a tribe, community, or an entire nation is the single most manipulated issue in human history. A few "thoughtful" financiers can easily ruin a country through credit manipulation and monetary debt leaving the commoners to fend for themselves. Like average Americans during the depression, they never know what hit them. There is great suspicion when the rich class seems to grow and run away with all the loot and leave little or nothing for the rest of us. This has been going on since the beginning of trade itself. It is not a result of capitalism but a result of money "manipulation".

The Federal Reserve caused the great depression by contracting the money by 1/3 from 1929-1933 after inflating it near the end of the roaring 20's. People suffered and lost their land. The Fed later injected much needed money and liquidity into the system making it available for the big war effort. It was not the war itself that got us out of the depression; the Fed simply printed the money that was lacking beforehand.

The war was won with great fanfare and celebration and the "fabulous fifties" followed suit with prosperity and new riches simply because we were the only economy left standing in the rubble. The middle class was born, created from the resulting prosperity and low regulation. Since the early 60s, wealth from this explosion has been systematically stripped away from us, year by year, little by little, without our knowledge. It now takes two wage earners to achieve what one could do in the fifties. Family life has been altered and the culture has declined as a result. In addition, the Fed has harbored and protected some of the worst financial criminals in history, including the IMF, the Bank of England, and the infamous BCCI International Bank used by the CIA and many other illegal money laundering operations before it was finally shut down in 1991.

Few and far between are the times when sound money is the rule and the common people develop their own prosperity. Although we need a system of exchange, credit, and barter, we have allowed these systems to be taken over by deceitful money men, credit experts and debt collectors for too long and too often in our history. Monetary corruption is the one conspiracy that is out in the open and yet incredibly hidden from public view. We just don't realize our own money can be our worst enemy. It's the elephant in the room that goes unnoticed. John Adams said a country can fall by the sword or by debt. The day will come when sound/ honest money will be understood by all people, I hope that day comes sooner than later.

NORTH AMERICAN UNION...George Bush met with the Canadian and Mexican presidents in 2005 about joint regulation of airlines, food and highways without congressional approval or discussion, it was called the Security and Prosperity Partnership of North America. The idea is to intertwine the three countries into one working unit, like what happened in Europe with the EU and the Eurozone.

The reason why both parties in the US have ignored illegal immigration is evidence that the global ruling class wants a new North American Union. The US middle class then pays the social cost of the Mexican poor coming across the border. Our education system is teaching diversity and the unification of all races, even changing history to make it appear that the white man was an illegal immigrant to America. President Clinton signed the NAFTA free trade agreement followed by President Obama announcing new streamlined trade laws to bring Canada and the US together under one roof. Multinational corporations have been pushing to end the sovereignty of the US to lower labor costs. New "inland port" cities of Kansas City and Denver will receive goods via the widened Panama Canal and Mexican seaports to avoid higher wage union controlled ports in Loa Angeles.

The NAU would include a group of overlords to determine policy in transportation, migration, water resources, and commerce. The rules of the NAU would supersede any existing law in each of the three countries. Ultimately, the European Union and the North American Union would merge. President Bush already signed a Trans-Atlantic contract with the EU.

The state of Texas has many patriots who oppose the massive new interstate freeway system being conceived to link Canada and Mexico. Although it is wise to keep travel and trade open to the three nations, it is also prudent to retain our sovereignty, identity, and cultural differences, and remain separate countries.

NSA, (God is Watching)... The National Security Agency is a secretive organization run by the Dept. of Defense. Using cryptologic intelligence, their mission is to collect and analyze foreign human induced data for the protection of the United States.

Since September 11, 2001 and passage of the Patriot Act, the push has been on to collect data and spy on the American people and store records of every citizen. They monitor emails, phone calls, and internet activity. In addition, massive digital storage facilities called

FUSION CENTERS run by the Dept. of Homeland Security are also collecting information on US citizens. There are 72 in existence and over a billion dollars has been spent to build them. These types of spying and data collection are against the Constitution of the United States and go against the very foundation of the country. It is an obvious violation of the fourth amendment.

A massive $2 billion data collection center is being constructed in Bluffdale, Utah for the NSA. It will become the nation's biggest informational storage locker, containing the words and images of a whole country, a covert memory bank of human activity. Each person will have a personal data trail of court records, traffic tickets, phone and text messages, social media postings, employment and health histories, google searches and more. The immediate effect is apprehension in society as we "self-censor" ourselves out of the fear of arrest or harassment by the government.

The NSA claims it will be able to stop crimes before they happen and infiltrate terrorist cells. It could be used for research projections and other useful applications. The problem is that any information collected on US citizens could be used against them.

A few NSA whistle blowers have come out publically to reveal a sinister story taking place. The situation has gone way too far. For example, if you were involved in an anti-government rally, you could be threatened by the FBI to stop protesting or they could leak your personal information to the public. Let's say you were caught posting anti-war statements in chat rooms over a five year period. You could be singled out and threatened. If your cousin was involved in a crime, *you* could put you in jail for *his* actions. Under the NDAA law, any person in the United States can be arrested and indefinitely detained for any reason without trial. It ends up to be a tremendous weapon for government to use against its own people, and a dangerous threat to personal liberty. Former NSA employee and whistleblower Thomas Drake said the according to the NSA in 2001; "we have opened up Pandora's box, we are going to turn the US into the equivalent of a foreign nation for purposes of dragnet electronic surveillance." This violates the 4th amendment of the United States.

Through the centuries, rulers have used the power of guilt to keep people in line. If a person chose to disobey the Lord, they would be judged accordingly. The miniature voice of God played on in the background, influencing decisions and directing proper action, always wary to obey God's law or be consumed with guilt. Contrary voices were that of the devil. If the "voice of God" wasn't strong enough, they could be imprisoned or hung for their crimes against the state. This method also compelled people to give up their lives in war for the "glory of God".

Today we have a new version of God's law. In addition to conscience and civic duty, the tool of *personal invasion* is used. Soon the government will be able to read your mind and predict your thoughts in a notorious web of digital control as all private information is compromised. This will lead to something more efficient than godly guilt. It will be the total control of the individual with no sense of self remaining. We will be complete wards of the state with no freedom, liberty or even self-awareness. Our lives will be directed in a data based totalitarian world with no chance of retribution or escape. All the horrors of George Orwell's 1984 will be among us if we don't somehow stand up and fight back.

PENTAGON PAPERS...In May of 2011, this document was fully disclosed to the public. In 1971 the New York Times published some of the leaked information before the Nixon administration put a stop to it. Sec. of Defense Robert McNamara commissioned the report in 1967 as information about Vietnam-US relations from 1945-1967.

The report proves that the Truman, Kennedy and Johnson administrations had every intention of escalating the war in Vietnam even though they said otherwise to the public. President Johnson campaigned in 1964 on the promise to not bomb North Vietnam; calling his opponent Barry Goldwater a trigger happy warmonger when all along Johnson was the one planning to bomb the little country.

POLICE STATE... "Those who would give up essential liberty to purchase a little temporary safety deserve neither liberty nor safety" ~Ben Franklin.

Highway checkpoints, Fusion center surveillance, TSA body searches at airports, home invasions, property confiscation, FIMA camps, and many other harassing events take place here in America every day. According to Wikipedia; "A police state is a state, such as the United States of America, in which the government exercises rigid and repressive controls over the social, economic, and political life of the population. A police state typically exhibits elements of totalitarianism and social control, and there is usually little or no distinction between the law and the exercise of political power by the executive".

What we have in this country is a piece of velvet covering the inner fist of the government. It has been that way for a long time. They run the show and anyone standing in their way is a threat. For many years, they didn't care what people said in small groups, or what types of discussion we engaged in, just so we stayed away from the media. Today, with the worldwide internet, we are able to communicate with many people instantly and spread information at lightning speed. Therefore, the real power that has been hiding in the shadows is being forced out in the open as they exert their will on the populace, protecting the power players that once lurked in the background.

The military and police are merging in an elaborate system run by the FBI. The CIA is encouraging or at least allowing drugs to infiltrate the US so law enforcement, banks and the judicial system can profit on its illegality. Any branch of the system is both a singular entity and also a part of the invisible web that covertly connects the monstrosity as a whole working in solidarity and in isolation creating a giant web of corruption and oppression.

The last line of defense we have is the local sheriff. Many local police departments are serving their communities with honor and loyalty while others have sold out and turned corrupt. In some areas children are taught to tattle on their parents and fellow classmates. Child rights laws have been put into effect. Databases are kept on children and their school records kept on file.

Peaceful assembly and protest rallies are now carefully monitored and even disallowed. Many have been shut down or invaded by police forces. Sometimes police pose as anarchists who intentionally cause damage just to close down a legitimate protest.

The ultimate reaction of the police state is martial law wherein the military takes total control in an emergency situation. It can be temporary or last for years as in the Philippian Islands from 1972-1981.

PROJECT PAPERCLIP...After the smoke cleared in WW2, 1800 Nazis and 3700 of their dependents were allowed to come to the United States under Project Paperclip, signed by Harry Truman in 1945. Truman's orders specifically stated that no Nazis or anyone connected to the Nazi Party would be allowed to come over. Instead, the Joint Objective Intelligence Agency changed the names and identities of some of the worst criminals, and brought them over under cover. Instead of being tried for war crimes, they were sent here with good paying jobs in rocket research, mind control and biological weapon systems. They lived a life of luxury here in the States when every last one of them should have been in prison for the crimes they committed against the human race.

Our government also betrayed up to 20,000 POWs left in the Soviet Union after WW2. It was better to ignore them versus negotiating their release. We also protected criminal Japanese biological specialists. The same thing happened after the Korean and Vietnam conflicts.

Public school teachers will not discuss "Operation Paperclip." Instead, they are told to carpet bomb students with misinformation about WW2; the Americans were the good guys and the Germans were the bad guys. We are taught about the Nuremberg trials where 23 war criminals were tried, convicted, and sent away forever, securing freedom for humanity, but it was not that simple...

With their new identities, the Nazi felons were encouraged to bring their expertise to the United States, working for us in the fields of rocket engineering and biochemical weaponry. V-2 missiles, the stealth bomber and the propulsion units of the moon landings and other cutting edge technology can be attributed to these imported Nazi war criminals. Wernher von Braun was a former SS officer and the mastermind of the NASA moonshots even though he was identified as a security risk. Others include Arthur Rudolph, operations director at Nordhausen, where 20,000 died, Kurt Debus- SS officer, and Hubertus Strughold the father of space medicine and overseer of human experiments at

Auschwitz. There were hundreds of others.

What does America really stand for? Do we stand for justice? Or will we trade justice for political expediency? Millions of ordinary people suffered and died brutally under Hitler's regime. Yet, our leaders chose to protect the guilty in exchange for bragging rights and notoriety.

NASA has gone on to deceive the American people as to its real intentions. Nazi technology may have included anti-gravity and other profound inventions. There are many who think the moon landings were a clever hoax, or at least some of the pictures were faked. Photographs of the lunar surface were used in more than one instance, depicting different landscapes. The current "Vision 20/20" is a way to militarize space and keep track of any dissenting and rebellious people around the globe. At some point all people and their communications will be monitored fully. To what extent was Nazi ideology imported to this country, and how much remains to this day?

PSYCHIATRY...For centuries, faith and religion set the terms of reality and the law of the land was set in place based upon whatever doctrine worked to keep the masses in order. The advent of individual freedom and the scientific revolution brought many people to question the authority of the church and shine the light of reason on its long held beliefs. The church was no longer in charge; they took their position on the sidelines, becoming a voluntary institution as it ought to be. The vacuum was then filled by a new religion, and that is Psychiatry.

Claiming to be scientific in its methods, much of what they do resembles a form of religion. Claiming man is nothing more than a primal-response machine, with no spirit, they have not only influenced the public school curriculum, but placed a heavy stamp on government and its policies. Although their research has brought us theories that have some useful applications, in general human beings have not benefitted. Shock treatments, medication experiments, involuntary incarceration, physical abuse, and loosely diagnosing mental illness has made us into kind of a robotic populace as we run to the doctor for every problem and challenge in life. In the past, the church preformed this function, now the psychiatrist has become the priest and his church is the office.

Puerto Rico 1967. A group of prominent psychiatrists met to discuss the future of drug use. They envisioned school children using drugs to speed up their learning to leave time for "character development." Total control of human emotional status was the goal by the year 2000.

Millions of school children are now on these mind altering drugs. 52 million children are screened for "mental illness" without the consent of parents causing an invasion of privacy.

The results are 1.5 million children on antidepressants are at risk of violent behavior and suicide. Education achievement has decreased. Violent crime is up 147% and drug abuse is up 2900%.

Psychiatry should be a voluntary option, but many times it's mandatory. The replacement for any religion old and new is freedom. Individual rights allow people to become critical thinkers who can then solve the problems of life on their own in whatever way is right for them. Freedom alone makes for the best of all possible worlds.

RACISM...I know it's odd to view racism as a conspiracy, but throughout history and today we find that a government or even a school system will intentionally pit one race of people against another. The populace becomes distracted, and overlooks what the government is up to and instead wastes time debating irrelevant issues that are conjured up from the old bag of totalitarian tricks. It is much easier for a nation to declare martial law or take away freedoms from the people if the people are fighting amongst themselves. The 1993 Rwanda massacre shows how easy it is to pit one group against another.

It is perfectly natural for all races, creeds and colors to relate with and become friends with each other. Children do this all the time until they are taught otherwise.

Racism is a learned trait coming from our own government. For example, black communities were once strong family bastions with a solid religious foundation. Since the advent of welfare, the black community has declined in the midst of free housing and public assistance, with crime and single parent households on the increase.

The Democratic Party has taken a stance as being the savior of the black race and the bringer of Civil Rights when in fact there was more Republican than Democrat support for the Civil Rights Act of 1964 which was watered down by President Johnson before it passed. Many southern Dixiecrat-Democrats were opposed to the legislation. Before that time, Republican Dwight Eisenhower had supported the Civil Rights Act of 1957 and sent troops to insure blacks were allowed in high schools while John Kennedy voted against the bill as a Senator. Martin Luther King Jr. and Sr. were registered Republicans.

Traditionally, up to the 1960s, blacks were Republicans and Democrats stood against any civil rights, going as far back as the Civil War. The Republicans pushed through amendments 13, 14 and 15 giving Blacks freedom, citizenship and the right to vote. The Republicans started the NAACP and Affirmative Action while the Democrats started the Ku Klux Klan.

It wasn't until the late 1960s the Democratic Party started to gain millions of black voters promising them government benefits and welfare. Since that time, the black race has gotten poor and fragmented, the families have dissolved, the high school dropout rate is high and the crime rate is higher.

So called experts then tell the media that blacks are "underprivileged" and need even more assistance which increases dependence and decline. We are told the blacks deserve repercussions (for slavery) and need more
funding for housing and food stamps. Educators say that blacks are unable to score well on standardized tests and need "extra" help getting into college. Race baiters and race hustlers then come along in the media and stir up trouble which increases hate crime and agitates the situation further. The definition of race baiting from Wikipedia is this;
"The act of using racially derisive language, actions, or other forms of communication in order to anger or intimidate or coerce a person or group of people."

On Feb. 26, 2012 in Sanford, Florida, George Zimmerman, a Hispanic man confronted Trayvon Martin, a 17 year old black youth. Zimmerman shot Martin and killed him after a scuffle. Even before the case went to trial, the race baiters were in full swing. One newspaper called Zimmerman a "white Hispanic" in order to bait the blacks against the whites. NBC News admitted to rearranging Zimmerman's quote to make it sound like Zimmerman was racist. President Obama said the "stand your ground" law should be reexamined as Jesse Jackson called for it to be repealed. Black leader Al Sharpton reacted by saying Martin was murdered. The New Black Panthers offered a $10,000 "bounty" on the capture of Zimmerman. On Facebook, a new page called "Justice for Trayvon" received 200,000 likes. Then, reactions came; A 78 year old white Ohio man was beaten by a group of blacks to "get revenge for Trayvon". On April 24th, a man chased some kids out of the street who were playing basketball in traffic. The kids went home and their parents, who were black, returned with brass knuckles and baseball bats. They proceeded to beat the man close to death.

The Tea Party, which began in 2007 as a grassroots movement to address the expanding federal debt, has been the target of race baiting many times as the media and even congressman have called the movement racist when in fact there is no racism. Race baiters have even infiltrated Tea Party rallies acting like racists to fool the public. Unfortunately, we will always have to put up with individuals and groups of people who push their agenda using the tool of division. Blacks who have attended Tea Party functions were pleasantly surprised to not find any trace of racism and made to feel like human beings and not members of a deprived race.

The only information in poor areas or projects comes from whatever they hear from social workers, radical preachers or the slanted media. It's no wonder there is so much hatred against white people and the so called rich. The media induced hysteria is designed to incite race riots and bad feelings between the races. It's designed to help divide the country between the blacks and the whites and also the rich and the poor. Martin Luther King was murdered because he taught us to look beyond race and judge people by their character, not the color of their skin.

The media continues overtly and covertly to "poison the wells," inciting bad blood between the races.

Native Americans are themselves kept on the poor farm which creates alcoholism and a loss of self-worth. They should be allowed to reclaim their heritage and traditions and occupy their own unique place in society. The government should stay out of their business and allow them to assimilate or stay as they are in peace.

Any race of people could have been victimized in this way. The fact is that no race is inferior or superior to another. It is a manufactured illusion.

Others in society suffer the same way. "The rich" is a subgroup where *class envy* is utilized. They are made to appear lucky, fortunate and privileged and "evil" in the eyes of the poor. The media gives the false notion that free enterprise "doesn't work" because the rich prosper while the rest of us have nothing when in fact the corrupt monetary system is what produces crony capitalism and ill-gotten wealth. Children are taught to study hard to get a good paying job. If they happen to achieve success, they are then labeled as the greedy rich who should be taxed more.

Faith can go either way. Centuries ago, when religion ruled everything, the heretic or witch was burned at the stake. Religious people are now in hot water as their beliefs and traditions are being challenged, debated and even mocked in the public square. As you can see, there are many ways to deceive the people when the people themselves are cunningly divided into opposing groups.

ROAD CONSTRUCTION...Professional architects and engineers have designed beautiful buildings, bridges and infrastructure across America. Cities have been planned and constructed as marvels to our ingenuity and imagination. Living amongst those winding pathways and landscaped boulevards is a monster in the form of road construction. This monster is costing the average taxpayer billions as it continually eats up and recycles roads and highways for no apparent reason. Suspect contracts are awarded to renew highways, tear down and build new bridges, and reroute roads for no good reason.

Left standing is old infrastructure, turning brittle and left in disrepair. Sewer systems are falling apart, bridges are collapsing, and people are wondering what's going on. Where is all the money going to?

Some of us can see the scam. A road is refurbished, paved over with tar that soon ends up cracking and falling apart, then the road is shut down again as they "resurface" the pavement in a never ending cycle of failure and fix. Many roads are intentionally designed without proper drainage beneath so they crack and heave under the pressure of frost and changing temperatures, causing pot holes and broken wheels. The public then demands something be done and funding is allocated for a "new" road. Many times a road will be "fixed" by applying a new layer of tar only to have it crack again. Duplication means more funding. The ancient Romans built roads that still exist today. What is the problem with American road building? There are many examples of well-built turnpikes and freeways that have lasted for fifty years or more under all types of traffic and weather conditions. Why not use our technology to build permanent roads, bridges and highways that never fall apart under any circumstances. Instead, government contracts work for the short term, building temporary structures designed to fail so they can demand everlasting funding that will keep them placing signs and barriers in our lives for years to come. Investigative reporters have shown workers taking multiple breaks during the day. Next time you see construction crews leaning on their shovels, give a honk.

SCIENCE...There are few words that embody more trust than the word scientist. Science has been a building block of civilization and progress for centuries, yet the avenues of *false* science are many.

I have covered the misleading topics of archeology,

psychiatry, eugenics, and global warming already.
The social sciences are also suspicious. Sociological research is often full of agenda driven statistics, graphs and reports. For example, a company may pay for a study that proves their products are safe and effective. Surveys may be taken to show support or disapproval for an issue like gun control. Research taken is many times invalid, unrepresentative, not standardized and slanted to obtain a false perception for public consumption. Any poll or statistic can be manipulated to achieve a desired outcome, and it happens often.

The field of science is a money based endeavor. Scientists are paid well to "discover" things that increase their employer's bottom line or their reputation. University scientists have agendas handed down from the upper administrators which may be political in nature. Soviet scientists always followed the will of the Communist Party.

True science is a stepping stone to a greater future; it is what the world craves and needs. The problem is that all too often half-truth and deception is all we get from the many levels of pseudo-science.

SECRET WARS...Craig Roberts explains that between 1951 and 1978 the United States involved itself in "stages coups, covert military action, popular revolutions, and assassinations conducted under the guise of national security were in fact motivated by the business interests of major corporations and the investment bankers that backed them." This was all done secretly in the name of stopping "Soviet expansion." This happened in Iran, Guatemala, Cuba, Africa and South America. Democratically elected leaders were taken out in favor of individuals more suited to American interests. In 1953 for instance, the CIA violently removed Mohammad Mosaddeq and installed the authoritarian Shah of Iran.

5.4 million citizens of Congo have died since 1998. The country is rich in cobalt, diamonds, gold and copper. The area has been intentionally destabilized by elements of the United States government and major corporations who fund both sides of an ongoing conflict. This also allows the looting of coltan that goes to the making of cell phones and video gaming systems. Uganda, Rwanda, and Burundi are given credit for the exportation of these minerals when all along, they were stolen from Congo. There is a huge human cost paid to have this cheap entertainment and luxury, the average American having no clue to the notorious activities going on around the globe.

SEX AND POWER... Sexual scandals and abuse have occurred in positions of authority for centuries. Many politicians have had careers ruined by public scandal. The Catholic Church is facing lawsuits stemming from the mistreatment of minors by Priests. The mainstream is becoming more acceptable to deviant sexual behaviors as time goes on. Human trafficking and governmental prostitution has become the norm in society creating millions of victims. At one time the media would cover-up for the president as with the JFK/ Marilyn Monroe affair. Later on, society would come to accept Bill Clinton's promiscuous lifestyle and shrug it off. This may be the tip of the iceberg for international pedophile rings of sexual predators in high places.

As far back as the early 1950s an Indiana University sex researcher named Albert Kinsey wrote the "Kinsey Report" to reveal his findings. In it, he claimed homosexuality and a host of other deviant sexual behaviors were perfectly normal. Children, he said, were sexual from birth. According to Dr. Judith Reisman's book about Kinsey, he used children from 3-7 years of age in his experiments, yet there is no outrage in the academic community. Kinsey said adult sex with children is normal. He went on to become the father of the sexual revolution.

In 2006, the Immigration and Customs Enforcement agency investigated and found 5200 possible cases of Pentagon employees viewing child pornography on work or home computers. The Pentagon only checked about 2/3 of the names.

"Conspiracy of Silence" was scheduled to air on the Discovery Channel in May of 1994. It was yanked off the air and bought out by unknown sources, a media blackout followed, all copies were ordered destroyed. The documentary exposed a group of religious leaders and Washington politicians who flew children to Washington D.C. for sex orgies in the 1980s.

Richard Nixon remarked that his off the record speech at the private Bohemian Grove, California in 1967 is what really propelled him to the White House. In 1942, the Manhattan Project took form at the Grove. This outdoor meeting place of Presidents and world leaders is full of pagan rituals, underage prostitution and homosexual behavior. This is not where national policy should be set.

SKULL AND BONES...In 1832, a Yale student by the name of William H. Russell traveled to Germany and joined a secret society group based upon the illuminati.
When he came back he and a few other students started a new group that became the most powerful secret society in American history, an act of vengeance for the anti-masonic stance of the college. They worshipped the goddess Eulogia, and made secret plans to rule and control the world. Since then, three members have become President; Taft, Bush 1 and Bush 2. Others include William F. Buckley, John Kerry, Percy Rockefeller and Prescott Bush.

Skull and Bones or the Brotherhood of Death has found its way into many of the big covert groups including the Trilateral, CFR, Federal Reserve, major research facilities, and other governmental institutions, spreading their influence on the power elites of the world. The members are encouraged to seek the highest offices after college to keep the authority of the "Bonesmen" intact. They threaten anyone that would write a book or otherwise give away the secrets of the club that is said to dominate many important positions in banks and institutions around the world.

The obvious shortcoming to this club is plain to see. Here we have a long tradition of self-created monarchs who are toying with the idea of running the world. Instead of uplifting humanity and supporting the natural rights of all people, they have chosen a path of self-degradation and personal consumption, turning themselves into little tyrants with no redeeming value, all for the sake of some global order mythology.

<u>STUDENT LOANS</u>... In 2010, the Federal government took over the student loan program from private lenders. The many years of tuition increases and bloated university budgets have broken the system. High school students are hooked into loans by means of bribery. The government gladly lends money to students who will face an uphill battle for years to pay it back, if they pay it back at all. They also receive a liberal arts education which solidifies the meaning and importance of state control.

Years before, college was something that families could afford; they sacrificed and saved for it. Little by little, as we have lost our money, savings and assets, the dollars that were once available for higher education are impossible to come by.

While the media complains about the cost of food, fuel,

and other things, there is dead silence on the rapidly rising cost of tuition. The reason is not hard to understand.

The university system houses the fraternity of social engineers who work with politicians to mold and develop young minds. Therefore, rising tuition will rarely be discussed by a president or in the media because college professors and researchers are the ally of the politicians and the media. Their simple solution is to dole out more grant and loan money which basically put students through for free. The problem is that graduating
students can't pay the loans back! The percentage of delinquent student loans has grown astronomically high. The time will come when the delinquent loans will have to be covered by the public, in other words, bailed out. Again, the middle class will be stuck with the bill as it was with the automotive and bank crisis. When that happens, the country will drop yet another notch down towards totalitarianism.

TRILATERAL COMMISSION...There are three centers of industrialized power; The United States, Japan and the European Union among other smaller countries. These are the members of this international cabal. They meet in various capital cities once a year. Jimmy Carter was one of the original members in 1973. It was founded by former head of the CFR David Rockefeller. When Carter became president, he appointed Zbigniew Brzezinski, who was the head of this commission from 1973-1976, to the post of national security advisor and National Security Council chief. The commission helped Carter win the election of 1976 by manipulating the media, academic centers and the bankers. George H. Bush, Bill Clinton, Henry Kissinger, Dick Cheney, Paul Wolfowitz, and Alan Greenspan are some of the big names in this group. The list continues to grow larger with the names of big media, newspapers and corporate sponsorship. While the Council on Foreign Relations relies on political influence, the TLC relies on economic influence to get its members into positions of high power and control to help create an international monetary cartel of power brokers.

In the words of David Rockefeller;

"We are grateful to The Washington Post, the New York Times, Time Magazine and other great publications whose directors have attended our meetings and respected their promises of discretion for almost forty years. It would
have been impossible for us to develop our plan for the world if we had been subject to the bright lights of publicity during those years. But, the work is now much more sophisticated and prepared to march towards a world government. The supranational sovereignty of an intellectual elite and world bankers is surely preferable to the national auto-determination practiced in past centuries."

-1991 Trilateral Commission meeting.

UNIONS...It was significant in American history when workers got together to represent themselves as one unit to the large companies they worked for. Problems in early factories and manufacturing plants included long hours, child labor, unsafe conditions and low pay. Today's workers owe a debt of gratitude to the unions that paved the way to better employment conditions for all.

Unfortunately, modern unions have turned into the very entities they used to complain about in the past. The average person now has to support massive public unions in education and government with little or no bargaining power. This leads to ever increasing pay and benefits the taxpayer must absorb with no checks on unproductive workers.

Private companies like Chrysler, General Motors, General Electric, and inefficient "green" groups get preferred treatment with stimulus packages and bailouts from Democrats that were elected using laundered money coming from forced union dues. In addition, unions demand high wages that cannot compete with foreign and non-union wages, thereby driving corporations out of the state or country which increases unemployment and steers the country into economic decline.

The marketplace should be free from crony capitalism and all workers should be allowed to work for what the job dictates, whether that be low or high wages.

UNITED NATIONS...The League of Nations came into being after WW1 led by Woodrow Wilson. It was created to stop any new war from starting and maintain world peace. It lasted for 27 years and proved to be ineffective in its mission. However, many worthy programs emerged from the League. The International Labor Organization worked to obtain a 40 hour work week and end child labor. The Heath Bureau worked to end malaria and yellow fever. The Slavery worked to end forced labor and the slave trade.

Many of these groups went on to become part of the UN as the League was liquidated in 1946; The United States was never a member.

"The age of nations must end. The governments of nations have decided to order their separate sovereignties into one government to which they will surrender their arms." (U.N. World Constitution)

The UN was founded in 1945 to replace the League of

Nations. Headquartered in New York City, the stated aim is to facilitate cooperation in international law, security, economic development, human rights and world peace, and provide a platform for dialogue. 193 nations are members. There are several organs and 17 specialized agencies of the UN including the World Bank, the IMF, World Health, and the Educational Scientific and cultural organization. There seems to be an agency that covers every aspect of human life. The problem is that the organization is basically unaccountable to the public.

The UN Commission on Global Governance published a report in 1995 called "Our Global Neighborhood" in it, there were some interesting recommendations for the future;
A system of global taxation;
A standing U.N. army;
A Court of Criminal Justice;
Expanded authority for the Secretary General;
An Economic Security Council;
U.N. authority over the global commons;
An end to the veto power of permanent Security Council members; And a new parliamentary body of "civil society" representatives.

Any governing body will always try to hold on to its power and expand itself if at all possible through the constant manipulation of the people it rules. The John Birch Society has kept a watchful eye on the United Nations for many years. Many are calling for the United States to pull out of the UN because of inner corruption. Unfortunately, the UN has become an instrument of international tyranny as its many arms of power overextend themselves.

They are now involved with limiting human population by financing abortion and sterilization and the promotion of homosexuality. More than 50 million abortions take place every year. The family is being

attacked in favor of being a "world citizen"
A *world school board* facilitating international education based on humanism is forcing itself on local school districts through the state and federal departments to regulate what is being taught to children.

Land use is being dictated by the Agenda21 plan and the biosphere programs. Even Mt. Rushmore is under attack, as the UN tries to provoke the United States into giving the famed carvings back to the "Indians."

Plans are to have guns confiscated and careful records kept of firearm owners. Proposals have been made to repeal the 2nd amendment.

The American standard of living will be required to be reduced to a "sustainable level" which means the
promotion of electric cars, light rail, and childless families to combat ozone and global warming (which in itself is a manufactured crisis).

Property rights fall to the wayside as governmental planners determine land use. Pantheism being the official religion of the UN which says that nature is God and human beings are no more important than anything else.

The US military is required to study the UN manuals on behavior and missions while wearing UN insignia on the uniforms. The plan is for the UN to have all military power as individual nations hand over their troops to the UN.

The American institutions of government shall remain a facade to reinforce the idea that we still have a Constitutional system when in fact there is a world government in force. Human rights are then passed down from higher authorities rather than the natural rights coming from God. Church organizations are being infiltrated by forces that undermine true faith and tend towards world government control.

The US should be out of the United Nations.

UNIT 731... The American government covered up a ghastly Japanese experimentation complex in Pingfan, Manchuria during WW2. Known as Unit 731, atrocities were committed on up to 10,000 Chinese, Russian and American prisoners. People were frozen, blown up, operated on and given deadly viruses for the purpose of perfecting biological weapons.

The knowledge gained from this experimentation helped to develop typhoid and plague outbreaks in China. 9300 biological balloon bombs were released in the prevailing winds over the Pacific Ocean, with 300 landing in America. One of the bombs landed near Gearhart Mountain in Oregon. A church group discovered the bomb on May 5, 1945. A pregnant woman and 5 children were killed when the balloon exploded. The press kept silent about the incident and the balloons.

General MacArthur made secret deals to protect and hire the Unit 731 scientists after the war to work for the United States and Japan in academic fields, scientific research, and other key positions. The promise was made to not prosecute these people as war criminals. Like some of their Nazi counterparts, these "scientists" avoided trial and lived out their lives in luxury when they should have gone to prison for life or executed.

Gen Ishii, who ran the top secret facility, was allowed to live out his life in peace as others around him went on to top level positions after the war including Governor of Tokyo, President of the Japan Medical Association, and head of the Japan Olympic Committee. Gen. Kitano, who later was in charge of Unit 731, ran the Green Cross Association after the war. Others attained senior university posts in fields of medicine.

A few surviving POWs from the camp came forward to collect benefits from the Veterans Administration. At first they were denied because there was no record of the terrible events that had been covered up by the US government. In 1993, a Congressional investigation declassified the records to finally reveal the horrors of this Japanese death camp. In Japan today, there is still denial that something like this ever happened.

VACCINATIONS…In 1796 Edward Jenner of England produced the first vaccine to combat smallpox which killed between 20-80% of infected adults and 80% of infected children. It killed 400 million people in the 20th century before it was eradicated in 1979. Louis Pasteur later developed vaccines that worked against rabies and anthrax.

Jonas Salk developed a polio vaccine in 1952. Eventually, polio was eradicated from most countries in the world. Obviously, vaccinations and immunizations have benefited the human race. The problem is that we have a very complicated science associated with the development and delivery of these vaccines. The average person is left to use these concoctions with utter faith and trust in the scientists that develop them. This leaves the door open for mismanagement, fraud and abuse on a large scale.

In 1957, Maurice Hilleman joined the Merck Company as the head of the virus and cell biology division. In a newly discovered taped interview, he admitted using SV40, AIDS and cancer viruses in vaccines that were then given to humans for experimentation purposes. Him and his colleagues are heard joking about the Russians not being able to compete in the Olympics because they would be "loaded up with tumors." He is also heard saying that it was too hard to develop vaccines using those "damn monkeys" and went on to say the transporting of the monkeys in cargo airplanes brought the aids virus to the United States.

The SV40 cancer causing virus was an unknown ingredient in the early polio vaccine. It was discovered in

1961 and no vaccines could contain this virus by law. However, the existing vaccinations and seed material for new vaccines containing SV40 were not destroyed, but given to children up to 1963, and the seed material may have made new batches that were administered up to the 1990s. The monstrous increase in cancer may be related to vaccines.

Bill Gates of Microsoft fame is deeply invested in the New World Order. He is concerned with overpopulation and the regulation of humanity as is the United Nations and groups like the Club of Rome. He has a plan to biometrically track all people on Earth. He wants to work through government agencies to force feed inoculations and vaccinations, some of which include sterility agents and other additives to reduce population growth. The profits are enormous in this scheme and the control of humanity fits right into the plan of totalitarian rule. The irony is that overpopulation is made worse by the governments own welfare system that rewards bad behavior. The more kids, the more benefits! If we lived in a free society which encourages responsibility, families would tend to only have children they could support, thereby reducing population.

The dramatic rise of autism worldwide makes me wonder if the planet is getting a population control lobotomy. If a large segment of the masses are unable to function and make their own decisions, they would be under the direct control of globalist totalitarians that are in a frenzy to reduce the sheer numbers of people on the planet. Ultimately, autistic people could be rounded up and destroyed if the right regime takes over, thereby eliminating the "time, energy and expense" of having to care for them.

Autism now affects 1 in 88 kids including 1 in 54 boys. In 1985, the rate was 1 in 2500. The young growing brain is extremely sensitive to chemicals. Vaccines having mercury preservatives are suspected in this rise of autism.

In England, the government requires 46 vaccine shots up to 18 years of age. Meanwhile in Rimini Italy, a family has been awarded 174,000 Euros after the Italian Health Ministry admitted that the MMR caused autism in their 9 year old son.

WAR...It seems to be part of our lives from birth to death. On any given day we hear about bombings, attacks, military maneuvers, and defense spending. Covered in chapter 6, war is a component of the powerful and the influential. In the past, those who commanded armies for the kings and rulers needed war for their very being and personal survival. Today, the military industrial complex needs a constant threat of war or better yet, blood itself to perpetuate its inner workings, as it lusts for money, land, resources and pure power. Common in war is the betrayal of the people who are hoodwinked into believing that the conquest is somehow necessary for the good and survival of their nation. Ordinary masses pay "protection" money to the state not knowing of the state's war addiction. Many times the same financiers who run the money system are the creators and perpetrators of a conflict and play both sides as in WW1. False flag attacks are a useful tool to start the war and continue it to its bitter end, before another one begins.

The "war on terror" is the latest in a long series of illusionary programs put forth by the government. After WW2, the so called "cold war" between the Soviet Union and the United States served a dual function to deceive both American and Russian people. Both sides were told the clever tale that the other side was "evil". It gave both governments 40 years of controlling power over its citizens, keeping them locked up in perpetual fear of nothing.

The Northwoods document in 1962 called for self-inflicted wounds to raise public support for an invasion of Cuba, staging attacks on a ship and airplanes among other things.

After the fall of communism, the search was on for a new enemy. Terrorism became a catch phrase and false flag terror attacks were executed on the United States by the United States. Evidence now shows that many of these terrorists have ties to the CIA. The effects of the war on terror include the draconian Patriot Act, the National Defense Act, and the federalization of airport security which subjects ordinary travelers to humiliating searches.

A vast majority of people have no interest in war and yet it rages on. For the good of humanity the cycle must end. Education is the key.

WAR ON DRUGS... President Nixon began the war and since then, almost 3 million Americans are behind bars. The country is still overrun with illegal drugs and associated crimes continue. The public schools of America are still the best place to buy drugs. Much of the crime that takes place is related to the illegal drug trade and the black people suffer disproportionately in prison. The border has become as violent as any foreign war zone.

The judicial system, politicians, and all levels of drug enforcement depend heavily on illegal substances for their jobs and well-being. They are not about to make drugs legal and lose their careers. In fact the CIA has been known to actually assist drug cartels and continues to rake in millions off the drug trade. American controlled Afghanistan keeps on producing high levels of opium. MK ULTRA, the CIA program of mind control mentioned earlier, has introduced dangerous chemicals into society, like LSD.

When the prohibition of alcohol was lifted, law enforcement looked for a new drug to go after. Marijuana was the target. This non-addictive benign plant has become the poster board of blame for all ills in society. It is blamed for everything from mental illness, to crime and for being a stepping stone to harder drugs. It's time the American people wake up to this madness and end the war on drugs because this supposed war is nothing but a war on the American people.

"the aggregate happiness of society, which is best promoted by the practice of a virtuous policy, is, or ought to be, the end of all government"

~*George Washington*

Chapter Six: The Agenda of War

"War is what we say it is"

A medieval observation says there is a power behind the throne greater than the king. That is true to this day. The agenda of war in the ancient past had much to do with conquering and maintaining control over territory and resources. A higher being was often cited as the rationale for conquest. When rulers started to learn about money manipulation, many wars that appeared to be one nation vs. another were really nothing more than a banker's trick of funding both sides and provoking conflict, then making the winner pay the losers' debt! These bankers would become rich and powerful in their own right and were then in a position to influence the destinies of nations. Future conflicts were hidden behind the motives of brute force, business interest, or the scrambling effort to take and secure resources.

Today wars are a complex web of all these factors. The tragedy of military service is that the common troops do not know who they are really fighting for and who the real enemy is. They are serving and dying in vain! The idea that they are defending the Constitution is laughable. They are defending corporate interests, dictators and central banks manipulating conflict behind the scenes. The war on terror has been stimulated by false flag attacks on our own selves including both 911 incidences, the 'Underware' Bomber and many others. Historically, the USS Liberty (by Israel), the Gulf of Tonkin, and all the way back to the Lusitania, USS Maine, and even Lincoln's move at Ft. Sumter were all self-inflicted wounds designed to bolster the military industrial machine.

The result is widespread violence, death and destruction based on lies. Yes there is a time to defend against aggressors, but those times are uncommon in the history of war. Most of the time war involves an unseen hand, provoking hostility and profiting from the conflict. The King or commander-in-chief is just a patsy that covers and protects the power play going on behind the scenes. The power play includes the lust for resources, money, land and the ultimate control over the souls of the enemy *and* the warmongers own people. Humanity has been transfixed by state religions and forced ideology. These forced beliefs fooled us into thinking the conquests are backed by the will of God or a benevolent government. Again, the development of credit and money took it all a step further where financiers kept a country or two under their thumb by using debt as a tool and a bargaining chip. In the human lottery of war, they would fund both sides to insure victory for themselves and send thousands of ignorant pawns to their death.

"History records that the money changers have used every form of abuse, intrigue, deceit, and violent means possible to maintain their control over governments by controlling money and its issuance."

~President James Madison

The House of Rothschild stated:

> *Give me the power to control the issue of a nation's currency and I care not who makes that nation's laws."*

This telling statement shows that any system was their victim, whether socialist, communist or capitalist. Money rules over all politics, because money is politics.

The truth about the REVOLUTIONARY WAR has been buried for a long time. Yes, the war had something to do with taxation and British oppression, but there was more to it than that. Ben Franklin went to London in 1764 and observed beggars and poor people all around. He told the British there were no unemployed in the Colonies, no poor, no beggars. It didn't take long for the Bank of England to pass the Currency Act which made it illegal for the Colonies to print their own money (which they viewed as an act of rebellion). The money supply was severely cut which caused devastation and unemployment in America, and the Colonies grew bitter against the British. Franklin explained; "the poverty caused by the bad influence of the English bankers on the Parliament which has caused in the Colonies hatred of the English and...the Revolutionary War." Alexander Hamilton and others observed the same thing.

The bankers made their move and the people knew what was happening, the drawing down of the money supply by the British caused depression in the Colonies which was the real reason for the unrest which led directly to war. (If our citizens in the 1930s would have realized just what caused the great depression, there may well have been a similar rebellion against the Federal Reserve System).

The story of NAPOLEON is another case in point. He did not trust the banking element. He bargained with Thomas Jefferson and raised 3 million dollars of gold through the Louisiana Purchase. This debt free money was used for his conquest of Europe. The Bank of England financed his enemies. The Duke of Wellington eventually forced Napoleon into exile with help from banker Nathan Rothschild who smuggled gold into Spain. Napoleon was forced to borrow money from Eubard Banking of Paris. Now the two bank sponsored forces would meet June 18, 1815 at Waterloo.

Nathan Rothschild was waiting in England for news of the historic confrontation. The outcome would make or break the finances of the country. His assistant delivered news of the outcome of the battle before Wellington's courier could get back to England. Nathan then pretended Wellington lost and sold huge amounts of British bonds. Word got out that Napoleon won and everyone sold their British bonds. Then Nathan secretly bought back the devalued bonds. The spoils of war went to the Rothschilds, not the people of either country.

Napoleon himself summed up the power of bankers;

"When a government is dependent upon bankers for money, they and not the leaders of the government control the situation, since the hand that gives is above the hand that takes...Money has no motherland; financiers are without patriotism and without decency; their sole object is gain."

The Rothschild's wealth increased by 20% overnight. Through their secret spy agency and messenger service they were able to keep tabs on inside information and benefit from the shadows.

A sideshow for the British was the WAR OF 1812. The Americans declared war because of forced British Impressment of sailors, French trade disruptions, British support of Indians, blockage of Canadian expansion, and defense of honor which was really the second war of independence for America. Andrew Jackson won important battles in the field and compare with his victory over the central bank later in life.

The United States was on the gold standard at the time. When the banks in Washington D.C. ran out of gold to back the money, peace negotiations went in the works in 1815. This shows how a money system backed in gold will halt a war in its tracks, benefitting the people. Even so, it took until 1834 to pay the debt of the war.

The charter of the central bank of the United States expired in 1811. James Monroe allowed it to lapse. The Bank of England needed America to be in debt for many reasons including its eye on commerce. Again we see the power of the bankers, using war to maintain their foothold on the people and using leaders like Henry Clay to fight for and prop up paper money.

There was no central bank during the MEXICAN-AMERICAN WAR, 1846-1848, which annexed territory from Mexico including New Mexico, the Texas area, and Alta, California. The United States forgave a Mexican debt of 3.5 million while paying 15 million for the conquered lands. To fight the war President James Polk easily financed three loans to cover the cost. There was no shortage of available funding. With no central bank around, the war was paid off right away rather struggling for years to pay off the interest to a bank.

America, with all its riches and prosperity, was a great threat to the Rothschilds. First of all the revolution brought an end to their money monopoly. The colonies

had their own currency (even though England went on to ruin it through counterfeiting). Then, the first and second central banks of the United States ended. Later, they tried to finance both sides of the CIVIL WAR but Abraham Lincoln refused to accept their loans at high interest. Lincoln later complained that he had to fight both the bankers and the southern army at the same time.
Otto von Bismarck of Germany said in 1876;

"It is not to be doubted, I know of absolute certainty that the division of the United States into two federations of equal power was decided long before the Civil War by the high financial powers of Europe. These bankers were afraid that the United States, if they remained as one block and were to develop as one nation, would attain economic and financial independence, which would upset the capitalist domination of Europe over the world."

France's army was then stationed on the Mexico border and the English in Canada. The hope was that no matter what the outcome, the U.S. would be in debt to European bankers. The London Times reinforces this viewpoint,

"If this mischievous financial policy, which has its origin in North America, shall become indurate down to a fixture, then the government will furnish its own money without cost. It will pay off debts and be without debt. It will have all the money necessary to carry on its commerce. It will become prosperous without precedent in the history of the world. The brains, and wealth of all countries will go to North America. That country must be destroyed or it will destroy every monarchy on the globe."

This should put to rest any lingering doubt as to who runs the world and who thinks they are superior to everyone else.

Interest free Greenbacks were then used to finance the war. In this case Lincoln was able to somewhat resist the banking influence but had to compromise by allowing the National Banking Act of 1863 which created national banks and their bank notes. This does not make Lincoln the "good" guy, just a little shrewder than the Rothschilds. A far more sinister plan was in the making for the citizens of the south. A northern invasion based on greed and profit protection.

Abraham Lincoln on the upcoming conflict between the states;

"My paramount objective in this struggle Is to save the union, and is not either to save Or destroy slavery. If I could save the union without freeing any slave I would do it; and if I could save it by freeing some and leaving others alone I would also do that. What I do about slavery, and the colored race, I do because I believe it helps the union."

Lincoln also thought the black race was inferior as proven in this quote;

"I will say then that I am not, nor ever have been, in favor of bringing about in any way the social and political equality of the white and black races – that I am not, nor ever have been, in favor of making voters or jurors of Negroes, nor of qualifying them to hold office, nor to intermarry with white people; and I will say in addition to this that there is a physical difference between the white and black races which I believe forever forbid the two races living together on terms of

social and political equality. And in as much as they cannot so live, while they do remain together there must be the position of superior and inferior and I as much as any other man am in favor of having the superior position assigned to the white race."

As we can see Lincoln was a racist and he laid out plans to actually ship the blacks out of America permanently. He also thought of the Indian as a nuisance and took steps to harass them also.

At the time, the evils of slavery were well known around the world and were being dealt with peacefully. Slave owners were being paid to set their servants free. If it wasn't for Lincoln, American ingenuity would have found a way to positively end slavery without a single shot being fired. As it was, Lincoln's dispute with the south sent thousands to their death fighting for something other than the evils of slavery. The Emancipation Proclamation was a last ditch effort to paint the war as a way to free the slaves. Many northern troops deserted at this time, frustrated that Lincoln suddenly changed his tone. He made good on his threat to set the blacks free if the South chose to secede.

Lincoln had used his time as a lawyer to further the interests of large companies and insure them a large share of public funding. As President, he continued this effort which included the large wholesale protection of the northern territory from the free trade "enemy" to the South.

Lincoln was a master of language. Frequently he would quote Bible verses or patriotic language to deceive the public and further his selfish interests.

Over 700,000 Americans lost their lives in a dispute that should never have happened. What is called the Civil War was a clash between the "Federal Union" and the "Confederate States of America". It was a war of northern aggression. Thomas Jefferson said this about secession...

"Every man and every body of men on earth, possesses the right to self-government" and "the tree of liberty must be refreshed from time to time with the blood of patriots and tyrants." and "If any State in the Union will declare that it prefers separation over union, I have no hesitation in saying, let us separate."

Lincoln called secession the "essence of anarchy." It was not anarchy, but loss of ill-gotten wealth in the north that threatened Lincoln as his crony friends. Tariffs were used by the North to protect northern businesses and public works projects. England reacted by putting a ban on southern cotton, pinching their economy. The free trade zone of the South threatened the profits of the northern companies that Lincoln defended as a lawyer and President. Lincoln threatened the South with higher tariffs in his inaugural address. Lincoln threatened the South in his inauguration speech that he was about to raise tariffs higher. The South only had 30% of the people but paid 80% of the tariffs. This left the South no choice but to secede from the union.

Lincoln cold bloodedly micro-managed the complete destruction of the South, sending his sadistic generals Sheridan and Sherman on a death march that burned whole cites and plundered the entire southern territory. After the war, the North continued the rampage by accumulating assets and forcing foreclosures of whatever was left standing. If the South managed to win the conflict, Lincoln and his high command would have been hung for war crimes. The Whigs of the North were more sympathetic with England while the Southern Democrat/Republicans believed in American expansionism and a weaker central government. The

Southern people may have actually saved this nation from British rule before the Civil War ever took place!

In school we are taught about "Honest Abe" the great President who freed the slaves and saved the union, one of the good guys. The truth is that he was something other than what we are taught to believe.

The SPANISH -AMERICAN WAR of 1898 was a conflict that started with the mysterious explosion of the American ship Maine in Havana harbor. This event was used as a pretext for war. About that same time the Populist movement in the U.S. was gaining momentum. It came about from a deep suspicion of the two political parties, a system that aligned itself with the power of big banking, namely Morgan, Carnegie, Rockefeller and Rothschild. The attack on the Maine was to get the public's attention diverted to Spain as being the real enemy. All along Spain maintained innocence on the
Maine's attack and years later, the United States admitted Spain had nothing to do with it. Spanish sailors risked their lives to save Americans on board the sinking ship.

William Randolph Hearst and his newspapers pushed for war with yellow journalism, creating lies and false scenarios about Spain. When all was said and done the bankers retained their power and America annexed more territory around the world including Puerto Rico and the Philippines, emerging as a world power.
It's no wonder Secretary of State John Hay called the conflict a "splendid little war."

THE RUSSIAN REVOLUTION is a popular subject but is not completely understood. Many scholars have no idea that big money from the west funded Lenin and his Bolsheviks allies. J.P. Morgan wired much needed cash and the Red Cross was set up in St. Petersburg as a front for the money men, the manipulators of the overthrow who funded both sides of the national conflict. The return profit was land and resources set aside in the Soviet Union to be owned by the bankers. The Tzar never knew who the real culprits were that sacked their country and kidnapped and killed them. The story of the Romanovs is not complete until the final chapter is written; the great powers behind the throne were bankers that ended their reign and changed the direction of the world forever.

WORLD WAR 1 was a war that never had to be. Alliances were drawn between the nations of Europe years before the first invasion in 1914. If Germany was attacked, Austria and the Ottoman Empire would defend them and likewise if Austria was attacked, Germany would stand with them. The Allies were bound together in similar fashion with the French, English, Russians and others bound together by treaty. Although these safeguards were put into effect, there was an overriding tendency to respect the rights of nations and not upset the cart for the good of all. When the Austrian King and his wife were assassinated, and Germany invaded Belgium, it put in motion the beginning of the war, or so they say. England had gone off the gold standard before that incident which makes you wonder if something was afoot. Why would a country go off a gold standard? Maybe it was a preparation for war. They knew it was coming.
 Meanwhile in America, Woodrow Wilson was elected under the notion that "I will not send our boys over there". He was a "peace" president.
During the war, the English Navy installed a blockade against Germany that literally starved the country. About 750,000 people died from lack of food. Then came the big turnaround, German U boats countered by sinking

the passenger liner 'Lusitania.' The ship went down quickly as illegally stored explosives went off in the hull. Germany had taken out adverts in American newspapers warning people not to board the ship. Many of these ads were not allowed to be published, an obvious conspiracy. The official inquiry under Lord Mersey was a cover-up that placed blame on the ship's captain. Years later Lord Mersey lamented that the whole Lusitania event was a "damn dirty business."

Many other ships were attacked. Although death tolls were lower than reported, newspapers and newsreels of the time sensationalized the incidents, building a groundswell of hatred against the Germans. It wasn't long before Wilson pressed for the United States to enter the war.

The short piece; "War is a Racket" written by Major General Smedley D. Butler USMC in 1935 is a short summary of how the great war was utilized by insiders to acquire land and take profits. He says;

"War is a racket. It always has been. It is possibly the oldest, easily the most profitable, surely the most vicious. It is the only one international in scope. It is the only one in which the profits are reckoned in dollars and the losses in lives. A racket is best described, I believe, as something that is not what it seems to the majority of the people. Only a small 'inside' group knows what it is about. It is conducted for the benefit of the very few, at the expense of the very many. Out of war a few people make huge fortunes."

He points out that 21,000 new millionaires and billionaires were made during WW1. None of these individuals garnered a rifle or dug a trench; but stood far from the battlefield and raked in the money.

Bethlehem Steel's profits went from 6 million to 49 million. Dupont made 58 million and United States Steel made over 100 million extra per year of the war. Not bad. Bankers, automobile manufacturers, clothing companies, and ship builders also made massive profits. The brief participation in the First World War cost us $52,000,000,000, of which 16,000,000,000 went to a very few individuals. It's is a heavy load for taxpayers to handle, and a nice return for the elites who push for and plan for war. War bonds were sold and cashed in for much less after the bankers turned a profit. The men who fought and died are scattered all over the globe in cemeteries and survivors ended up in hospitals or mental homes. Many bought useless war bonds and others were swindled into paying for their own equipment and uniforms in the war itself.

The European bankers and industrialists had told President Wilson they could not pay back the 6 billion dollars owed to America if they lost the war, so they needed us in it even though Wilson ran his campaign on staying out of it. The servicemen were told it was a war to end all wars and the purpose was to make the world safe for democracy, but neither came true. The war made the world a safer and more fertile ground for profiteering.

In the 30s, Butler watched the build-up to WW2 as the "mad dogs" once again ran loose through Europe. Butler advocated keeping our ships close to America and limiting the great profits of industry to reduce the lust for war in the future. He said that the next war would be advanced by horrible inventions of science. He was correct as all the warring nations of WW2 experimented with chemicals and people to further their ungodly knowledge of destruction.

The history of WORLD WAR 2 is ripe with conspiracy. The complicated alliances between nations and the sheer

passion for conquest darken any easy conclusion as to why it happened. It was more than just a fight between the Axis powers and the allies, tyranny vs. freedom. The fact is that our own government allowed major companies of the United States to trade, fund and assist Nazi Germany before and during the war.
First of all Hitler devised a way to justify his aggression. In Feb. 1933 Nazi Hermann Goring coordinated an attack on his own building, The Reichstag. The resulting fire was then blamed on a mentally unstable man named Marinis Van der lubbe who was said to be working for the Communists. This event sparked the "temporary" suspension of civil rights in Germany and justified upcoming invasions. This matches what Lincoln did with Ft. Sumter and Bush after 911. American companies were waiting in the wings with oil, machinery, and communications networks to assist Germany throughout the war.
The "fraternity" consisted of leaders of industry and high ranking government officials according to the book; "Trading with the Enemy" by Charles Higham.
Standard Oil supplied high octane fuel, Ford supplied trucks, ITT helped with Nazi communications and bombs, and Chase Bank held millions of dollars in gold for Germany. Yet, we sent our sons to fight and die for the cause of freedom just as American corporations raked in ill-gotten dollars and maintained their web of trade. Declassified documents tell a story of treason that absolutely shocks the prism of history.
England and Germany established the BIS, Bank for International Settlement which ended up laundering gold and money through Swiss accounts. Chase Bank, an American institution owned by the Rockefellers, froze the assets of French Jews and many ended up in death camps for lack of money to leave the country. Chase also offered discounted Marks in trade for dollars to Nazis

living in America if they wanted to bring the loot to Germany.

Collaboration between the Paris Chase Bank and the Nazis continued throughout the war with the full knowledge of its New York base. Other American banks did the same. Eventually some Swiss banks paid reparations to holocaust victims.

Another Rockefeller interest was Standard Oil, but had no interest in patriotism to the United States. The German Air Force could not fly without Standards tetraethyl lead additive. The substance was purchased in England, sent to Germany, and the Nazis were able to bomb London using English fuel that in fact was paid for by the British Royal Air Force! Standard Oil tankers supplied German submarines with gas that sank American vessels. Even though the Americans were running short of rubber, Standard cut a deal with Hitler to supply Germany with what they needed. They
supplied the Germans with high octane fuel to bring their spies, diamonds and currencies across the Atlantic on giant planes owned by the L.A.T.I.

Since they went through Brazil, there were no inspections or searches. Nelson Rockefeller claimed he had no knowledge of these activities. A report in 1941 said that Standard Oil did not have any ships torpedoed by the Germans. A sarcastic R.T. Haslam, vice president of Standard said that Germany has produced a fine gasoline, "equivalent of our own".

Did our government know? Executive order 8389 allowed transactions with the enemy if specifically authorized. While a fuel shortage caused gas lines in the United States, Germany *and Japan* had all the fuel they needed.

IBM gave their services to Hitler after 1933 and through the war. The coordination, cataloging and identification of prisoners aided the 3rd Reich in the systematic roundup and gassing of millions of Jews. The complicated made simple by an automated punch card service provided by IBM against the Jewish people.

ITT entered into actual contracts with branches of the German military, supplying things like switchboards, radar equipment, and other items necessary to carry on war against the allies. On April 21, 1943, it was announced at an ITT shareholders meeting that 13 percent of its operations were for the Axis powers.

Ball bearings were essential for the Nazi war machine. A Swedish bearing company called SKF was a major producer. It also had branches in the United States, Norway and Germany. 60% of its product was used by the Germans. When word got out at the SKF plant in Philadelphia that some of its production was going to Hitler, a great protest was held, but 8000 workers went back to work reassured that none of the production was reaching the enemy. That was a lie. The Americans lost 60 planes in an attempted bombing of the SKF factory in Germany because information was leaked of the impending attack. In 1944, Norwegian SKF workers destroyed their whole factory, disgusted that Sweden was collaborating with Germany.

Winthrop Chemical Company and Bayer distributed Milk of Magnesia and aspirin to the Germans.

Many of Hitler's "radical" ideas were imported from the United States. In 1907, Indiana became the first state to adopt forced sterilization for the "feebleminded". Many other states considered the same type of law that discriminated against mentally handicapped and even unwed mothers. Hitler looked at Abraham Lincoln as a great hero. Lincoln was able to smother states' rights and build a strong central government that trampled the Constitution.

Hitler admired Henry Ford and was greatly influenced by his book called "The International Jew" (1927). He had Fords picture in one of his offices. The Ford Motor Company continued to operate independently from the US government. They refused to build engines for England but supplied Germany with tanks, and 5 ton vehicle supplies.

General Motors also had connections with the Nazis. In the mid-1930s, GM committed to the production of tanks, armored cars and trucks for the 3rd Reich. The company was awarded $33 million for destruction of their plants in Germany by the United States government after the war, even though the General Motors-Opel plant manufactured German military aircraft.

Obviously, there was a complex grid-work of industry and alliances that existed apart from the war effort. President Roosevelt had to juggle the demands of these industries while fighting another battle with the Axis powers.

There is no question that Roosevelt and Churchill knew about the pending Pearl Harbor attack. America and Japan both needed to enter the war for various reasons. The commanders at Pearl Harbor have gone on record saying they were not given critical information concerning knowledge of the Japanese plans that were deciphered about the impending attack. See the book "Infamy" by John Toland.

I contend that the Third Reich survived and flourished after the official surrender. Their corrupted ideology was simply transplanted in America as 10,000 of them were given protection after the war. They continued their experiments for the CIA in mind control and the Aerospace industry for rocket engineering. The ideology goes on in the form of psychiatric experiments, medications, and public school curriculum.

This is not to say we should change our whole attitude about the war. It was necessary to defeat the rouge axis powers and stop tyranny in its tracks. The allies did that and put a temporary stoppage on the spread of totalitarianism. However, we must keep in mind that elements from America influenced Hitler before the war and we absorbed ideology, science and leadership from Germany and Japan after the war. During the war many of our businesses were more than happy to continue the trade and technical assistance to Germany. It was not a neat division between us and them, there was a little too much of them in us!

The shocking aftermath of WW2 is never discussed. After all, we won and there was celebrating to do! The truth is that the Russians were not about to give up their American and British POWs without a trade that benefited them. They wanted captured Nazi scientists in exchange for the prisoners. Knowing that the American people would never stand for this, an elaborate lie was conceived. It was told an all-out effort was made to recover prisoners and that Russia had sent them all back. Anyone not showing up was listed as missing in action. The truth is that the prisoners were intentionally left in the Soviet Union, basically sacrificed for the sake of "national security." The Red Army held an estimated 344,000 allied servicemen and over 1 million displaced persons after the war. Although the official version states only a few scattered individuals were left in Russia, up to 20,000 were abandoned forever and their fates unknown.

There is a real problem with the KOREAN WAR. It was never meant to be won but served the purpose (again) of streaming billions of dollars into the coffers of the banks and the pockets of government officials. Evidence exists that most American military operations were forecast

and broadcast to the North Koreans so they would know ahead of time where and when attacks would be made. The Soviet Union and the United Nations received information from the United States government and then warned the Communist forces. General MacArthur explains; "There was some leak in intelligence, it was evident to everyone. (Brigadier General Walton) Walker continually complained to me that his operations were known to the enemy in advance through sources in Washington. Information must have been relayed to them, assuring that the Yalu River bridges would continue to enjoy their sanctuary and that their bases would be left intact. They knew they could swarm down across the Yalu River without having to worry about bombers hitting their Manchurian supply lines."
MacArthur eventually became fully aware of the treason from his own government so he broke out on his own.
On September 15, 1950 MacArthur landed at Inchon and wiped out the Red Chinese and the North Korean positions. Harry Truman relieved MacArthur of his command at that point. The United States was not allowed to fully defeat the enemy and had to settle for a compromise. Korea remains divided to this day. Thousands died in a war that was never a war. 8000 POWs were left behind.

The 2005 film "Why We Fight" centers around the farewell speech of Dwight D. Eisenhower on Jan.17, 1961, where he warns of the increasing influence of the "military industrial complex" and the vastly expanded arms industry. This complex will be looking for war and expecting war or talk of war at all times to continue its heavy handed existence into the future. His warnings were true and prophetic.

The VIETNAM WAR killed 50,000 Americans and up to two million Vietnamese civilians.

August 2, 1964. The North Koreans attack the USS Maddox in the Gulf of Tonkin thinking the destroyer was providing support for South Viet Nam operations. Two days later on August 4th, there supposedly was another attack on the same ship. This second attack influenced Congress to pass the Gulf of Tonkin Resolution which committed a large American military force to the region, and bombings began soon after. Released documents have shown that the second attack never took place but was used as a pretext to war anyway. Sec. of Defense Robert McNamara has admitted in the film "The Fog of War" that the August 4th attack did not happen. The confusion on that day in 1964 was good news to Lyndon Johnson as he opened up a full scale war on North Vietnam. The U.S. was looking and yearning for conflict and they got it.

As with the Korean War, victory was not the intention. While American men were suffering and dying, and getting infected with agent orange, our own CIA was waist deep in drug smuggling, raking in 3-4 billion dollars per year while ignoring the 2 soldiers per day dying from heroin overdose. Money was being laundered in the rubber industry and the military was simply not allowed to win the war, which, again was not really a war at all.

June 8, 1967, during the 6 day war between Israel and the Arab Nations, the American vessel U.S.S. LIBERTY is dispatched to the Mediterranean Sea. At 2:00 PM the ship is attacked by two unmarked aircraft and two Israeli torpedo boats. The Liberty requests air support from the nearby 6th fleet but is turned down by orders from the White House. The admiral called to verify the order and President Johnson said; "I want that god dam ship going to the bottom". Three hours into the attack a Russian spy ship appeared on the scene and the Israel attack had to be stopped. The Liberty then limped to safety. President Johnson had ordered the ship sunk in order to blame it on Egypt. That would give the U.S. the excuse to take over the Middle East. The plan failed and a cover-up ensued. Israel called it a terrible mistake and had to pay reformations. 34 Americans died and 174 were wounded. Captain William McConagle and his crew were told to "shut up' after the incident or face time in prison or death. Years later an Israeli pilot said they knew it was an American ship all along. The official cover-up continues to this day.

THE COLD WAR. The fifty year period after WW2 was a time of basically scaring the people of the United States (and the Soviet Union). We were taught to hide under desks at school, build fallout shelters and give large amounts of tax money towards a massive military buildup to deter the Communists. Likewise, the Russian people were taught that the "imperialist" Americans were the bad guys.
The Nazis that came over to the U.S. after WW2 exaggerated the power and force of the Soviet Union for their own job security as they worked in research and military technology. According to Mark G. Brennan's article "The Cold War Fraud" The support for this thesis now appears in a two-volume study, undertaken between 1965 and 1985, on Soviet intentions. In the study, prepared by the BDM Corporation, readers learn from interviews with former Soviet military officers, strategy analysts, and industrial specialists, that American officials "[erred] on the side of overestimating Soviet aggressiveness" and underestimated "the extent to which the Soviet leadership was deterred from using nuclear weapons." Furthermore, the study claims that the American authorities' ineptitude in judging Soviet military intentions "had the potential [to] mislead ... U.S.

decision makers in the event of an extreme crisis." Unsurprisingly, the study confirms the role of the military industrial complex in perpetuating the decades-long state of panic. The text shows how "the defense industrial complex, not the Soviet high command, played a key role in driving the quantitative arms buildup" and thereby "led U.S. analysts to ... exaggerate the aggressive intentions of the Soviets."

The terrible results of this time period are measured in the suffering of the people of Russia and the downgrade of the quality of life here in America. The heavy hand of both governments stifled human creativity and also created poverty and misery around the globe. During this period of time, there were great developments, great achievements and a general advancement in the cause of humanity. However, it was in spite of the hand of big government, not because of it. How much greater it could have been if "they" just stepped back.

The fall of Saigon occurred in 1975 as the final helicopter airlift rescued the last civilians from the defeated city, the final chapter of the Vietnam War. The United States went through a 15 year period of relative peace until 1991. The engines of war having refueled for a high tech televised invasion of Iraq.

THE GULF WAR. The American people were told that a massive buildup of tanks and Iraqi military equipment was taking place in and around Kuwait, a small oil producing nation to the south of Iraq. Years after the war was over, overhead photos from the Soviet Union during that time period showed no activity on the ground.

Fifteen year old Nurse Nayirah, (daughter of the Kuwait ambassador to the U.S.) gave what turned out to be a staged event, a false tear filled testimony on worldwide TV. She cried about Iraqi soldiers stealing babies out of incubators. This helped fuel public opinion in favor of a

U.S. invasion. Iraqi leader Saddam Hussein was built up with firepower and arms by the U.S. during the 1980s. He was basically our own creation to fight the neighbor Iran. Some of our own ammunition and chemical weapons were used against us during the conflict. We intentionally created a monster which we conveniently had to destroy.

Millions watched on CNN cable TV as the new high tech weapons were deployed on the country of Iraq. Bagdad was bombed by "smart" precision strikes and it wasn't long before the Iraqis were forced to surrender. The Americans stopped short of taking the country. That was left for another time. The aftermath left soldiers having to deal with Gulf War Syndrome disease from chemical and bio weapons and oil smoke. A 1993 study concluded that 205,000 Iraqis died as a result of the war and its aftermath. That includes 3500 civilians and 111,000 due to post war adverse health effects. The U.S. suffered about 300 military deaths. There is no question that the web of big oil property leasing had more to do with this conflict than "liberating" the people of Kuwait. If we are a nation concerned with liberating the oppressed, why did America do nothing when 900,000 good people of Rwanda were being systematically slaughtered in 1994?

This military operation on a Middle Eastern country had many negative side effects. One is that the beehive of hate was stirred up. Islamic militants chose to strike back with terrorist attacks and bombings centered on military and civilian targets. America was faced with fighting a new kind of war, a war where the enemy is no longer in plain sight but lurking on any street corner or behind any tree. This meant the military industrial complex would be a full time machine, a 24/7 military monster that never sleeps and never dies, a jokers dream for the power brokers of the world.

What better way to incite war and get the attention of the American people than an attack on the famed New York City? Not once, but twice! There are direct CIA connections to the World Trade Center bombing of 1993 and a myriad of questions surrounding the 911 attack. These two incidences and the 1995 Oklahoma City bombing were major events meant to begin new wars and increase legal scrutiny on the American public through the Patriot Act and the creation of Homeland security. They are all discussed in Chapter 5.

THE AFGANISTAN WAR. This country has a long history of occupation by foreign powers. The Soviet Union battled here for geo-political reasons starting in 1979. The war was so costly that it led to the fall of the Soviet empire. To battle the Soviets, the CIA under President Carter set up covert operations to aid the insurgents a full five months before the actual Soviet invasion. Osama Bin Laden left his home in Saudi Arabia to fight the Soviets with American assistance. He was trained by the CIA. America spent 3 billion dollars in the resistance movement. The great war on terror had its origins here, where our own government virtually created the enemy that we fight today. Bin Laden, the supposed mastermind of the 911 attacks, was a creation of the American military.

October 2001, the American coalition launches operation "Enduring Freedom" to battle the Taliban and Al-qaeda. This follows the assassination of Northern Alliance leader Ahmad Shah Massoud on Sept. 9 and the Sept. 11 attack on the United States. It ends up to be America's longest war which still rages on in 2013.

The US Geological Survey has run images over Afghanistan revealing unique and high price metals and potential high profile mining opportunities. General Petraeus said there is "stunning potential here." Lithium, iron, copper, cobalt and gold are there for the taking. Will these resources be used to help Afghanistan or be plundered by foreign companies?

In 1998 oil companies were calling for a new government in Afghanistan to allow a pipeline to run across the nation. I suspect the 911 attacks were planned far in advance by inside sources to achieve this and other goals.

93% of the world's opiates come from Afghanistan. The world's supply of heroin and opium originate from here. It is obvious that there will be a US occupation in this country indefinitely. It is a highly strategic location and the natural resources will supply American affiliates for years to come. As the war on terror propaganda rages on, we the people are snookered into believing the conflict is about killing terrorists when all along, it's all about supplying corporations and drug dealers with ill-gotten riches.

THE IRAQ WAR. Saddam Hussein and the weapons of mass destruction! That was the battle cry for the invasion of Iraq. Democrats and Republican alike waved the banner.

Shortly after the 911 incident, George W. Bush had a private meeting with his defense secretary Donald Rumsfeld. The discussion centered on devising "creative" options to justify invading Iraq. He wanted to be seen and remembered as an accomplished President, and out of the shadow of his father. He envisioned the invasion long before September 11th. The supposed reason was "to disarm Iraq of weapons of mass destruction, to end Saddam Hussein's support for terrorism, and to free the Iraqi people." The real reasons were for capturing large basins of oil production, the protection of Israel, the buildup of the military security police complex and the neoconservative lust for revenge. The cover story was to "free the Iraqi people," hunt down terrorists, and rid the world of Saddam Hussein and his weapons of mass destruction.

Saddam Hussein was a creation of America to begin with. He originally worked alongside the CIA in the 1960s. His war machine was originally funded with help from the United States. After the rebellion in Iran in 1979, the American backed Shah was deported and Hussein was used by the United States as a weapon against the new Iranian regime. Jimmy Carter encouraged Iraq to attack Iran. The war waged on for 8 years and killed over a half a million Iraq and Iranian people.

The decade of the 90s saw the United States losing interest in Saddam Hussein; he was driven back to Bagdad in 1991. In late 2000 Hussein converted all of Iraq's dollar assets to Euros which angered the financial centers of the United States. By the year 2000, his usefulness was over, and his country was basically confiscated by the United States in the Iraq War. Hussein was captured and eventually executed.

CIA whistleblower Susan Lindauer spent a year in prison to stop her from telling the truth about the Iraq war. It turns out Saddam Hussein offered to retire in exile and proposed that Iraq purchase millions of American cars in a ten year period, anything to avoid invasion. George Bush and the military went in anyway, at the cost of millions of lives and the destruction of the Iraq government all for the sake of resources and control.

The war officially lasted from 2003-2011 although permanent bases have been built there and a military presence remains. Estimated deaths range around 109,000 with 66,000 civilian casualties. The money saved in Iraq now has gone on to be spent in Afghanistan. Expenditures there went from 2.2 billion to 5.7 billion dollars.

WAR PROFITEERING is at its highest level since WW2. There are more private contractors in the field of battle than military personal. Their contracts are worth over $400 billion. One third of all Pentagon contracts go to just five companies; Lockheed Martin, Northrop Grumman, Raytheon, Boeing and General Dynamics. They were hired to go into Iraq and Afghanistan to beef up the infrastructure and rebuild the nation. Huge monetary awards and blank checks were doled out to "preferred" companies. Just like WW1, war is indeed a racket.

Just one example of corporate fraud occurred with the Dick Cheney supported company of Halliburton. This oilfield service company operates in more than 70 countries. It received a 7 billion dollar Iraq oil infrastructure contract through obvious connections with the government. Halliburton was caught overcharging the Pentagon for fuel deliveries which led to the US Justice Dept. opening up criminal investigations into fraud, waste and abuse. Hundreds of millions of dollars are said to have been defrauded from the American taxpayers.

The Pentagon's inspector general admits that the military cannot account for 25% of what it spends. The Pentagon admitted to losing 2.3 trillion dollars according to a CBS report in January of 2002. As the military rages on, they invent new wars and stage more false flag attacks while assaulting the taxpayer's pocketbook in the process.

In the book, "Dreams from My Father"
BARRACK OBAMA shows how he adopted his father's ideals of anti-colonialism even though his relationship with him was very limited because of divorce. With roots in Kenya, one of the first things Obama did as President was sent back a bust of Winston Churchill to England

because it was the British who stifled a rebellion in Kenya in the 1950s.

For many years, Obama grew up and hung around individuals who looked at the United States as colonialists. His friends in college were socialists and even communists;

Among those were David Axelrod, Bill Ayers, Rahm Emanuel, Rev. Jeremiah Wright, and Frank Marshall Davis and many others. His mother was a communist sympathizer and his father favored 100% taxation of the rich in his writings. Alice Palmer traveled to the Soviet Union to attend Communist Party functions, she is the state senator who hand-picked Obama to run for her seat. As we can see, Obama had many bitter relatives and friends who disliked America and what it stood for.

He learned to gain support from mainline voters by creating a vibrant personality. Instead of coming across angry and bitter, he was agreeable, happy and always smiling.

Obama is not completely wrong in his beliefs. The IMF and their associated corporations *have* looted poor countries through the years. The problem is that Obama holds a grudge against the entire free enterprise system, wrongly blaming it for the turmoil in the world. He seeks to downgrade the United States and punish the country for its transgressions, ignoring the great history of capitalism and how well people live in places like South Korea, Japan and Hong Kong.

The so called Arab Spring in 2011 came under Obama's watch. He was responsible for ousting Libyan leader Gadhafi and Egyptian leader Mubarak. Obama's little wars and drone attacks in Yemen, Pakistan and Syria are allowing very radical elements to take over countries that were at least manageable in the past. Obama promised to slow down and end the wars. Instead war in general has escalated under his watch. This leads to a rather odd partnership. His anti-colonial attitude combined with existing military willingness to start up new conflicts is a perfect fit in the globalist's game plan of bringing about America' decline. The average family lost 40% of their net worth from 2007-2011.

Barrack Obama, with all of his anti-colonial sentiments, is either unwittingly or wholeheartedly beefing up the war machine and its business allies.

On Set.11, 2012 a heavily armed attack occurred on the American embassy in BENGHAZI, Libya. At first, the Obama administration told the public the attack was the spontaneous reaction to an anti-Muslim video on YouTube. How dumb does the President think we are? It was a coordinated terrorist attack that killed the ambassador and three members of his diplomatic mission. It has come out that the embassy requested extra security but was turned down by the White House. On top of that, drone cameras in the sky allowed the situation room to view the hour's long attack in real time. The nearby CIA annex was given the "stand down" order, but two Navy Seals went to the scene against orders and saved some lives. The plot thickened later when former General and CIA director David Petraeus had to resign over an affair he was having with his biographer. Or did he have to resign because of what he knew about the attack? What is obvious here is that the military, the CIA and the president are hiding something. Was this a false flag attack or maybe a stand down to allow for greater death and damage?

It is true that Al-Qaeda was originally developed by the United States to fight the Soviet Union. Terror techniques were taught by the CIA as we basically built a monster that would come back and bite us. Furthermore, we actually provoke the monster and encourage it to do so. Al-Qaeda is being used in combat missions for and against America. The war on terror is filled with smoke, mirrors and deceptions, all in the name of deceiving you and me.

PAT TILLMAN was an NFL football player who gave up his career in 2002 to join the Army Rangers to "fight for his country" after the 911 attacks. He died from "friendly fire" in the Afghan mountains in 2004. The Army first announced he had been killed by enemy fire, which was a lie. They later had to admit he was killed by his own fellow soldiers. He had been waving and shouting that he was Pat Tillman, yet, he was fired at repeatedly and finally shot in the head. His brother Kevin was told the lie first, then his family and then the public. The Army burned his uniform and journal days after the incident. The cover-up went through high ranking Army officials all the way up to Donald Rumsfeld. A Silver Star award to given posthumously to Tillman by Gen. McChrystal even though he was not technically worthy of it. The Army wanted to portray him as a great hero when all the while Tillman himself was starting to question the merits of the Iraq War. He thought it "was a mistake and going to be a disaster".

One of his first missions in Iraq was a rescue mission for a POW named Jessica Lynch. Tillman believed it was a public relations stunt. Special Forces knew the Iraqi enemy had fled the building where she was kept so the rescue was simple enough. Lynch said she was never a heroine because her rifle had jammed and she was knocked unconscious. The Army falsely claimed she had knife and gunshot wounds and had endured rough interrogation, none of which was true. The entire event was staged for public consumption. After events like that, Tillman became suspicious of his entire tour of duty. He saw the inner corruption first hand and he didn't fit the mold of the American war hero patriot. Was he murdered because he knew too much and was becoming a liability?

BLOWBACK. Millions of innocent people have died because of the misguided policies of America. Wikipedia defines blowback as "an espionage term for unintended consequences of a covert operation that are suffered by the civil population of the aggressor government. To the civilians suffering the blowback of covert operations, the effect typically manifests itself as "random" acts of political violence without a discernible, direct cause; because the public—in whose name the intelligence agency acted—are ignorant of the effected secret attacks that provoked revenge (counter-attack) against them" Studies have shown that "blowback" is a real concern. Ron Paul has spoken in depth about blowback and garners more support from the military troops than any other candidate because he tells the truth.

Internal military studies have agreed with Robert
Pape's assessment; "Over 95% of all suicide terrorist attacks around the world since 1980 have in common not religion, but a clear strategic purpose, to compel modern democracies to withdraw military forces from the territory that the terrorists view as their homeland or prize greatly." Not only that but many terror attacks are pure theatre put on by our own agencies to spark public attention.

The American people should understand Pape's statement and work to defund the aggressive military forces we have around the world. The military industrial complex is alive and well in today's world, and is out of control. It must be suppressed and brought down to size until it only deals with legitimate matters of defense. The war on terror is a war on the American people. We have lost our money, we have lost our rights and we have lost our soldiers. This will go on indefinitely until such a time when the American people wake up and put a stop to it.

Here is a partial list of war and holocaust victims, a full listing would take up many more pages;

US Civil War- 700,000, Spanish American War - 220,000,
WW1- 20 million, Soviet Revolution- 5 million,
Chinese Civil War- 2 million, Manchurian War-1.1 million,
Soviet Union Ukrainian War-10 million,
Stalin's purges- 13 million, WW2- 55 million (with German holocaust and Chinese revolution), Chinese Civil War #2- 1.2 million, India/Pakistan- 1 million,
China Tibet- 1.2 million, Korean War- 3 million,
Mao's leap forward-38 million,
Mao's Cultural Revolution- 11 million, Vietnam-3 million, Ethiopian civil war- 1 million, Congo/Zaire war- 3.8 million, Khmer Rouge- 1.7 million, Menghitsu- 1.5 million, Sudanese civil war- 2 million,
Soviet Union Afghanistan-1.3 million, Gulf War-85,000, Rwanda-900,000, USA Afghanistan-40,000,
Iraq USA war- 160,000, Armenia holocaust -1.5 million Christians, Mexican revolution -1 million,
3 million per year die of malaria since the DDT ban.

Alexander Solzhenitsyn was right when he said that "a state of war only serves as an excuse for domestic tyranny", the numbers don't lie.

In conclusion, those of us who are lucky enough to avoid the ongoing waves of war and murder should be grateful. Humanity has endured not only the horrors of war but the systematic killing and murder of millions of innocent bystanders in holocausts, ethnic cleansings and genocides. The casualty list is truly horrifying. Many of us cast it aside and go on with our lives. Please understand that often war is for profit, the calculated plan undertaken by political and financial crooks. They work behind the scenes, "poison the wells" and deceive well-meaning people. We then send our sons and daughters marching off to war in a patriotic trance totally unaware that the conflict originated from plotting power brokers whom they will never see or hear. The real tragedy is the troops do not know who they are fighting for and why they are fighting.

Some of us can claim ignorance, but those of us good people who know the truth and do nothing must take responsibility. The corruption of government is proportional to the apathy of its own people.

The "Big Lie Theory" of propaganda is attributed to Hitler's own Joseph Goebbels; "If you tell a lie big enough and keep repeating it, people will eventually come to believe it."

We now live in a world order that does not allow sovereign nations, only the illusion of them. Hence WW3 is unlikely to take place. However, bloodshed and war will still exist worldwide in one form or another as a diversion. "Terrorists" are now the contrived enemy.

There is an age old desire for global conquest that is alive and well today. Hopefully, humanity will wake up soon and put war in its final resting place.

*"we cannot make war without trade
or trade without war"*

~Jan Pieterzoon   1670

Chapter Seven: False Flag Deception

"throw down your guns, we have been misled"

False flags attacks, or staged events, occur when a nation attacks itself as an excuse to go to war or increase domestic oppression.

We all remember the kid who made a mess and pointed his finger at someone else. "I didn't do it, he did!" Maybe these same kids grow up to become deception artists. Deceit happens in everyday life and in all areas of government and finance. The intentional "mess" is created to get a desired reaction.

Many broken barn windows in rural America during the depression were repaired by the very hoodlums that broke them under cover of darkness, a way for tramps and con men to make some extra cash; first they commit a crime, then they show up the next morning and fix their own mess-with pay.

If a school district desires more money for administrative benefits and pensions, they will first create a diversion. They make a claim in the media that they need more funding. They may threaten to increase class sizes, turn off the air conditioning or eliminate a popular activity in an effort to "save money." Then they come to the public with a levy. The voters cheerfully vote yes to a new levy or tax "for the good of the students". I would call that false flag education.

The Federal Reserve creates economic disasters to increase its power and position. Bankers have run railroads and auto manufacturers into debt just to receive bailout funds.

The Panic of 1907 was started with a rumor by JP Morgan that two major banks were going to become insolvent; this led to a six week run on the banks. The public foolishly demanded financial reform and they got it in the form of the Federal Reserve Act, an economic false flag.

Environmental false flags happen frequently, the theory of global warming scares people with threats of flooding oceans and worldwide drought.

The field of science can use their fatherly influence to induce panics on society; The "dangers" of high Cholesterol for example.

War offers a great opportunity for false flag attacks.
America has engaged in attacks and planned attacks against itself to appear the victim and then play the savior role. War then becomes the health of the state to the detriment of its people. Joseph Stalin said; "The easiest way to gain control of a population is to carry out acts of terror. (The public) will clamor for such laws if their personal security is threatened."

In today's world, you should ask yourself the question as to why Islamic terrorists go after so many American interests and burn American flags. Even the Madrid and London bombings were linked to the United States being our allies. Why do they target us? It's because the American military targets their countries. As far back as 1953 in Iran, this country has been bullying and manipulating the Islamic world. Moreover, since 1991, large scale terrorist attacks have been followed by the spilling of blood and death to serviceman and innocent civilians. There is evidence that many of these terrorist attacks including 9/11 originate in the bellows of our own government. All the while, the state gets more power, the military industrial complex gets bigger, and the average citizen loses more of their rights and privacy.

FORT SUMTER provided Lincoln with an easy target to entice the first shot, starting the first hostilities of the Civil War.

THE USS MAINE was sunk; Spain was falsely blamed by America, starting the Spanish American War.

THE LUSITANIA was torpedoed by a German U boat, swinging the will of the American people towards war in WW1.

PEARL HARBOR was a sitting duck when Hawaiian commanders were not filled in on an impending attack after Japanese codes were broken, and enemy planes showed up on radar.

NORTHWOODS OPERATION, James Bamford who wrote "The Puzzle Palace" and "Body of Secrets" uncovered some very interesting government documents for state sponsored terrorism. Northwoods had the approval of the Joint Chiefs of Staff in 1962, although it was later rejected by President Kennedy. In 1992, Congress made many top secret documents available because the movie "JFK" spurred interest in the subject.
  As a way to frame Cuba, Northwoods proposed innocent American people to be shot, refugee boats to be sunk, urban terror, hijacked planes, sunken ships, and airplanes shot down. The goal was to get public support for a war against Cuba.
  Related to this operation is "Operation Mongoose"

which intended to "Provoke, Harass or Disrupt Cuba." "Operation Bingo" which was to make it appear American facilities in Cuba were under attack.
"Operation Dirty Trick" which would blame Cuba if astronaut John Glenn were to crash his Mercury spacecraft.
~An OAS (Organization of American States) attack to be blamed on Cuba. Jamaica and Trinidad were possible targets.
~Bribing one of Castro's commanders to attack the US.

The GULF OF TONKIN incident in 1964 was used to escalate the Viet Nam conflict.

The sinking of the USS LIBERTY in 1967 was designed to create an all-out war in the Middle East.

WTC BOMBING/1993. On Feb.26, 1993 an explosion ripped through the basement of building 1 at the World Trade Center in New York City killing six and injuring 1042 people with a half billion in damage.
  The FBI had knowledge of a terror cell and infiltrated it with an informant. They provided a safe haven to build the bomb. The plan was to substitute harmless power for the explosives and then arrest the terrorists, but the FBI had other plans.
  On October 28, 1993, Dan Rather reported on CBS News that "the FBI might have known of the plot in advance and may have stopped the bombing that killed six people". CIA-paid operative Ehmad Salem secretly recorded many of his conversations with FBI agents after he became suspicious. He agreed to supply fake explosives to the bombers but was overruled by FBI agents. The real bombs were delivered to the scene.
  Law enforcement was given credit for uncovering the plot and putting the offenders behind bars. Khalid

Sheikh Mohammed admitted blame for the attack after his sons were abducted by the government and he endured waterboarding torture. Later, incriminating transcripts were not allowed in the court proceedings

Since 1990, the FBI had plans and documents relating to the bombing. The truth is that our own government allowed the explosion and may have masterminded the entire event, and then took credit for the cleanup.

OKLAHOMA CITY BOMBING. Soon after the explosion at the Alfred P. Murrah building in 1995, President Bill Clinton deflected blame to the so-called far right elements in the country. He said; "We hear so many loud and angry voices in America today whose sole goal seems to be to try to keep some people as paranoid as possible and the rest of us all torn up and upset with each other. They spread hate. They leave the impression that, by their very words, that violence is acceptable." He was aiming suspicion at Rush Limbaugh and various white supremacist groups. He credited the bombing as helping his reelection campaign.
There are a few things wrong with this explanation as shown in the film "A Noble Lie".
 -The truck bomb would have blown outward in a circular motion, yet the damage to the building was at a right angle.
 -There is evidence of more than one bomb, as witnesses testified on TV.
 -Local TV station 4 was bought out by the New York Times because they told the truth. Journalists fired and blackballed from future employment.
-Threats against grand jury and whistleblowers and refusal to allow relevant witnesses at trial.
-The book; "The Final Jihad" was written in 1994. After the bombing, the copyright date was changed to 1996. The story shows fore-knowledge of the actual events. It is

about someone setting off a bomb in Oklahoma City and being picked up later by a state trooper. The character's name was Tom McVeigh. The author (who is the brother of the Oklahoma governor) was told not to talk and he later said the story was written after the bombing.
-The Murrah building was chosen partly because it had a day care center and with the horrid images, would increase public sentiment for passage of the anti-terrorist bill which had previously failed to pass in spite of the '93 Trade Center bombing. After the Oklahoma massacre, it passed.

WTC/911...By the year 2001, the CIA, FBI, NSA, Dept. of Defense and many other intelligence agencies were spending billions to track, define, and spy on the country and its so called enemies abroad. Information was extensive on terrorist activities, especially after the 1993 bombing. How could an elaborate terrorist plot involving the hijacking of planes and diverting them into tall buildings be overlooked? Why was there an Air Force stand down on that day? How could three tall buildings crumble and fall at the speed of gravity without the use of carefully placed detonators? How could solid steel girders melt when jet fuel could not reach the required temperature to melt them? Why was the crime scene cleaned up so fast and all the debris shipped off to places unknown? Why was the Patriot Act written before 2001? Building 7 housed many top secret documents and files, why would it happen to free fall downward in a cloud of dust without being hit by an airplane? Why did the FEMA show up one day before the attack?
  Al-Qaida was an invention of the CIA and Osama Bin Laden, a former employee of the United States. Yet they are blamed for the incident.
  Zacarias Moussaoui took a flight training class in Eagan, Minnesota in 2001 before the attack. He was

interested in flying planes straight, not landing or taking off. The FBI was notified but took no action to this obvious threat. Why?

The government is very compartmentalized, and they don't communicate well with each other. It is not logical to claim the entire government had prior knowledge of the impending attack. It is reasonable to think however that there was inside information in one or two intelligence agencies, the awareness of something big in the making, something imminent, something horrible, and it was then "allowed" to happen.

Why were all the films of the Pentagon attack confiscated? Why did witnesses watch parts fall from the sky of the doomed Pennsylvania airplane? Where are the bodies?

By 2013, professional architects, engineers and others have banded together to question the official version of events on September 11, 2001.

What role did our own government play in this disaster and why it was allowed to happen? If our intelligence was breached and taken by surprise, why is there no investigation into its incompetence? Why is there a complete lack of blame and reprehend? These are just a few of many questions that linger on. There are many books and videos on this subject, including "Loose Change."

THE MADRID BOMBING. March 11, 2004 exactly 911 days after the 911 attack on New York City and three days before the general elections, coordinated explosions rattled the commuter train system of Madrid killing 191 and injuring 1800 people. It may have been the work of an Israeli Mossad false flag operation which means it was a false flag attack gone wrong. The attack was blamed on al-Qaeda hoping the Spaniards would re-elect Jose Maria Aznar and continue to support the United

States in the Iraq War. The plan backfired as the voters overwhelmingly elected socialist Jose Luis Zapatero who pulled the Spanish troops out of Iraq within two weeks of his election.

THE LONDON BOMBING. On July 7, 2005, Peter Power was leading a training drill "based on simultaneous bombs going off precisely at the railway stations where it happened this morning", when he had to switch the drill to a real life event. 52 people died and 700 injured in four actual explosions, three trains and one bus. Was it coincidence that the real thing was happening at the same time as a practice drill?

For an hour and a half, the authorities told the public there was a power outage when in fact bombs were detonated. The four CCTV cameras at the exact sites happen to not be working that day. Witnesses said there were no Muslims with backpacks seen aboard the trains and bus. Four stooges may have been used in the drill and were killed. The official story was that the four terrorists had exploding devices in their backpacks, when all along, the devices were professionally installed under the trains.

THE UNDERWARE BOMBER. Umar Abdulmutallab confessed to attempting to detonate plastic explosives on board Northwest Airlines flight 253 from Amsterdam to Detroit, Michigan. The media spin is that Al-Qaeda supplied him with the bomb and trained him. He actually worked for the CIA and Saudi Intelligence. Immediately after the incident, Homeland Security and the media began pushing for worldwide body scanners, obviously, a manufactured event from the start.

Attorney Kurt Haskell witnessed Umar as he tried to board the aircraft; "On Christmas Day 2009, my wife and I were returning from an African safari and had a connecting flight through Amsterdam. As we waited for our flight, we sat on the floor next to the boarding gate. What I witnessed while sitting there and subsequent events have changed my life forever. While I sat there, I witnessed Umar dressed in jeans and a white t-shirt, being escorted around security by a man in a tan suit who spoke perfect American English and who aided Umar in boarding without a passport. The airline gate worker initially refused Umar boarding until the man in the tan suit intervened. The event meant nothing to me at the time. Little did I know that Umar would try to kill me a few hours later as our flight approached Detroit."

Obviously, the CIA gave Umar a defective bomb, and the FBI made sure he was allowed to board the plane. He was used as a Patsy to implement more government policies that serve to reduce our rights and take away liberties.

AURORA THEATRE SHOOTING. On July 20, 2012 a mass shooting occurred during the midnight showing of "The Dark Knight Rises." 12 people were killed and 58 injured. James Holmes was said to be the lone gunman even though at least one witness claims to have seen someone else prop open the emergency door after a phone call. Witnesses claim there were smoke bombs coming from opposite sides of the theatre. Holmes was arrested outside of the building, dressed in black with a gas mask. His apartment was rigged with wires and explosives set to go off when the police arrived, yet he warned police about it. The original movie trailer had a theatre shooting which was removed after the event. Did he act alone? Where did he get the know how to rig complex explosive traps? Where did he get the money to buy thousands of dollars' worth of guns and equipment?

Holmes was a PHD candidate in neuroscience at Colorado University. Billy Kromka, a fellow student said;

"It was just shocking, because there was no way I thought he could have the capacity to do commit an atrocity like this," He may have been involved with mind-altering research.

He was obviously on heavy medication after his arrest, and later on in court hearings, unable to speak. Fellow Inmates herd him scream and yell that he was "programmed to kill." This harkens back to the MKULTRA techniques of mind control that the government has admitted to using in the past.

Robert Holmes, James father, is employed by FICA and the creator of computer algorithms that have the potential to trace any transaction to its original source, thereby showing the guilt of professional financial thieves that threaten International banking and the economy. Could this be a set up to silence Robert Holmes and prevent high finance criminals from going to jail? What about raising public sentiment for gun control?

Another twist is the medical nurse who treated many of the victims. Jennifer Gallagher had the advantage of hearing details of the shooting and their version of what happened.

She was in a group picture with President Obama when he visited the victims. Later, while on vacation in Iowa, she mysteriously drowned late at night. Was she silenced?

Obama's former chief of staff Rahm Emanuel has said, "You don't ever want a crisis to go to waste." The government is good at creating a crisis to encourage the passage of more laws that take away privacy and liberty.

SIKH TEMPLE SHOOTING. August 5, 2012, just before services around 10:30 AM, six people died and four wounded when supremacist Wade Michael Page attacked the Sikh Temple in Oak Creek, Wisconsin.

However, witnesses say that; "Between ten and ten-thirty, four white males who were dressed darkly, dressed in all black clothing, came in and opened fire on our congregation." The temple leader said he saw two suspicious men looking around the area before the shooting occurred.

Who are we to believe? The eyewitnesses or the media who would have us believe the shooting was the work of a lone gunman with ties to white racists groups? Again, the never ending narrative about gun control headlines the event and the facts are thrown under the bus.

FEDERAL RESERVE BUILDING. October 2012, Agents arrested a 21 year old Bangladesh man after he tried to detonate explosives at the NY Federal Reserve Building. The entire episode was set up and run by the FBI. There was no actual bomb. Yet the media gave credit to the government for thwarting another terrorist attack.

CYBERWARS. The technology of today makes it rather easy to create threats against nations and organizations through hacking and deception. A small group of antagonists can pose as spokesman for a country. They can give off false threats and actually pit one group against another causing confusion and disinformation.

BOSTON MARATHON BOMBING. April 2013, two explosions rocked the finish line of the famous footrace. A month earlier, the animated TV show "Family Guy" depicted a car *running over people* at the finish line of the Boston Marathon and a cell phone setting off two explosions earlier in the episode, probably an odd coincidence. Like the London Bombings, the riot police happened to be involved in a training drill before and during the actual explosions. When the FBI asked the public to send in film footage and pictures of the event, much of it showed up at the Alex Jones' site Infowars.com. These pictures show suspicious activity of many people including government officials and Middle Eastern looking men on the scene. One "person of interest" who was a bloodied witness to the explosion was deported out of the country with Obama's assistance, covering up a possible Saudi connection. The story suddenly changed. Finally, two Russian/ American brothers named Tsarnaev were declared the suspects and a manhunt ensued. The older brother was killed and the younger arrested in serious condition. The mother and the father of the two boys claim their sons were set up. The FBI first claimed they had no earlier contact with the older brother, and later, they admitted there *was* earlier contact with him, in fact they were being watched a long time before the bombings and also during the event. Perhaps they were hired for drill work and then framed as the "patsy's".

If you think this bombing could not have been a staged event, remember the *Northwoods* operation where the government planned actual attacks on its own people to further a political agenda against Cuba back in the early 60s. The pressing need of the many security agencies of government is to increase domestic spying. Whenever an "event" like this takes place, there is always a call to increase public surveillance. The event is used as a pretext for more law and more police state activity.

Many CIA whistleblowers have come forward to reveal the reality of false flag operations. Susan Lindauer, a former CIA Asset, has come forward after spending time in jail to discuss 9/11 and the Patriot Act, forcible drugging and indefinite detention. John Kiriakou was delivered a 30 month sentence for revealing the details of American induced torture tactics. Chip Tatum who worked for US intelligence, discussed the CIA drug transactions before his disappearance.

"we are on the verge of a global transformation. all we need is the right major crisis and the nations will accept the New World Order"

~David Rockefeller

Chapter Eight: Generational Football

"all the worlds of men and only one earth"

The Burr Street Gang was a collection of young boys who hung around St. Paul back in the 1930s. They would ride their bikes for miles, through the endless alleys and city streets, bumping along block after block. Back then, there was so much stuff to do around town you wouldn't want to be caught inside the house for very long. It was an innocent time, when misunderstandings rarely led to serious disputes, and even then a push and shove would suffice instead of knives and guns. Drug abuse and mass media were not a factor in the neighborhood. It was a simpler time when hopping a freight car or jumping in a lake on a hot day was thrill enough.

My Dad was one of those guys. He and his pal Louie and others knew each other their whole lives. It was a bond that carried them through war and peace, good times and bad, a lifetime of friendship. They were part of the so-called greatest generation, the values were strong and the morals high. Patriotism was expected and few people thought twice about serving their country. The family and neighborhood bonds were intense and the sense of community threaded deep across the country.

The axis powers were viewed as a threat to the well-being

of this harmonized world. The depression left people feeling stronger in spirit and the American people were not about to let a foreign speaking band of thugs walk in and take them over. Joining up was an easy decision. They went to war with determination and courage, but the fight wasn't easy and many did not return to enjoy life in the fabulous fifties, when America was left standing alone.

The year was 1944, my Dad was impatient; he joined the Marines to "get it over with fast". He trained at Camp Pendleton, went to Hawaii and then on to the "island". After the battle, his division went back to Hawaii to prepare for the invasion of Japan which never happened. Instead they occupied part of Japan for a while and then sailed to San Diego until the war was over.

  The journey was long to Iwo Jima, across nautical miles of open ocean and foreboding waves. The men reflected on their lives and prepared for the worst. Dad told himself he was going to die and was ready for it. At last the smoking island came into view. The desolate place was rumbling with explosions, rocked by continuous and maddening bombardment that went on for weeks. The Japanese were dug in, hidden deep beneath the ground in tunnels and caves, anxiously waiting for the inevitable invasion of the angry Americans who had been attacked on that peaceful Sunday at Pearl Harbor.

  The "Japs" were family men themselves; they sent letters home just like we did. They bled the same, they died the same. They were not a whole lot different than us.

What is the force behind it all? What measure of man convinces another man to overcome and kill someone else who is the same as himself?

It was February 1945; landing on the island was pure misery. There were no rocks or trees to hide behind. Marines were digging themselves into the loose red sand that encompassed the place. Many that made it ashore were mowed down immediately. My Dad jumped into a foxhole and watched as some of his fellow Marines and friends were torn apart.

He was in the 5th division, the one that suffered the most casualties, 9276 to be exact. It was called "the spearhead" because its job, as an infantry division was to isolate the highest point on the island called Mt. Suribachi. This is where the famous raising of the flag took place. Dad watched from below as the flag waved. He was part of the 26th regiment that fought on in spite of high losses. The 26th alone started out with over 3000 men and had just over 1400 left after it was decommissioned to reserve status. A regiment was considered ineffective at 30% casualties. The 26th fought on in spite of close to 50% losses. They were nick-named "the professionals."

One evening a group of war weary marines were assembled to ask for volunteers. Communication wires were urgently needed to be strung across dangerous territory in the darkness of night. My Dad was one who accepted the challenge. He was later awarded the Bronze Star for courage.

I remember him as a guy who never backed down in the face of adversity. He was kind to strangers but stout when he has to be. The Iwo experience stayed with him for life. He always downplayed it though, saying you have to move on. He moved on but was still able to beat me in a foot race when he was 50 years old!

It is a long way from that island in 1945, to the carefree suburban existence where I grew up in the 60s. I had the same lifetime comradery with friends that he had and observed strong family life, but we never had a real threat to our existence as they did in the 40s. The cold war, fallout shelters and nuclear bombs were more of a thing for kids to joke about than to take seriously.

I was raised in what I would call a "libertarian" household. Mom worked extremely hard around the house, keeping it clean, making meals and just always being there for us. She was the glue that kept us together and went on to be a loving Grandmother for my own family. I and my brother and sister were taught to work hard, be honest, think ahead, plan in advance, help others in need, never take what does not belong to you, live a clean life and leave the world a better place than you found it. These values were also important in my Dad's view of politics. In that time, the Democratic Party represented more of the working class, mainline sort of person. Through the years the party has drifted from its core, taken over by special interests like feminism, animal rights, environmentalism, and big welfare. Although my Dad would never admit it, the party had left him. He stubbornly continued to vote for and support anyone with the DFL label, even though the party had long ago sold out to the big interests and big money, representing the very thing he claimed to stand against.

I was never much interested in politics early in life. It was always a dull and boring experience in public school. That was not by accident; the schools avoid controversy and make the subject uninteresting for a reason. *Don't get the kids whipped up*, they just might learn the nature of the game.

Finally, in college I learned about conservative philosophy. For the first time, I actually thought about the nature of politics and the tremendous importance of individual rights. It felt great to vote for Ronald Reagan who ushered in a new era of freedom and liberty. Although much of that was wordplay, it got me thinking. Dad was disappointed that I took that position. Whenever we discussed an issue he became short sighted, abrupt, narrow minded, and sometimes angry. I was willing to explore new ideas and think in different ways but my Dad harbored some kind of deep resentment towards the very rich, the well off, the wealthy, whatever you want to call it. People in expensive cars and mansions seemed to be a target for his resentment. To this day I don't know where this attitude came from, maybe a cultural phenomenon. Democrats would go on TV and say things geared towards his personality type. They would reassure him of their interest in taking care of the "little people" the working poor and that we must tax the hated rich class. I still can't get over the fact that he referred to himself as one of the "little people". What a thing to call himself after all he'd been through! He was far from a little person; he could measure up to anybody in terms of hard work and honesty. Actually no one is a "little person" and I frown on the Democratic Party for picking this term to apply to their followers. Dad should have peeled away the layers of the phony two party system, and realized the corruption and double dealings that took place on both sides. He was probably aware of this but his inner drive to divide people into classes kept the belief alive in his mind for so many years.

Sometimes he would go to a poor part of town with a TV set to give away. It was hard to find a person to take it. He didn't understand the people there were not really *that bad off*. The system had given them plenty of benefits including TV sets and cable service, a steady monthly income, food stamps and a place to live, but it came at the expense of his middle class neighbors, not the rich. A broader view of history shows that the poor got getting better off since the application of free enterprise and capitalism. Now that system has turned to crony capitalism which leaches from the middle class.

The early eighties brought me to more realizations about the world. A great monopoly existed in politics. My studies and thoughts started to circulate on the Libertarian Party and its principals. It had great meaning because of the way I was raised. Ironically, my parents raised me under libertarian principals and never realized it. Yet, in talking with my father, he made it sound like I had joined a religious cult. From then on, we never saw eye to eye on the subject. We argued many times and got nowhere. It was unfortunate in many regards. What could have been a learning experience for both of us ended up many times leaving me feeling uptight up and bitter. I will chalk it up to the fact he was very argumentative and was driven to take the opposite side of almost any position I would take. He told me the most irritating statement again and again; "there you go, sticking up for the rich again". I heard that my whole life, a mantra of the liberal left.

My view is that there should be no limits on honest wealth, but there should be sanctions on dishonest gains. Dad never divided these two groups. He lumped them all into one "rich" band of thieves.
For a long time, I believed we had a true free market and the stocks would always rebound. I thought we had capitalism here and I supported the system. Later on, I realized the system had a lot of crony capitalism, corporate state fascism and a central bank run amuck. Certainly the rank and file Democrat is right in a sense but they don't want to admit that their own party is an integral part of the corrupt game. They point their

fingers at the wrong crowd while placing blame on the wrong people, Dad fell within that group.

Others had the same impression of good old Charlie. On one hand, he was very friendly and made people feel at ease and other times he wanted nothing but a good conflict. To put this all in perspective, the generation of the greatest generation was a very stubborn generation! The accomplishments of their time cannot be overstated; on the other hand, they had trouble seeing their own flaws and drawbacks. There was a certain amount of "sweep it under the rug" mentality about things that were upsetting.

Some of their cherished beliefs and institutions may not be so perfect after all. That includes party, church, and leadership. All in all we have a generation to be proud of, but with some distinctive flaws.

Dad was an avid newspaper reader, all the way to the end. One day I pulled out an old newspaper from the wall of my house. It was from 1939. It was loaded with good articles and in depth information, and was a bigger size than today's papers. This was the avenue of coverage for years. In those days the paper (a trusted friend) would show up on the doorstep every morning and evening. The paperboy would even get a gift at Christmastime. News of the outside world revolved around it. It was respected and cherished. However, things changed with the advent of cable TV and the internet. Suddenly we didn't have to depend on the nightly news or the paper for good information. We had more than just 3 TV networks to rely on. On my weekly visits to Dad's place I was armed with something new, a source that trumped the paper! I had news coming right off the wire; I knew the score of the game right away, and the latest newsbreaks. I knew the weather in faraway states and was able to communicate with people around the world in real time. I was getting political opinions that never showed up on TV.

Dad just couldn't get himself to trust it and still depended on the good old newspaper. Oddly enough, Dad listened to talk radio. He was a dedicated listener of Rush Limbaugh, Shaun Hannity, and Jason Lewis. For years he told me Rush won't last long. I ask him why he listened to him and he said he has to "keep up with the enemy". Somewhere along the line, the conservative message must have had an effect on his thinking.

After the financial collapse of 2008, I knew there was something deeply wrong, and I discovered the world of conspiracy. I took advantage of this new internet streaming source, the information highway! I went to my Dads place armed with new and exciting articles and opinions coming from every which way. I argued in favor of people like Ron Paul and Jesse Ventura. Little did Dad know that Ventura won the Minnesota governorship with the help of the internet. Ron Paul had the biggest single day money donation through the internet. Alex Jones ran numerous information packed articles a day that would never appear in mass media. It was a new world and yet Dad couldn't see it, or didn't want to see it. I found myself telling him about the Federal Reserve System, global governance, hidden and unknown history, environmentalism, 911 and many other things. He never believed what I was saying because it wasn't in the newspaper. I would have to go back home and print the information and bring it over the following week. He would read through my documentation and scribble in his own comments and then hand the stuff back to me like a graded test. I told him things like Castro was emptying his jails and sending people here, an environmental group called Elf knocked down a TV tower in Washington, Mexicans learning how to conquer

America in schools, rich people keep on giving in bad economic times, more Republicans voted for the Civil Rights Act, Democrats want to nationalize 401K plans, newspapers and networks are owned by big corporations, most Americans favor an audit of the Fed, Obama wants to ban conspiracy theories and regulate the internet, the global warming myth, LBJ lied about the Viet Nam war, Harry Truman tried to seize the steel industry, and Lincoln believed blacks were inferior and wanted them out of the country. Dad was especially touchy about historical issues even though he prided himself on his enlightened view that the Bible should be taken with a grain of salt. Dad would simply not believe anything I said until I showed it to him in black and white! One time he said; "I look through your stuff and can't believe what I'm reading"

 The only time we agreed on anything is when I brought over a little book about the corrupt banking system. He thumbed through it and said it was probably true. A very rare moment of agreement!

 Even watching a baseball game had its conflicts. In one game a pitcher was about to throw a no-hitter. The final batter hit a ground ball and was called safe at first, thereby spoiling his no hit bid. The instant replay showed he was indeed out! The next day there was an outcry by a few sportswriters to declare the call wrong and award the pitcher his no-hitter. I was not in favor of this because the rules state any call at first base is the final judgment of the umpire, right or wrong. Dad angrily disagreed. He said the pitcher "deserves" his no hitter, no matter what the rules say. This incident displayed a fundamental difference between the two of us. I did not "feel bad" for the pitcher like Dad did. He felt the pitcher had a bad break and it was up to some higher authority to straighten it out for him. I felt (as the pitcher did) that we must abide by the rules and move on in life, and not depend on "the government" to bail him out. Ironically, when I was a kid, Dad taught me this same lesson; take care of your own problems. This ended up being our last argument. Even though he had trouble breathing and speaking, he felt the need to make his case known.

What I found in Dad was a man who was proud of his life and what he accomplished even though new technology and information began speeding by his traditions and old ways, threatening the bedrock of his world. Or maybe he was just being stubborn for the sake of it, or maybe a little of both. It's tough to hoist a sail into the winds of change.

Someday all *I* believe may be questioned by those smarter than me. I may sit in the same position as my Father and feel like refuting every new thing I hear. The blinders may go on me like they were on my Dad. At that point, maybe I'll be a little more tolerant and open minded. After all, every new generation needs a lift off and a prayer from the last, that's how we got to where we are today.

Looking back, I can see how we attach ourselves to the time in which we live. How invisible forces can mold the way we think and behave. We become the religion of ourselves and sometimes the religion is hard to overcome and step out of. Some may avoid conspiracy theories because they threaten us. I say we should put our suspicions aside and march on!

I prefer to remember a loving Father who would toss me a football or play catch with the baseball for hours, a guy who would build snow slides and take us fishing, a Dad who was always there with good advice when things weren't going well. And finally, a guy who left the world a better place than he found it.

Words from Dad's favorite poem;

> "Let me live in my house by the side of the road
>   Where the race of men go by-
> They are good, they are bad, they are weak,
> They are strong. Wise, foolish- so am I.
> Then why should I sit in the scorner's seat
> Or hurl the cynics ban?-
> Let me live in my house by the side of the road
> And be a friend to man.

"think positive"

CKD 1923-2010

Chapter Nine: The Green Anchor

"the earth shall survive man; long after we are gone, there will be clear streams and blue skies"

The year was 1973. I rode with my brother in law and a friend to the headwaters of the Mississippi River at Lake Itasca Park in northern Minnesota. The Chevy Blazer rounded forested bends and curves as we eagerly approached the beginning of this long and powerful waterway. When we got there, what we saw was not very impressive in size. A tiny stream flowed out of a quiet, pristine lake. It was hard to believe this was the mighty river of Tom Sawyer, paddleboats and all the glorious folklore! On this day I not only saw the little stream, but I became aware of another more sinister thing, litter.
My brother in law looked around in disgust and began picking up papers, cups and various scraps that tourists threw by the shoreline. He wondered why people would drive all this way and then reward the park with their garbage. All three of us pitched in and cleaned the area before we left. Since then, needless to say, I do not litter.

Back then, a commercial on TV caught my attention. An old Indian man walked beside an urban waterway, stepping over trash and old tires. A tear rolled down his face. America had entered a new era. Ecology was a new buzzword at the time, in school we would study the environment and man's effect on the world. Back then, a problem was identified (as in water or air pollution), and rectified with complaints, lobbying efforts and passage of fair regulations and laws to deal with the issue. Rivers were cleaned up, hazardous waste removed, scrubbers put on factories and better fuels and more efficient cars were produced that lowered smog levels and made our world a better place to live. Unfortunately, since that time, environmental science has gone south; it has been corrupted and turned into a tool of research dollars and political advancement.

Julian Huxley, along with Godfrey Rockefeller and Prince Philip, were three of the founders of the World Wildlife Fund in 1961. The "Panda Bear" WWF is a strong force in wildlife and environmental protection. Unfortunately, they have been an obstacle to human progress and advancement. The group ignores the well-being of people in third world situations and seeks to "protect" areas for ownership and occupation of a select few who eventually would inherit the land as their own personal playground.

Enviro-terrorism, eco-fronts, and carbon credit rip-offs are accurate terms to describe the forces of environmental extremism and UNESCO (United Nations Education Social Cultural Organization). These and other groups are not about being good stewards of the earth. They are hijacking the environmental movement for their own selfish ends. Maurice Strong wrote the introduction to a Trilateral Commission article entitled "Beyond Interdependence: The Meshing of the World's Economy and the Earth's Ecology" in which he said "This interlocking is the new reality of the century, with profound implications for the shape of our institutions of governance, national and international. By the year 2012, these changes will be fully integrated into our economics and political life." Their plan was to mix not only science and politics, but to include another diabolical element; *Eugenics*. The movement we normally associate with the Third Reich had its name changed and transformed into new organizations. The ideas of Hitler never died; the metamorphosis of his race plan has appeared in these new fronts, Planned Parenthood being among them.

  Julian Huxley and Max Nicholson were big supporters of eugenics and racial purification. Huxley was president of the Eugenics Society when he co-founded the WWF, and he also headed UNESCO. He believed in race science and taking control of the "human herd." He knew it would be difficult to bring back Nazi ideology, but UNESCO has worked to make the unthinkable thinkable again. This was done and is done secretly mixing the highly energized and emotional environmental movement with eugenics and human population reduction. The next time you give money or time to what you think is a good cause for the Earth, think twice. If you still can't wrap your head around this line of thought, consider the following quotes:

"It doesn't matter what is true, it only matters what people believe is true"   -Paul Watson, co-founder of Greenpeace

"We've got to ride this global warming issue, even if the theory of global warming is wrong, we will be doing the right thing in terms of economic and environmental policy"
  -Timothy Wirth, President of the UN Foundation

"Unless we announce disasters, no one will listen"
-John Houghton, chairman of IPCC

"The only way to get our society to truly change is to frighten people with the possibility of catastrophe."
-Professor Daniel Botkin

"No matter if the science of global warming is all phony...climate change provides the greatest opportunity to bring about justice and equality in the world."
-Christine Steward, Canadian Environment Minister

"The only hope for the world is to make sure there is not another United States. We can't let other countries have the same number of cars, the amount of industrialization, we have in the US. We have to stop these third world countries right where they are."
-Michael Oppenheimer, Environmental Defense Fund

"Giving society cheap, abundant energy would be the equivalent of giving an idiot child a machine gun."
-Prof. Paul Ehrlich, Stanford University

"I suspect that eradicating smallpox was wrong. It played an important part in balancing ecosystems"
-John Davis, Earth First! Journal

"A total population of 250-300 million people, a 95% decline from present levels, would be ideal."
-Ted Turner, founder of CNN & major UN donor

"If I were reincarnated I would wish to be returned to earth as a killer virus to lower population levels"
-Prince Philip, patron of the World Wildlife Fund

"Isn't the only hope for the planet that the industrial civilizations collapse? Isn't it our responsibility to bring that about?"

-Maurice Strong, founder of UN environmental program

Obviously self-proclaimed elitists think they know more about the value of human life than anyone else. They want the earth for themselves and fly around in private jets, use vast amounts of energy, live in lavish homes and own their own islands. They enjoy the good life while other people starve and exist in poverty. They talk about equality and human rights on one hand, then discuss ways to degrade and lower the quality of life for millions on the other. Their positions of wealth and power make it possible for them to concoct environmental fables to fool the general public. Most of the followers have no idea who they are working for and where the money goes. The general public cannot discriminate the fine line between an honest cause and a corrupt organization, another example of the need for the public to be informed. It is alarming that this doctrine of phony environmentalism is put forth and backed by the public schools of America.

The truth is that cheap, clean energy should be made available for the entire human race. There is plenty of it to last for centuries. This will raise the standard of living higher for all people in all countries, and move the human race to unheard of levels of advancement and civility. Instead, we have poverty leading to crime, immorality and destitution. The poor people of the world are intentionally denied the basics of liberty and opportunity, all for the sake of energy savings and population control. *Every human being deserves the chance to be prosperous and live a good life.* We all deserve food and we all deserve oil. It should not be reserved for the privileged few who selfishly want the world to themselves. In regards to overpopulation, a free market system, where people have direct control over their lives, would produce families who are self-controlled. They would not have any more children than they could pay for themselves. Now we have the poor and dependent procreating without regards to any financial or moral standard.

To be good stewards of the earth we need to become self-governing and prosperous, we don't need to lie to people and keep them in perpetual poverty. We are going to need the efforts of all people to scientifically search for and find alternative fuels and new discoveries that will improve our lives in an honest way. I am for the development of new ways and means to live. Lying to people, creating endless wars, using false science, and devising ways to eliminate and degrade people will not solve anything, it simply increases human misery. These false-flag environmentalists need to be rounded up and exposed for who they are. They are self-indulgent narcissistic criminals who have no desire to actually help out the human condition other than their own.

A case in point is their desire to obtain national parks, public property, and historic sites for their own jurisdiction.
United Nations International biospheres like those occurring around national parks are a way to obtain and hold land formerly devoted to public use. The term biosphere can be seen on national park signs in the United States. They have slowly taken charge of public lands and instituted new policies like raising fees, closing trails and campgrounds, and introducing wildlife

designed to scare away visitors. Slowly, international forces are taking over what was once private property and national park property from the American people. Tibetan folks were driven off their land to make way for a biosphere in the Wolong Nature Preserve. On a local level, Big Marine Lake in Minnesota was the sight of the forced removal of the Shady Birch resort making way for a state park. A small example of what happens on a daily basis. Residents in northeastern Minnesota successfully repelled the United Nations in their attempt to create a buffer zone around Voyagers National Park which would have eventually extended to cover all of the Boundary Waters Canoe Area. These examples may seem like normal ways the government uses to protect wildlife and obtain land for the public good, until you find just what they are really up to! For one thing, even though American taxpayers pay for the upkeep of the parks, the ownership is slowly being handed over to the United Nations. The UN slowly absorbs the land and seals it off to public use with the use of biosphere buffer zones and rings of non-use. It removes any existing private property, and commercial occupants.

In California and elsewhere, developers have masqueraded as environmental groups to purchase and "protect" public lands. As soon as the deals are sealed, buildings go up and the land is fully developed. What was once an open space for the public turns into malls, townhouses or office buildings all in the name of protecting the environment?

The line has been blurred between valid efforts to preserve and maintain the planet and sublime efforts to confiscate and take control of our public and private property. This alone should be disturbing enough to anyone that supports any degree freedom and liberty.

In April 1975, Newsweek magazine ran an article

designed to scare the public and make it easy for certain research organizations to make an extra buck. In the article, a scientific "consensus" concluded the world is heading into a new ice age. The charts, measurements, and opinions of prominent climate experts and meteorologists had proven this to be a fact! "The Cooling World" story laid out the scenario of ever colder temperatures ahead, leading to progressively longer winters, shorter growing seasons, and more deaths due to exposure. It was nothing more than a cheap horror movie in the making. Through the years they have changed the story, modified the plot, and devised new ways to pull the wool over our eyes. Acid rain, asbestos, the ozone layer, and many other scare tactics were invented to demonically mix truth with fiction to obtain power, money and control over the American people.

As I explained, many ecological organizations have ties to international groups that have nothing to do with the environment. They are a smokescreen for a massive globalist agenda. The real loser is the Earth itself as good causes collide with bad agendas. When well meaning do-gooders mix with hard edged politicians and puppet masters, bad things can happen.

~The Smoke and Mirrors of Global Warming~

One of the greatest frauds perpetrated on the American people and the world is the concocted fable of global warming. Man-made carbon emissions creating a "greenhouse effect" in the atmosphere that warms the planet and raises temperature, melting the ice caps and eventually flooding coastlines. Never mind the fact that carbon dioxide is a trace element and human induced carbon dioxide is even more of a trace element in the atmosphere. Never mind that a gradual warming would create more farmland to feed the poor among other advantages. The global warming theory has all the tools necessary to make for long lasting religion based on faith and guilt. Since global warming would cause massive flooding, more severe storms, and melting glaciers, this theory is more adaptable and useful than global cooling, and *it sounds scarier!* The United Nations could blame America for its insatiable appetite for fossil fuels. Then lay a carbon tax on industry, not to stop carbon dioxide, but to "penalize" the company and make it pay carbon credits. In other words, it's a fancy way to steal the assets of the American people with higher fuel costs, and a generous flow of money going to people like Al Gore and his friends in research, college funding, and the United Nations, a simple but fiendish plan to siphon power away from the individual and move it to the oligarchs.

After a few years however, it became obvious the physical world was not cooperating, the Earth was not warming! The catch phrase then turned to "climate change". Using the term climate change, they wouldn't have to keep the lie going about ever increasing temperature... too hard to prove. Plus researchers were caught fudging the numbers. In fact, the Earth cooled from 1940-1980, and there was no suitable increase since then. Carbon emissions were seen as unimportant. Now, all they have to do is utter the phrase *climate change,* which has in fact been happening for millions of years. Blame every bad thing on *climate change,* a jokers dream! The casual observer in all this has got to wonder why we have seasonal change; winter and summer. Is it caused by carbon dioxide or the sun? We would safely conclude *the sun* is the largest contributing factor for weather and climate change and human emissions have nothing to do with it. In fact, carbon dioxide is an essential element of life, the more we have the better. CO_2 enables lush greenery in the Amazon rainforest to the tall trees and vegetation of North America and around the world. Carbon Dioxide is a life giver, not a culprit. I have not heard any Global warming scientist say there are any advantages to a warmer climate; it's always negative forecasts about flooding and hurricanes. The truth is that a warmer world would create more farmland, a longer growing season and a chance for new population centers to develop. A colder earth would remain inhospitable for human activity in many regions. The point is that the so- called science of global warming is in fact a fraud and an agenda driven movement.

The global warming religion reminds me of the time when ancient Greeks would set sail in the restless Mediterranean Sea. A fierce storm would come through and capsize their ship. In response they would condemn and ridicule those who offended the Gods for causing the storm. Today, when a drought, tornado or hurricane hits, the doorstep of the "climate change deniers" is stormed with fiery torches and accusations! There even is legislation being presented stating that climate change denying is an act of "mental illness." Once again, as in the ancient past, human beings are blaming each other for the weather and condemning each other! History repeats itself!

What it shows here, very plainly, is that science can be a dishonest or even deadly profession. All scientists are not like the professor on *Gilligan's Island*, wholesome and honest. They can be corrupted for the right price or an ideal which they believe. For example, the American eugenics experiments were modified by the Nazis and then after the war, these same individuals worked for the CIA under the mind control program MKULTRA. Millions of innocent people died in the cause of this backward science.

The book "Silent Spring" written in 1962 by Rachel

Carlson was responsible for the eventual banning of the pesticide DDT. Since the ban, 3 million people contract malaria and 1 million die every year from the disease that DDT once controlled. Also bed bugs have returned to America after being practically eliminated by the use of DDT. As it turns out, the chemical was not harmful but beneficial; another example of bad science giving bad results.

In fact, many of the "green" proposals in energy, ethanol, and light rail are full of corruption from the start. Wind companies put up their monstrous fanning blades (killing millions of birds) with subsidies from the government. Saving energy is not so much the intent as modifying human behavior, and of course the wealth and fringe benefits are enormous. Without federal assistance, they would go broke because solar and wind energy are not viable and would never survive in the free market. Real estate investors collude with light rail organizers to buy land along proposed routes, not for the public good but to make loads of money while forcing a 19th century form of transportation on to a public who has no interest in it. The question is who is running off with the cash? Farmers accept money to grow ethanol which destroys engines and takes more energy to create than it saves. Again, who gets the money? Americans are fooled into trusting every scientific survey or poll and especially trusting of UN research scientists. The real word for global warming is global government which is the hidden agenda. Globalism cannot be forced upon America so it skillfully disguised behind green sounding terminology. Internationalism is meant to sound like a good thing but is really a way to loot the country and deprive us of our assets. Why else would our own government give the United Nations billions every year if there was no conspiracy?

It has been said a consensus of scientists support the theory of climate change. Most of the support comes from scientists specifically paid and connected to this research area. They support it because they rely on grants to study the theory. They have a vested interest in keeping the grant money flowing to them. Most scientists outside this research field say that carbon dioxide is *not a threat* to humanity and over 30,000 of them have signed a petition on the internet supporting that conclusion.

The earth cooled from 1940-1980 and warmed slightly from 1980-1996. Since then, according to the International Climate Change Conference sponsored by the Heartland Institute, the Earth has gone back to cooling which flies in the face of the global warming theory. Much of this natural trending comes from the movement of heated and cooled ocean water and natural sun release cycles, not the burning of fossil fuels. A vast majority of scientists in the world do not support the theory of climate change and/or global warming as caused by human activity. In fact, if all human activity stopped, it would have no effect on the weather and climate, it is what it is.

Be forever wary of any scientific movement that crawls across the land like a new religion; it could very well be another way to scare, swindle and fleece us.

Don't allow the gloom and doom crowd to hamper your lifestyle. Your activities are good for the economy and good for the country. America is still a vibrant nation and the hope of the world. Our way of life benefits all people.

"never does nature say one thing and wisdom another"

~Juvenal, Satires

Chapter Ten: Music, Walls, & Wiring

*"our future as a race of individuals;
in this we are then judged"*

My house is not only a home, but a source of personal history. I have a long past here, a place of growth since the age of 15 when my parents divorced. Although my career stalled out in 1986 when I gave up architectural drafting, I have since delved into other things. I have gone from a simple minded teenager riding little Hondas and playing catch in the street to a high school, college and vocational graduate, armchair philosopher and part time writer, poet, amateur drummer, song writer, carpenter, plumber, mechanic, HVAC guy, roofer, tile and carpet installer, deck builder, siding installer, drywaller, electrician, fence builder, and truck driver, among other things including the father of 2 sons (one autistic), husband, friend, acquaintance and relative to many. It's been a never ending quest to find myself and seek some kind of goal or accomplishment. There is a driving force in life to overcome obstacles and challenges, and above all, work at something. Some of us are so unambitious that we become despondent, depressed and are apt to fall into chemical addiction and mental instability, falling into the trap of some categorized disease where psychologists lurk. Fortunately, I have kept my body, mind and soul active in life to avoid pitfalls and keep my faith in the world and humanity.

Although I take advice and ideas from others, I rely on myself to overcome obstacles. My Father told me a few times that there is nothing you can't overcome, just have the will power. I do not seek the guidance of a counselor, preacher, or anyone else for that matter. The answer exists and always has existed within. Seeking answers from anywhere else is a reliance on others and their reality. I prefer to survive in the hard world of the internal. Though the answers take longer to find and the road much tougher, once I reach a destination, life is real and concrete, permanent and everlasting. The sun shines and the skies remain blue, and nothing can destroy it. At that point can I enjoy family, friends, and life in general, and be of service to humanity.

The one thing we are bombarded by every day is our own thoughts. I have found that thoughts take the form of many things. They make you feel a full range of emotion. The idea is to have control over how you react to those thoughts, to accept them and not avoid them. We must learn how to live with ourselves, our thoughts and all the manifestations of the brain. Every thought has a purpose and a lesson even though they may be frightening or fearful. Every pleasant thought is the result of hard work and patience. Thoughts should be allowed to come and go like the wind and the rain, the sun and the darkness. Allow yourself the full range of being, endless flash cards of perception which lead to wisdom and growth. Thoughts come to test us often, to see our reaction and judge how well we rationalize them. We can answer the riddles of thought by *not avoiding* their approach but accepting their loud or small voices. It is your own brain in action, not to be confused with mental illness which is largely a sham, but its natural function. Sometimes confusion is the best way to measure the power of the mind. How you will overcome it, tame it and then use it in the future.

The new world order depends on you being afraid of your own thoughts and self. They train you in school and in the media to be a part of and dependent on the reality of others and not to live as an individual. No critical thinking is allowed! They tell you how things are and to avoid dissention of any kind. Your very thoughts are trained to depend on the thoughts of those around you and them dependent on you, a circle of closed minds operating on limited experience and cautious thinking, unknowing of the silent elites who turn the cage and run your life.
  Those who are a part of the new world order should realize you too are under the control of others. You cannot be an individual when you rob other people of their own individuality.

By now you may wonder what happened in my life to get me to this point. Why me of all people?

A series of events, both fortunate and unfortunate...

It feels good to be mechanical, changing the oil on my car or tightening a screw into a finished piece of wood. Spinning a circular saw and seeing the wood dust fly in the air or hammering a nail soundly home. I can stand and stare at a project for a long time, planning silently the process and ramifications of the complicated scheme in my mind, making sure every possible angle has been evaluated. The neighbors must wonder what I'm doing, staring at the house, my eyes running down the overhangs and across the window lines. Sometimes I get what I call "shooting thoughts" that come out of nowhere. I might be installing a piece of siding and stand back and look at my progress. My mind begins to wander. I wonder about the average person, people that seem to be up on current events but not at all conspiratorial. They think all there is to politics is what's on TV or what they learned in school. They have no sense of something hidden, something amiss. I call them political atheists. They believe all there is to politics is the obvious and observable; there is nothing beyond that point. Their idea of a conspiracy is how bad the other party is messing everything up. The concept of God is analogous to this. If I say there is no God, it means the observable is all there is. Existence is only what we can see in front of us. But wait; religious scholars will tell you then about faith, faith in the unseen and the unknown, the idea of a force that created everything and works behind the scenes, but yet is everywhere and in everything.

I maintain there is also a force in politics, *unseen and unheard*. A system developed over the centuries that remains out of sight and yet retains control of us. They offer what they call freedoms, but are nothing more than parameters. In reality we are on a very short leash. They manipulate whole societies without so much of a whisper of suspicion from the common person.
Sometimes in the break between the whining screw gun and the pounding nails, shooting thoughts come to me out of nowhere, or is it a subtle message from the matrix?

During and after high school we all had old cars to drive and more so to work on. Nothing was more satisfying than taking a sputtering old ugly car and fixing it so it runs smooth and shines like a polished agate. I popped a

Black Sabbath tape in the old 8-track machine. Whatever depression or frustration hung over me, the droning dark chords of the band would galvanize my gloom and I rode out the storm. Who needs medication; therapy or drugs when you have the blasting thunder of Black Sabbath to drown out and destroy all things negative? What the Beatles did for me as a kid, the Moody Blues and Black Sabbath did for me later. Sabbath would slay the gloom and the Moody Blues would be like a ray of light after the storm had passed.

Then I discovered the Doors. Jim Morrison obviously saw deep into life and demanded something more, something beyond the normal. The same thing I was looking for. I found I was not the only one. Rock and poetry became fused into a wall of sound.

In 2003 we decided to add on to the house. My brother Ken came to town for a month and framed in the walls and roof, then it was up to me and a few others to complete the job. Well the job was finally completed in 2010, seven long years!

In 2005 a group called Sabotage played in the background as I tackled the duct system and furnace of my new addition, the "Beethoven's last Night" CD played on and on, getting me through the cold nights, struggling with the dim lighting and icy temperatures. Cutting sheet metal and spinning little screws through my cold breath.

By 2009, I was faced with the shear drudgery of that new hallway. I had to wire it, cut the sheetrock, and mud the seams with drywall compound, a messy and gooey job. Then *sand the drywall*. This is the most awful job there is. The white dust got all over everything and all over the house. The kitchen countertops become white, like a snowfall. The very air swirled with dust. My face became pure white, and then, as I struggled to the top of the ladder, the phone rang. The job required two days of this hellish torture. The only thing that got me through the ordeal was the Animals CD. The Absolute Animals, 'House of the Rising Sun', 'When I was Young' and other songs played over and over, I agonized through the process of laying the laminate floor and finally cut and installed the final trim pieces. I did it! The Animals led the way through the agony and brought me to the finish line. I was actually enjoying the work! It was Eric Burdon who really got the job done, not me.

Designing, measuring, staining, and cutting the steps and the railing of the oak stairway was yet another interesting battle. This time is was Mariska Veres and 'Shocking Blue' who came to the rescue. I played their greatest hits CD for months. Mariska was there for me day in and day out. It was 'Forever Changes' that got me through the bedroom construction and a lot of old folk artists like Burl Ives giving me enough of a boost to nail the last piece of trim in the otherwise endless project.

How do you occupy your life? What construction project do you perform in your mind? How do you go about labeling and naming the hours and minutes? How do you escape from the clutches of "them"?

We are all but ghosts, caught in some invisible framework of time, trapped in a wavelength unseen, torn between who we are and what we are told we are. Faint feelings we have, of lives in the past, molded and carved by the smiths of old earth. We look through their mirrors like hideous glimmering windows in space, distorting what is true and not true. Here we shall remain, gliding swooping, searching and dragging our chains down the corridors of eternity, ever stagnating in the wisdom of the vast and throbbing cosmos.

We are indeed 'One Nation Under Them' unless we boldly break the deception of their grip and the stronghold of their power.

*"beneath a river dwells a force, untouched by the clock
it feels the rumble of pounding rapids overhead
and lives on until the raging waters dry to a mere trickling
snake in the sand.
it remains still beneath the sun and the moon
waiting for us to harness its power
and launch ourselves to greatness"*

Chapter Eleven: Matters of Faith

"There are patterns in the universe we must endure like life and death, and the question of existence. We also endure the jokes we play on ourselves and all forms of human error and deception"

For a long time, organized religion ran everything, politics, government, culture and human thought. Over time, it yielded its authority to sovereign nations, and now, global corporations are the primary movers.
Faith is now an option and no longer mandatory. The government stays out of religion, and we can now take it or leave it.
 In this age of social media, gaming, cable TV and distraction, faith has taken a back seat to contemporary life. Old style churches are out, and newfangled, updated mega worship centers complete with coffee shops and rock bands are in, leaving the old buildings behind as crumbling shells of the past. The church no longer holds all the cards as millions of the former faithful have left to seek alternatives in the vast pop culture on the outside. Yet, an old fashioned Christian revival may be on the horizon. Eventually the mental fatigue of the media, the distractions, and the stress of modern living take its toll on the mind and body, and we long for simpler times.
2013 marks the advent of Ben Carson, who spoke at the National Prayer Breakfast with President Obama looking

on in dismay. Carson, a pediatric surgeon, calmly laid out the plan of how the country is being taken apart and put in decline, the government is...

1. Creating division among the people.
2. Encouraging a culture of ridicule for basic moral principles.
3. Undermining the nation's financial stability with crushing government debt.
4. Weakening the morale and funding of the military.

"It appears, coincidentally, that those are the very things happening right now," Carson noted.

I used to look forward to Sunday school. It was an important day as church parking lots filled up with neighbors. For me it was a time to dress up and spend a couple of hours among friends studying Bible stories. Everybody was accepted for who they were. No judgments, no expectations, just a time to get away from it all and learn a few scriptures and sing gospel songs. It was a "feel good" time before going home to a nice roast beef dinner; a perfect prelude to the opening kickoff of the Vikings game. My good friends went to different churches and it was fun to come home and compare notes. Life was good and the communities were strong. The snow fell, and melted, the sun shined, seasons changed and the world was a stable place.
  Becoming a teenager meant questioning everything including God. My life was no longer predicated on the Bible. Youth classes meant being around old friends that now snuck outside to smoke cigarettes and showed little interest. Honest questions about evolution were being dismissed.
The whole thing changed and it was time to move on. It was time to question faith itself. It was the beginning of a

long period of unraveling reality and reassembling the world again, piece by piece. There comes a time in everyone's life where you have to accept the ultimate challenge and that is to kick out the stool you are standing on and stand alone.

The exit of faith means you have to replace it with something. For many of us, it means a sudden loss of stability leading to a life of transient pleasure. Fleeting happiness, loneliness, depression, drugs, all the things the old sermons warned against. The tools of survival are not given to us in school so we have to find them on our own. Some of us find them and some don't. The good news is that there is never a reason to give up on yourself and doubt the world. The answer can be found somewhere through the thicket of your own life and that answer is never the same as someone else's.

The rise of Atheism has its merits, but many radical atheists seek to whitewash all of society. They want to remove all religious symbols in the public square and rewrite what America means by eradicating religion and faith and taking over the school curriculum with their own brand of religious humanism.

The founding of America bears a huge stamp of Christianity and to deny that fact is a mistake. In church we are asked to make an *individual* decision about Jesus Christ. The very idea that GOD IS BIGGER THAN GOVERNMENT is the foundation of this country and the beginning of the age of individualism. To make it out to be something else and redesign the United States into a nation of unbelievers is reckless and dangerous. To me this would be exactly what people complained about when *religion* ran everything. After all, Julian Huxley has stated that humanism is a "religion without revelation". John Dewey called humanism, "our common faith". The Supreme Court in 1961 ruled that humanism is a religion. The public schools are based on this premise. Psychiatry underscores the idea that man has no spirit or soul. What we have in effect is the false doctrine of humanism replacing the false doctrine of original sin, one belief leading to another.

Humanism claims to be scientific but is in fact a false science. Psychiatrists actually vote on the next mental illness the same way a quorum of priests decided who was a witch. Radical Atheism wants to institute the very same totalitarianism of thought. This is not good.

It all comes down to the realization that people are in the midst of their own personal realms of reality and there will never be a time when we all think and act the same. In fact, if we ever got to that point, humanity would stagnate. Reality itself is an agreed upon illusion that changes as people change.

The Bible is a sorted collection of books assembled hundreds of years ago under the direction of church authorities. The Dead Sea scrolls and other ancient documents found in the 20th century prove that there are many writings not included in the finished Bible. Thomas Paine's book, 'The Age of Reason' points out many inconsistencies in 'God's word'. For instance; why would the Lord turn one of his own children into a pillar of salt? The first chapter of Ezekiel describes what some interpret as a spaceship landing and taking off. The Book of Revelation is so symbolic it would take another revelation to find its actual meaning. The books of the New Testament were actually written long after the actual characters in it lived, so none of its supposed authors actually wrote anything. So where does that bring us?

The Bible is one of the few records we have of a history of a people we would not otherwise understand. It has tremendous value and has been a cornerstone of human thought and action for 2000 years. The faith of

Christianity in all of its forms is a way of life for millions. Its believers will not waste time debating their faith with non-believers. *Jesus rises above the confusion.*
In fact, debating faith has never led to any solid conclusions. It is a circular argument which many times results in feelings of bitterness and anger. It's better to simply explain what you think and allow others to do the same. In a free society, there is room for everyone.

Sometimes the answer to the riddles of life is to not ask any questions. I feel that perception is an open book and we each fill the pages on our own. Indeed, we are self-governing Gods. I prefer the acknowledgement of the unknown and the acceptance of its great mysteries. The halfhearted explanation of it through religion falls short so I just ride on the waves of existence. True science is a trial and error bridge that leads to a better life and has not failed us yet. Someday the spirit world will be scientifically explained if we can get beyond this era of war and ignorance.

Images of failing churches say a lot about society. They are being vandalized, boarded up, and fenced off. Even the ones that remain open have wire mesh on the windows and multiple locks on the doors. What a sad replacement to God. Is this what we want? Is this a better system? Is society better off now? Think about it. The church in poor neighborhoods used to be the hub of activity, the place where volunteers would work long hours to help out their fellow man. Now, the poor areas are filled with street tramps, gangs, drugs, sex, violence and people living without any purpose but to rob their neighbor or collect welfare benefits. I prefer the old days in that respect.

Interestingly enough, I am not a person of faith. I am also not a doctor, but we need doctors, and we need churches and religion, not to be in control of everything but to provide viable options. Prayer at public meetings is a good thing, it signifies that there is a force or at the very least, natural rights that are higher than any government. Support faith, even if you have none because it is that attitude which puts individualism above and beyond the state rule. Josef Stalin made this observation about America; "America is like a healthy body and its resistance is threefold: its patriotism, its morality and its spiritual life. If we can undermine these three areas, America will collapse from within."

No matter how learned we become, humanity still must live in a state of ignorance of many things including life after death. Faith happens to be a door that some of us walk through and enter a room that satisfies our yearning of the unknown. But it is not the only door and not the only room.

One thing to remember is that much if not all of what we see, hear and interpret is the object of someone's own creation to begin with. Do not lose your grip, those of us who stand in the rain, outside of the crowd are symbols of normality in some other plane or maybe in our own past or future. We are each the master of our own plan and the ultimate state of a person is for every person to have their own state! This is the essence of a free society. A society of individuals will always trump a planned, collectivist utopia. In order for humankind to advance, the individual must advance. If there are limits placed on individual freedom, we as a whole suffer the consequences. We have to change the power of circumstance determining destiny to our very decisions determining circumstance. It all starts with the realization that cause and effect are not part of some destiny or master plan that we fall into at birth. Things do not happen for a particular reason, we make reasons out of the random things that happen. Each one of us is a separate universe living amongst all the worlds of ourselves combined. Indeed, *all the worlds of us and only one Earth do we live.* I submit it is a wiser choice for us to seek a greater light than to make the best of darkness. Do not accept the state of this world, the poverty, the gloom, the hopelessness. It is brought upon to us by the dark side of our own selves.

What is it that drives life on to new beginnings and new horizons as our forefathers sleep in the dust? The answer is the unexplainable instinct for survival and purpose, the instinct that cannot be removed by any force or power.

The closest thing to God or Caesar is what you see in a mirror, you are the answer. We don't travel to heaven; we carve ourselves out of eternity. In our wanderings we become not lost, but wise. The narrow minded remain in the background, afraid of the wind that blows truth down dark streets and back alleys, only to stop and swirl at their closed doors.

Maybe we are like endless waves reaching the shoreline of life again and again. Spiritual truth is simply not a tangible item. Instead, we must search for what is useful and only a free mind can unlock the secrets that we need.

Human history could have gone in many different directions. What we see and hear today is a product of our random actions through time wherein we manipulate the scenery and props for the acting we perform in our minds.

It boils down to a collection of individual decisions that were made on the run without thinking much about the ramifications of the future. Do not allow the state or some high authority to do the thinking for you, because then, it is they who determine perceived reality and govern the flow of the world.

I have recollections often of childhood and I may someday gain as much of what I had when I was young. Children greet everyone with a smile; the rich, the poor, the good, and the evil alike. What happened along the way and why were we taught to discriminate and judge people? Children have no need to *believe* because they don't ask probing questions that inspire a craving for God. They simply accept the wonders of life without explanation. They wonder and wander in the glory of not knowing or wanting to know. Now think of who you were as a child and what you've now become.

Don't judge others- because the faces you see in the crowd are your own self in other forms. Where you were born and how you were brought up determine your base of operations, but hopefully not your direction. At some point you have to take the wheel and drive your own life. Finally, leave the world a better place than you found it.

> *"this above all: to thine own self be true,*
> *and it must follow, as the night the day*
> *thou canst not then be false to any man"*
>
> ~William Shakespeare

Conclusion...

Among the globalists, there is one attribute that stands out, and that is eternal patience. They are perfectly happy to wrestle control from us in small increments. They are insidious to the point of setting plans in motion that won't come to fruition for many years after their own deaths. They are both well aware of and unknown to each other, but they all share the same lust for the ultimate domination of all people.

The same Kings and rulers that yielded the sword and publically burned us at the stake are now the ones who smile at us on television and walk the steps of the capital. Now is the time to wake up and take action to protect yourself and your family from the forces of the ages who have not died, but live on in new forms.

This book is designed to expand reality. It is not meant to be a full documentation of conspiracy theories. I encourage you to extend your understanding of these and other subjects that you may come across in life. Keep in mind that history is a fascinating account of someone's viewpoint and will never be completely accurate. There will be distortions and lies, but also the promise of new knowledge which is the real power we have. I hope your quest includes an open mind and the desire to discover hidden doors in your life and the world around you. Self-examination will develop your vision, sharpen your focus and increase your faith in the future, with a healthy dose of suspicion thrown in. The truth is like gold; it's hard to come by but it's worthwhile once you hold it in your hand. No matter where you are or what you do, life can be rich with fascination and adventure if you allow it to happen.

  Somehow we all made it this far! The human race has accomplished great things in spite of those who conspire against us. Good luck and keep thinking!

> *"Self-education is, I firmly believe,
> the only kind of education there is"*
>
> *~Isaac Asimov*

"Behind the ostensible government sits enthroned an invisible government owing no allegiance and acknowledging no responsibility to the people"

~Theodore Roosevelt 1912

One Nation Under Them

Additional copies available online

Recommended media...

G. Edward Griffin Jesse Ventura Ron Paul Alex Jones
Judy Shelton Naill Ferguson Shelton Richman
Charlotte Isebyt Thomas J. Dilorenzo
James Bamford Richard Trainor
George Orwell John Perkins James Bamford
Richard Trainor Irwin Schiff Peter Schiff Craig Roberts
The Proverbs Thomas Jefferson Adam Smith
Edgar Allen Poe Washington Irving Edwin Tunis
Andrew Jackson Charles Lindbergh Sr.
William Jennings Bryan James J. Hill Jim Murphy
Dr. Caroll Quigley Matt Taibbi
Friedrich von Hayek Ayn Rand Aldous Huxley
Ludwig von Mises Robert Toland
A sign for Cain As we go marching Hitlers Professors

Whistleblowers...

James Manford Chip Tatum Wayne Madsen William Binney Daniel Elsburg Amber Lyons Jeselyn Radack Tom Fife John Kiriakou Thomas Drake Robert Baer Bruce Riedel Susan Lindauer Jeffery Sterling James Risen Sibel Edwards Robert Steele Russell Rice